The
Cram Sourcebook

Volume Three

A History of the Cram Family in America from the Eighth Generation to the Present

by

Michael A. Cram

HERITAGE BOOKS
2021

HERITAGE BOOKS
AN IMPRINT OF HERITAGE BOOKS, INC.

Books, CDs, and more—Worldwide

For our listing of thousands of titles see our website
at
www.HeritageBooks.com

Published 2021 by
HERITAGE BOOKS, INC.
Publishing Division
5810 Ruatan Street
Berwyn Heights, Md. 20740

Heritage Books by the author:

The Cram Sourcebook: Volume One
A History of the German von Cramm Family, and,
English and Scottish Branches of the Cram Family

The Cram Sourcebook: Volume Two
The First Seven American Generations of the Cram Family, Descended from
John Cram Who Was Granted Land at Muddy River, Boston, in 1636

The Cram Sourcebook: Volume Three
A History of the Cram Family in America from
the Eighth Generation to the Present

Cover Photo: The Wilbur Irvin Cram [16163461] homestead in Loup County, Nebraska (1886). It
featured flowers in window boxes, canaries in cages, and a neat picket fence around the well-built sod house.
Family members pictured are: (l to r) Fred Franklin, John Edwin, Wilbur Irvin, his wife Honor (Filby),
and Albert Irvin. Information concerning the family may be found on page 426.
(Photo courtesy of Nebraska State Historical Society.)

International Standard Book Number
Paperbound: 978-0-7884-0460-3

Author's Preface to Volume Three

The Reference System

I discussed my use of the reference system in the introduction to Volumes one and two, but I shall repeat it here for those who might not have access to those works. In order to cross reference many related individuals, I employ a numbering system commonly known as a "Modified Henry System," enclosed in brackets. A reference number has been assigned to each member of the Cram family who is identified by name, no matter how long the life span. Unnamed children have no number. The system is flexible, allowing for the addition of numbers in any family as further genealogical research is done. Whenever possible, I have tried to number individuals in birth order.

In listing United States family members, the numbering system begins with John Cram, the first member of the family in America, as [1]. All members of the Cram family listed in Volumes two and three are directly descended from this one man. I have continued the numbering system unaltered to the present day.

Sources of Information for United States Ancestry

I attempt to reference all my sources, quoting text verbatim whenever possible. Much of my research was done in the library of the Western Reserve Historical Society in Cleveland, Ohio, and the New England Historic Genealogical Society (NEHGS). Special mention should be made of the work of Ardis King, volunteer for the NEHGS, who over a three-year period arranged the files of Elmer Cram [1524332122] into a resource for genealogists. This book does not exhaust the material in the manuscript of Elmer Cram, so I suggest that researchers do their own study of his files at the NEHGS, using Mrs. King's index volume as a guide. Original sources are cited in the text when appropriate, and a substantive list of sources may be found in the Selected Bibliography at the conclusion of this volume.

Changes or Additions to this Work

I ask researchers who would like to make corrections or additions to the information found in this work to contact me through the publisher. Since events in our lives are never predictable, if I cannot be located, I recommend that you forward your information to the New England Historic Genealogical Society in Boston, Massachusetts. They hold the manuscript of Elmer Cram, and the papers of Daniel Cram and have the most complete collection of Cram family information that I have been able to find.

MICHAEL CRAM
[152593A23]

Eighth American Generation

family of Lucius Wayland CRAM [15232142]

Lucius Wayland CRAM [15232142]
b. APR 6, 1827
d. DEC 9, 1898

m.1. MAY 5, 1850

Harriett Maria DAVIS
b. APR 17, 1831
d. 1904

m.2.

Ada L. CUTTING
b.
d.

1. Charles Wayland [152321421] b. MAR 2, 1851.
2. George Henry [152321422] b. APR 2, 1853.
3. Sarah Estelle [152321423] b. FEB 14, 1857.
4. Edwin Lincoln [152321424] b. MAR 1, 1860
5. Lucius Samuel [152321425] b. MAR 26, 1863.
6. William Grant [152321426] b. MAR 9, 1865.

Charles Wayland CRAM (1849-)
[152321421]

Charles Wayland was born in 1849 according to file 29 of Elmer Cram. The Annals of Meredith, NH, state that he was b. in Manchester MAR 12, 1851. Elmer states that he married Ella BROWN, but that is believed incorrect. In file 59, describing his son, Elmer notes that Charles married Abbie M. DRAKE.
     Their Child:
        1. Charles H. [1523214211] b. NOV 6, 1876 in Holderness; Charles was in the bakery business for a time, he was connected with two lumber companies, and later owned a furniture store; he also owned 25 acres of land on what was called "Hilltop" near Meredith where he had a colony of overnight campsites; he m.1. Mable E. SIMPSON of Haverhill, MA., d/o Charles W. & Euola (Wedgewood) Simpson, in 1896; he m.2. Martha N. HALLIHAN of Rhode Island on OCT 29, 1904; she was b. JUN 23, 1879; the first marriage entry is from the Annals of Meredith, NH., and the second is shown in Elmer Cram's file 59 without explanation of source or the disposition of the first marriage;
           Children by Martha Hallihan (Eleventh Generation):
             1. Gladys [15232142111] b. 1905; d. 1906.
             2. Unnamed infant; b. 1910

George Henry CRAM (1853-1938)
[152321422]

George was born APR 21, 1853 in Meredith, NH., and died DEC 13, 1938 at Lakeport, NH. He married Emily Farnsworth MARSTON, daughter of Samuel and Lucinda (Farnsworth) Marston of Pembroke, ME., on AUG 1, 1883. She was born MAR 21, 1857 and died SEP 15, 1928.
     Their Children:
        1. Laura Estelle [1523214221] b. OCT 6, 1886; d. FEB 22, 1935; m. Carlton A. HAMBLET in AUG, 1927; no children.
        2. Harriett Lucinda [1523214222] b. OCT 15, 1888; m. Guy L. SMITH, s/o Milton & Maude (Tucker) Smith of Plastow, NH., on OCT 8, 1914. He was born AUG 21, 1891.
           Their Children:
             1. Evelyn Marston Smith; b. FEB 2, 1916; she was a registered nurse at Faulkner Hospital in Jamaica Plains, NY.

2. Lois Maude Smith; b. JUL 31, 1918; d. APR 11, 1941 in
a Laconia, NH. hospital.
3. Olive Louise Smith; b. JAN 31, 1925.
3. Maude Augusta [1523214223] b. NOV 21, 1891; m. Lee S. PRINCE, s/o Frank &
Ruth (Batchelder) Prince on JUN 28, 1917; he was b. in 1888, and d. in 1940.
4. Ruth Marston [1523214224] b. JUN 28, 1895; m. Ray H. PRINCE, s/o Charles &
Martha (Gookin) Prince of Salisbury, NH., on MAR 8, 1920.
Their Children (in the 11th generation):
1. Ray Howard Prince; b. JUL 29, 1922.
2. George Harland Prince; b. OCT 8, 1924.
3. Charles Albert Prince; b. DEC 4, 1930.

Sarah Estelle CRAM (1857-1927)
[152321423]

Sarah was born in Meredith, NH. on FEB 14, 1857, and died in 1927. She married Moses Elgin
CHAPMAN, son of Moses and Margaret (Harawer) Chapman of Danvers, MA. on MAR 10, 1875. The
wedding took place in Center Harbor, NH., and the couple resided in Meredith where Moses was a farmer.
Moses was born FEB 24, 1852. He served in the Civil War, enlisting AUG 18, 1862 and serving for three
years as a sergeant in Co. I, 10th New Hampshire Volunteers. He took part in the battles of
Fredericksburg, Chancellorsville and Gettysburg.
Their Children:
1. Hattie Estelle Chapman; b. FEB 17, 1878 in Danvers, MA.; m. Frank L. Turner of
Epson, NH.; he was b. NOV 3, 1875 in Rochester, MA.; they resided in Short
Falls, NH.
Their Children (in the 11th generation):
1. Marion Frances Turner.
2. Ethel Whitman Turner.
3. Charles Donald Turner
4. Clyde Turner.
2. Alice C. Chapman; b. JUN 20, 1881 in Danvers, MA.; m. William Josiah
Kingsbury, s/o Rev. Josiah Weare and Mary Hill (Jackson) Kingsbury of
Tamworth, NH., on JUN 20, 1900; he was b. NOV 10, 1866 and d. JUL 9,
1936 in Derry, NH.
3. Harold Earl Chapman; b. FEB 6, 1892 in Stoneham, MA.; m. Jessie May Stanton on
JAN 10, 1924; she was b. JUL 9, 1904 in Saranac, NY.; resided in Derry, NH.
Their Child:
1. Harold Earl Chapman, Jr.; entered the U.S. Navy in JAN, 1942.

Edwin Lincoln CRAM (1860-1935)
[152321424]

Edwin was born MAR 1, 1860 in Roxbury, MA., and died JAN 29, 1935. He married Cora E. HOWE on
Nov 8, 1887. She was born in St. Johnsbury, VT., and died in Lakeport on APR 11, 1889. He married
second Lillian MERRILL, daughter of Daniel and Martha J. (Bagley) Merrill, on SEP 22, 1890. She was
born DEC 7, 1866 in Thornton, NH., and died MAR 2, 1947. During WWII Lillian knitted 140 sweaters,
24 pairs of mittens, 11 pairs of beanies, 13 helmets, and 40 scarves to be disbributed by the Red Cross. She
and her husband were members of the First Baptist Church of Laconia, NH. where he served for several years
as a deacon.
Their Children (all born in Lakeport, NH.):
1. Carl Edwin [1523214241] b. APR 2, 1889; m. Alice BABB, d/o George M. & Jennie
(Roycraft) Babb; she d. JUL 15, 1939; they resided in Concord, NH.
2. Prof. Frank Merrill [1523214242] b. JAN 19, 1892; not married; served as the
organist of the Unitarian Church at Concord, NH.; he lived in Lakeport, NH.
3. Harlan D. [1523214243] b. AUG 14, 1895; m. Effie Emerline PAINE, d/o Edward S.
& Lucy (Jones) Paine of Lakeport, NH., JAN 22, 1922; she was b. APR 19,
1894; they resided at Stoneham, MA.

4. Esmond [1523214244] b. JUN 6, 1904; m. Pauline CLAUS on JAN 1, 1936; they lived in Boston, MA.
5. Oscar [1523214245] b. AUG 26, 1893; m. Lettie SWEET, daughter of Elkin Sweet of Franklin, NH., on JUN 7, 1916; she was b. OCT 29, 1894.
Their Children (in the 11th generation):
1. Madeline [15232142451] b. DEC 27, 1919.
2. Milton [15232142452] b. MAY 7, 1921; he was a student at the University of New Hampshire in 1939.

Lucius Samuel CRAM (1863-)
[152321425]

Lucius Samuel had his name changed to Samuel L. Cram. Samuel was born MAR 22, 1862, according to John G. Cram (or MAR 27, 1863, according to Elmer Cram), in Roxbury, MA. He married Nellie F. PRESCOTT, daughter of Rufus E. and Adaline F. (Sanborn) Prescott of New Hampton, NH., on NOV 28, 1883 at Lake Village, NH. She was born SEP 22, 1845, and died MAY 24, 1935 in Belmont, NH.
Their Children:
1. Harriett M. [1523214251] d. MAY 24, 1935; m. David BICKFORD, of Center Harbor.
2. Herbert E. [1523214252] b. JUl 19, 1889; not married.

William Grant CRAM (1865-1936)
[152321426]

William was born in Roxbury, MA. on MAR 19, 1865, and died NOV 7, 1936 at Lakeport, NH. He married Georgianna F. PATCH, daughter of Frank and Mary (Osgood) Patch. She was born in 1867 and died JUl 24, 1937. Their children included three boys and a daughter, but only information about their daughter remains.
Their Child:
1. Helen [1523214261] b. JUN 15, 1890; m. Milton J. WALKER, s/o David P. & Lydia Ann (Hazeltine) Walker; he was b. MAY 25, 1866; they resided in Contoocook, NH.

References:

Annals of Meredith, NH. (pp. 147, 164-165)
Bible records of John Franklin Cram of Dorchester
Genealogy of the Edward Chapman Family of Ipswich, ME. (p. 33)
Prescott Genealogy (p. 551)
Records of John G. Cram
Records of Samuel L. Cram of Belmont, NH.
Unpublished manuscript of Elmer Cram (files 29, 59, & 219)

family of Albion Parris CRAM II   [15232244]

Albion Parris Cram II [15232244]
b. OCT 28, 1838
d. SEP 25, 1917

m.1. _____   1. Melville Fletcher [152322441] b. APR 8, 1861
                                        2. Nellie Albina [152322442] b. SEP 17, 1862
Susan M. FLETCHER
b. FEB 5, 1842   3. Carroll Albion [152322443] b. JAN 27, 1868
d. NOV 8, 1864   4. Benjamin Ralph [152322444] b. NOV 21, 1869
                                        5. Charles Maurice [152322445] b. FEB 15, 1872
m.2. MAY 6, 1866 _____6. Archer Parris [152322446] b. MAR 25, 1875
                                        7. Margaret Estelle [152322447] b. DEC 31, 1878
Lora Viola WALKER   8. Marie Gertrude [152322448] b. AUG 18, 1884
b. FEB 26, 1848   9. Lora Alberta [152322449] b. OCT 26, 1889
d. APR 15, 1915

Melville Fletcher CRAM (1861-1923)
[152322441]

Melville Fletcher was born APR 8, 1861. He died in Berkley, California on NOV 23, 1923. His wife was Ida ----.

Nellie Albina CRAM (1862-)
[152322442]

Nellie Albina was born SEP 17, 1862. She married first Orman F. FRENCH. She married second Rev. Harry PURRINGTON, a Baptist clergyman. They resided in Mechanic Falls, ME.
    Their Child:
        1. Gertrude French; m. Frederick Packard; resided in Montclair, N.J.
            Their Child:
                1. Robert Packard.

Carroll Albion CRAM (1868-1874)
[152322443]

Carroll Albion was born JAN 27, 1868 and died JUN 2, 1874.

Benjamin Ralph CRAM (1869-)
[152322444]

Benjamin Ralph was born NOV 21, 1869. He was a merchant in Mt. Vernon, ME. who lived in the old Cram homestead owned by his father and grandfather. He held many town positions and was a member of the state legislature. He married Caroline A. STEVENS, daughter of James Lincoln and Delia (Hopkins) Stevens, on SEP 2, 1896.

Charles Maurice CRAM (1872-)
[152322445]

Charles Maurice was born FEB 15, 1872. He was a graduate of Stanford University and George Washington University Law School in Washington DC., and became an attorney in Boston. Charles lived in Cambridge, MA.

Archer Parris CRAM (1875-)
[152322446]

Archer Parris was born MAR 25, 1875. He was an attorney in New York City who lived in Mahwah, New Jersey. He married Olive REED, daughter of George D. and Sarah (Haynes) Reed of Haynes, VA., on SEP 2, 1908. He held an honorary degree from Bowdoin College and was a graduate of George Washington University Law School.

Margaret Estelle CRAM (1878-1933)
[152322447]

Margaret Estelle was born DEC 31, 1878 and died in Seattle, Washington on AUG 14, 1933. She attended Colby College and Mt. Holyoke. Margaret married Edwin Prilay WHITING, son of Roscoe and Sarah (Prilay) Whiting, in Mt. Vernon, ME. on AUG 22, 1907. The family later moved to Seattle, WA. where Edwin practiced law.
> Their Children:
> 1. Edwin Cram Whiting; b. JAN 9, 1909; m. Olive Marjorie Knapton of Seattle on MAY 14, 1932.
> 2. Dorothy Margaret Whiting; b. OCT 14, 1913

Marie Gertrude CRAM (1884-)
[152322448]

Marie Gertrude was born AUG 18, 1884. Nothing more is known about her.

Lora Alberta CRAM (1889-)
[152322449]

Lora Alberta was born OCT 26, 1889. She married Magnus Tate CRAWFORD, son of George and Abbie (Tate) Crawford of Louisville, KY., in Seattle, WA. on JAN 11, 1916. Magnus was an electrical engineer with the Puget Sound Power and Light Company.
> Their Children:
> 1. Walker Crawford; b. JUL 20, 1919
> 2. Newton Craig Crawford; b. MAY 12, 1923

References:

Genealogical Outline of the Cram, Walker and Weekes Families (pp. 9-13)
Unpublished manuscript of Elmer Cram (file 22)

family of James CRAM [15241132]

James CRAM [15241132]
b. JUN 4, 1803
d. MAY 22, 1872

1. Nancy Jane [152411321] b. APR 2, 1827
2. David Smith [152411322] b. MAY 17, 1829

m. APR 15, 1826

3. Lydia Ann [152411323] b. AUG 24, 1832
4. Sarah Elizabeth [152411324] b. JUL 3, 1838

Dorothy SMITH
b. MAY 19, 1804
d. DEC 25, 1872

5. Mary Abigail [152411325] b. MAR 27, 1841
6. Dolly Maude [152411326] b. APR 3, 1844

Nancy Jane CRAM [1827-1897)
[152411321]

Nancy was born APR 2, 1827 in Brownfield, ME. and died in Lewiston, ME on NOV 6, 1897. She married Rev. Levi BRACKETT, son of John and Fanny (Cobb) Brackett, on DEC 25, 1852. He was a Baptist minister who was born at Westbrook, ME. on NOV 27, 1813 and died at Lewiston on DEC 29, 1890. He is buried at Brunswick, Me. Nancy graduated from Parsonsfield Seminary in 1852 in preparation for teaching. Her beginning salary was $1.25 per week.
   Their Children:
1. James R. Brackett; b. APR 1, 1854 at Raymond, ME.; he was Dean of Colorado University.
2. Levi Smith Brackett; b. MAR 14, 1856; d. AUG 15, 1856.
3. Levi Fairfield Brackett; b. JUL 11, 1858; d. JUN 22, 1860.
4. Anna Maria Brackett; b. MAY 18, 1861; m. AUG 10, 1898 to A. L. Dennison; he was b. APR 13, 1867; they resided in Exeter, NH.; he was a teacher, a graduate of Bates;
      Their Children:
   1. Theodora Dennison; b. OCT 11, 1899.
   2. Mary Leon Dennison; b. JAN 11, 1904 in Bath, ME.
   3. Harry Dennison; b. JUL 22, 1905.

David Smith CRAM (1829-1897)
[152411322]

David was born MAY 17, 1829 at Brownfield, ME. and died NOV 6, 1897 at Lewiston. He served in the Civil War, enlisting on SEP 21, 1864 in Company A, Maine Volunteers. He was present at Lee's surrender at Appomattox courthouse. David's farm at Brownfield (which he inherited from his father) was well known in the area. The Lewiston Journal of OCT 24, 1895 noted: "David Smith Cram and his son Alvin of West Brownfield, Oxford County have finished their harvesting and are well pleased with their corn crop of 202 bushels. Some of the ears were 14 inches long and a large number were over a foot long. For a farm that tourists call 'run down' this is a pretty good showing."

David married first Marcia Ann WENTWORTH, daughter of Augustus and Mary Ann (Lougee) Wentworth, on MAR 18, 1858. She was born at Brownfield on APR 16, 1839 and died there on JAN 28, 1873. He married second Almina BROWN, daughter of Samuel and Sally (Linscott) Brown on OCT 22, 1873. She was born at Brownfield on MAY 6, 1843 and died there on MAY 12, 1910.
   Child (by Almina):
1. Alvin G. [1524113221] b. JUL 1, 1879; m. Laura E. GUPTILL, d/o Harrison and Lousena (Pendexter) Guptill of Cornish, ME. on DEC 25, 1898; she was b. JUN 22, 1876 and d. MAR 7, 1947 at Greenwood, ME.
   Their Children (11th Generation):
   1. Eva A. [15241132211] b. FEB 27, 1905 in Brownfield; m. Earl ROGERS, s/o Arthur & Amy (Mayheu) Rogers on SEP 6, 1930; he was b. JAN 16, 1906 at Orleans, VT.
   2. Grace [15241132212] b. JUL 7, 1906 in Porter, ME.; m. Hilton SHIBLES, s/o Bark M. & Grace (Kelley) Shibles on SEP 21,

1930 in Fryeburg, ME.; he was b. SEP 8, 1901 at Haverhill, MA.

Lydia Ann CRAM (1832-1877)
[152411323]

Lydia was born at Brownfield, ME. on AUG 25, 1832 and died at Oakland, CA. on DEC 7, 1877. She married Calvin Joy CRESSEY on OCT 18, 1854 at Oakland, CA.
> Their Children:
>> 1. Frank Cressey
>> 2. Cora Cressey; m. Cash Crowe; she d. in 1928.
>> 3. William Cressey

Sarah Elizabeth CRAM (1838-1917)
[152411324]

Sarah was born JUL 3, 1838 at Brownfield, ME. and died DEC 20, 1917. She married first Samuel S. HILL, son of Truworthy and Almira (Wheeler) Hill, on FEB 23, 1859 at Snowville, NH. He was born on SEP 29, 1830 at Canterbury, NH. and died JAN 28, 1862. She married second Alvin SNOW of Snowville, NH. There was no issue from the second marriage.
> Their Child (10th Generation):
>> 1. Ida Hill; m. Everett Stanley
>> Their Children:
>>> 1. Harry Stanley; m. Daisy Drew, d/o Clement Drew.
>>> 2. Grace Stanley; m. Walter Drew, brother of Daisy (brother & sister married brother and sister).

Mary Abigail CRAM (1841-1928)
[152411325]

Mary was born MAR 27, 1841 in Brownfield and died JUN 11, 1928 at Conway, NH. She was married on MAR 26, 1860 to Orlando Azro BLAKE, son of Benjamin and Almira (Rogers) Blake of Brownfield. He was born JUN 112, 1837 at Brownfield and died there on OCT 22, 1914.
> Their Children:
>> 1. Elmer Ellsworth Blake; b. JUN 27, 1861; d. DEC 26, 1946; m. Rissie Chandler, d/o William & Frances (Bishop) Chandler; she was b. OCT 9, 1870 at Dracut, MA. and d. JAN 20, 1943 at Brownfield.
>> Their Children (11th Generation):
>>> 1. Hector Chandler Blake; b. DEC 12, 1889; m.1. Minnie Alexander, d/o Fred and Georgie (Trumbell) Alexander, on JAN 13, 1913 at Fryeburg, ME.; she was b. JUN 12, 1893 at Denmark, ME and d. DEC 30, 1913 at Brownfield; m.2. Ethel Claire Grey on OCT 3, 1914, d/o Smith Grey; she was b. OCT 7, 1889.
>>> Child - by Minnie:
>>>> 1. Roland Alexander Blake; b. NOV 18, 1913 at Brownfield, ME.
>>> 2. Helen Rosille Blake; b. MAR 5, 1892 at Fryeburg; m. Winfield Scott Head, s/o John and Hattie (Drew) Head, on DEC 21, 1916; he was b. at Eaton, NH. on NOV 16, 1885;
>>> Their Children (12th Generation):
>>>> 1. Florence Agnes Head; b. APR 19, 1918 at Eaton.
>>>> 2. Samuel Blake Head; b. OCT 12, 1919 at Eaton.
>>>> 3. Zoe Head; b. DEC 26, 1924 at Eaton.
>>>> 4. Bruce Head; b. at Eaton, NH.; d. FEB 11, 1946.
>> 2. Edward Henry Blake; b. FEB 14, 1864; he had infantile paralysis and was never able to walk.
>> 3. Nellie May Blake; d. at the age of five years from scarlet fever.
>> 4. James Blake; d. young.

5. Carlos Cram Blake; b. FEB 14, 1873 at W. Lebanon, ME; m.1. Lura Mary Clough, d/o Rev. Newton and Sarah Ellen (Smith) Clough, on AUG 14, 1894; she was b. APR 2, 1875 at Grantham NH.; divorced OCT 15, 1912; m.2. Nellie (Parmenter) Bean; There were six children fathered by Carlos; only three survived to adulthood;

Their Children:

1. Mildred Halita Blake; b. DEC 17, 1900 at Brownfield; m. Albert W. Coleman, s/o Albert and Mildred (Hearn) Coleman, on JUL 7, 1925 at Saco, ME.; he was b. SEP 16, 1900; he was a graduate of Wentworth Institute;

Their Child (12th Generation)

1. Newton Clough Coleman; b. JUN 11, 1926 at Biddeford, ME.; he was 1944 graduate of Herbert Hoover High School in Glendale, CA.; attended Milford CT. Prep School.

2. Stella Elizabeth Blake; b. NOV 27, 1902; d. 1918, she drowned.

3. Leland Newton Blake; b. SEP 4, 1904 in Brownfield; m.1. Mary Lenfest, d/o Dougal Louis Lenfest of S. Weymouth on MAY 12, 1928; m.2. Lorrine Maher (a divorcee) on MAR 14, 1937.

Child by Mary:

1. Lura Ann Blake; b. FEB 2, 1931 in Biddeford.

6. Walter David Blake; b. MAR 16, 1876.

Dolly Maude CRAM (1844-1847)
[152411326]

Dolly was born APR 3, 1844 and died MAR 12, 1847 of scarlet fever.

References:

Brackett Genealogy (p. 200)
History of Canterbury, NH. (p. 146)
Records of MIldred Halita (Blake) Coleman
Unpublished manuscript of Elmer Cram (Files 80 and 146)

family of Nathan Bailey CRAM [15241137]

Nathan Bailey CRAM [15241137]
b. OCT 11, 1818
d. MAR 24, 1899

m.1.

Elizabeth TARBOX
b. DEC 19, 1818
d. MAY 3, 1869

m.2.

Catherine LOMBARD
b. APR 24, 1823
d. JUN 14, 1886

1. Lucy Ann [152411371] b. JAN 1, 1845
2. Col. Edwin James [152411372] b. OCT 17, 1846
3. John Arthur [152411373] b. JUL 10, 1848
4. Emma Maria [152411374] b. NOV 9, 1850
5. Hattie E. [152411375] b. JUL 10, 1852
6. Eva Carrie [152411376] b. NOV 9, 1855
7. Frank Sumner [152411377] b. JUL 29, 1857
8. Ella L. [152411378] b. OCT 16, 1861
9. Fred Ellsworth [152411379] b. OCT 8, 1864

Lucy Ann CRAM (1845-1865)
[152411371]

Lucy Ann was born JAN 1, 1845 at Parsonsfield, ME. and died FEB 18, 1865, of typhoid fever. She was a school teacher at Parsonsfield.

Col. Edwin James CRAM (1846-1906)
[152411372]

Edwin was born OCT 17, 1846. After attending district schools, he completed his preparation for college at Limerick Academy and Westbrook Seminary. He matriculated at Bowdoin in 1869. He earned his Bachelor's degree in 1873 and his Master's degree three years later. He began teaching at common schools at the age of 17, a calling which he followed at intervals every year up to the close of his college course. In 1874, after being the head of Winthrop High School two terms, he was elected Principal of the Kennebunk High School, a position he held for seven years. He then commenced reading law with Strout, Gage & Strout in Portland, and after three years' study was admitted to the Cumberland bar in APR, 1884. In JUN of the same year he opened an office in Biddeford. He achieved a good measure of success at his chosen profession. In DEC, 1884 he was appointed Recorder of the Biddeford Municipal Court. According to the History of Parsonsfield, ME., his temperance habits were without question, having never used either liquor or tobacco in any form. He died JAN 22, 1906.

John Arthur CRAM (1848-1874)
[152411373]

John Arthur was born JUL 10, 1848. He prepared for college at Limerick Academy & Westbrook Seminary, graduating from Bowdoin with honors in 1873. Like his brother, he also commenced teaching at 17, continuing the practice at intervals up to the time of his graduation, when he assumed charge of the Wells Free High School. However, after two years his health failed. Although a man of strong constitution, and of marked athletic skill and power, long and persistent application to study and teaching had brought on pulmonary trouble, which, with brain fever, ended his earthly life on JUL 19, 1874. According to the History of Parsonsfield, ME., "He was a successful teacher, a young man of the highest integrity and honor, and in his death all felt that bright prospects were blasted."

Emma Maria CRAM (1850-1865)
[152411374]

Emma was born NOV 9, 1850, and died JAN 9, 1865, of typhoid fever.

Hattie E. CRAM (1852-1865)
[152411375]

Hattie was born JUL 10, 1852, and died JAN 4, 1865, of typhoid fever.

Eva Carrie CRAM (1855-1921)
[152411376]

Eva Carrie was born NOV 9, 1855 and died MAR 15, 1921 at Southern Pines, NC. She married Edward Everett SAWTELLE on AUG 10, 1876. He was born JUL 8, 1852.

Frank Sumner CRAM (1857-1926)
[152411377]

Frank Sumner was born JUL 29, 1857 and died FEB 15, 1926 at Limerick, ME. He married Cora Lizzie COUSINS, daughter of Abram & Elizabeth Dam (Small) Cousins of Limington, ME. She was born JAN 7, 1866 in Limington. Frank was a photographer.
   Their Child (in the 10th generation):
       1. Abram Cousins [1524113771] b. JUL 1, 1895; d. DEC 6, 1918.

Ella L. CRAM (1861-1862)
[152411378]

Ella was born OCT 16, 1861 and died MAY 1, 1862, at Southern Pines, NC.

Fred Ellsworth CRAM (1864-1922)
[152411379]

Fred Ellsworth was born OCT 8, 1864 and died DEC 28, 1922 (or 1923) in Melrose, MA. He married Lillian Isola EDES, daughter of Charles & Louisa (Storrer) Edes, in 1885. She was born in Brownfield, ME. on OCT 15, 1864 and died in SEP, 1919 in Melrose. He was a school teacher at Parsonsfield, ME.
   Their Children (in the 10th generation):
       1. Charles Arthur [1524113791] b. SEP 20, 1888; m. Hermine KANIA in 1925;
           Their Children:
               1. Lillian Ellsworth [15241137911] b. JUN 30, 1925.
               2. Richard [15241137912]
       2. John Frederick [1524113792] b. FEB 8, 1890; m. Elizabeth Gertrude MILLER, d/o
           Ferdinand & Caroline (Damon) Miller of Germany, on SEP 14, 1925;
           Their Child:
               1. Fred Ellsworth [15241137921] b. MAR 28, 1927.

References:

History of Parsonsfield, ME. (p. 69)
Unpublished manuscript of Elmer Cram (file 145)

family of Ebenezer CRAM [15241171]

Ebenezer CRAM [15241137]
b. AUG 8, 1809
d. MAR 24, 1877

           1. Henry Osbourne [152411371] b. JUL 27, 1836

m.1. JUL 11, 1833   2. Calvin Libby [152411372] b. JUN 28, 1844

Eliza Ann EDGERLEY
b. OCT 16, 1817
d. AUG 27, 1854

m.2.

Mary L. RICE

Henry Osbourne CRAM (1836-1912)
[152411711]

Henry Osbourne was born JUL 27, 1836 at Buxton, ME. He passed his boyhood days in his native town, attending Saco High School and upon graduation entering Bridgton Academy, graduating with honors.

Henry Osbourne was for many years engaged in the hotel business in partnership with his father as proprietor of the Elm House which stood on the corner of Federal and Temple Streets (in Portland, ME.) in 1864. Two years later, on JUL 4, 1866, the hotel was destroyed in the great fire of Portland. The Crams next managed the Commercial House, which was erected on the corner of Fourth and Cross Streets after the fire. After three years they sold out and became the proprietors of the United States Hotel in Market Square (now Monmouth Square) for two years.

Next they moved to Detroit, MI. where they ran the Biddle House, one of the largest hotels in that city. From there they went to East Hadden, CT., and thence to Baltimore, MD., later returning to Portland, ME. where Henry became chief clerk of the United States Hotel until he retired. According to his obituary in the JAN 11, 1912 edition of the Portland Evening Express, "He was a man of quiet and retiring disposition, always strictly attentive to business and his acquaintance with the traveling public, with whom he was always popular, was very wide."

The obituary went on to describe the circumstances surrounding his death: "Mr. Cram had been in rather feeble health for a number of years, but had been able to be about most of the time and last night he retired feeling in his usual health and spirits. This morning Mrs. Cram shortly after arising, found that he had passed away. He had been subject to fainting spells and the cause of his death is attributed to heart trouble."

He married Frances Ellen Van BIBBER, daughter of Capt. Nelson and Jane (Johnson) Van Bibber. They were wed on APR 6, 1867 at Portland, ME. She was born at Falmouth, ME. on DEC 25, 1847 and died APR 23, 1919.
        Their Children:
                1. Blanche Osbourne [1524117111] b. MAR 5, 1876, at Baltimore, MD.
                2. Paul Henry [1524117112] b. JAN 26, 1879, at Portland, ME.
                3. Harold Edgerly [1524117113] b. JAN 27, 1884, at Portland, ME.

Calvin Libby CRAM (1844-1845)
[152411712]

Calvin was born JUN 28, 1844 at Greenwood, ME. and died SEP 17, 1845 at Standish, ME.

References:

Portland Evening Express (JAN 11, 1912 issue)
Unpublished manuscript of Elmer Cram (file 89)

family of Rev. James Oliver CRAM [15241179]

James Oliver CRAM [15241137]
b. SEP 9, 1833
d. JUN 17, 1904

m. NOV 5, 1863

Lydia A. KELSEY
b. OCT 23, 1841
d. APR 11, 1917

1. John Levi Cramb [152411371] b. 1864
2. Charles Stevens Cramb [152411372] b. 1866
3. George Henry Cramb [152411373] b. 1867
4. Albert James Cramb [152411374] b. 1869
5. William Frederick Cramb [152411375] b. 1871
6. Frank M. Cramb [152411376] b. 1873
7. Edgar Myron Cramb [152411377] b. 1876
8. Lewis Oliver Cramb [152411378] b. 1878
9. Mary Emma Cramb [152411379] b. 1880
10. Levi Kelsey Cramb [15241137A] b. 1882
11. Arthur Benjamin Cramb [15241137B] b. 1885
12. Myra Alphonsine Cramb [15241137C] b. 1887

Dr. John Levi CRAMB (1864-1942)
[152411791]

John was born NOV 6, 1864 at the home of his grandfather, Levi Kelsey in Mondota, Illinois. He died AUG 8, 1942 at Sidney, Nebraska, and was buried at Denver, Colorado. He married first Dr. Tens I. CLEMMONS on MAR 30, 1885 at Fairbury, IL. She was born DEC 26, 1862 and died OCT 13, 1919. John married second Mrs. Ida J. (Cummings) DUNKEN on DEC 31, 1925.
    Children (all by his first wife):
        1. Harry Lee Cramb [1524117911] b. NOV 15, 1886 near Fairbury, NE.; d. AUG 25,
           1889 from the effects of burns.
        2. Floy Lenora Cramb 1524117912] b. JUN 9, 1888 near Fairbury, NE.; d. NOV 30,
           1959; m.1. her first cousin, Lorren F. CLEMMONS; they divorced; m.2.
           Michael T. PLASKETTE on AUG 8, 1919 at San Diego, CA.; no children.
        3. James Travis Cramb [1524117913] b. SEP 15, 1890 near Fairbury, NE.; d. OCT 20,
           1918 of flu-pneumonia; m. DEC 10, 1912, to Lena B. ZASEKA, d/o William
           Zaseka; she was b. MAR 3, 1892 and d. DEC 31, 1924;
           Their Children (in the 11th generation):
               1. Travis Henry Cramb [15241179111] b. JAN 20, 1914 at
                  Denver, CO.; m. Katherine Terese WINKEL, d/o
                  Joseph & Terese (Rush) Winkel of Austria; she was
                  b. at Sheboygan, WI on SEP 5, 1913;
                  Their Children:
                     1. Gloria Jean Cramb [152411791111]
                       b. JAN 26, 1944.
                     2. Paulette Lillie Cramb [152411791112]
                       b. AUG 8, 1947.
               2. Willis Clemmons Cramb [15241179112] b. SEP 27, 1915
                  d. JAN 12, 1920.
        4. Ruth Alphonsine Cramb [1524117914] b. AUG 6, 1893; m. AUG 27, 1918 to
           Joseph H. POTTS;
           Their Children:
               1. Joseph H. Potts, Jr.; b. AUG 27, 1920.
              2. Floy Irene Potts; b. DEC 26, 1922.
              3. Willis Dana Potts; b. OCT 1, 1925.

Charles Stevens CRAMB (1866-1869)
[152411792]

Charles was born APR 18, 1866 at Wheaton, Illinois, and died SEP 20, 1869 after being run over by a load of hay.

George Henry CRAMB (1867-1930)
[152411793]

George was born DEC 14, 1867 in Channahon, IL., and died JUN 30, 1930 at Fairbury, NE. He married Elizabeth T. PEARSON on FEB 27, 1893 at Fairbury, IL. She was born DEC 10, 1868 at Motherwell, Scotland, and died OCT 30, 1958 at Fairbury, NE.

    Their Children:

1. Martha Lydia Cramb [1524117931] b. JAN 15, 1894 near Fairbury, NE.; d. NOV 26, 1948; m. JUN 16, 1915 to Carl F. STARK, Jr.; he was b. APR 23, 1892;
    Their Children:
    1. Donald Richard Stark; b. MAY 17, 1917; m. Ann Fowler.
    2. Lewis E. Stark; b. MAY 10, 1920.
2. Lee James Cramb [1524117932] b. SEP 17, 1895 near Fairbury, NE.; d. OCT 21, 1960, unmarried.
3. Ethel Theresa Cramb [1524117933] b. DEC 30, 1896 near Fairbury, NE.; d. DEC 22, 1948.
4. Marie Elizabeth Cramb [1524117934] b. APR 18, 1901 near Fairbury, NE.; m. Glenn CORNELIUS; they were later divorced.
5. Kensey George Cramb [1524117935] b. MAY 10, 1910; d. OCT 21, 1960.

Albert James CRAMB (1869-1905)
[152411794]

Albert was born NOV 13, 1869 at Sandwich, IL., and died at Fairbury, NE. on MAR 7, 1905. He married Lulu M. LYNDE, half-sister of the author Francis Lynde, on NOV 9, 1898. She was born DEC 17, 1878 and died AUG 29, 1965.

    Their Children:

1. A daughter, dead at birth.
2. Norman Lynde Cramb [1524117941] b. OCT 22, 1902; m. Dorothy E. BUMGARDNER on JUN 27, 1905;
    Their Child:
    1. Gwendolyn Lee Cramb [15241179411] b. SEP 20, 1929.

William Frederick CRAMB (1871-1953)
[152411795]

William was born OCT 23, 1871 at Mendota, IL., and died JAN 23, 1953 at Fairbury, NE. He married Cora H. GARNSEY on DEC 26, 1894. She was born NOV 20, 1874 and died JUL 3, 1965. He became editor of the Fairbury Journal.

    Their Children:

1. Pauline Cramb [1524117951] b. DEC 10, 1900; m. Harold L. NUCKOLLS on JUN 22, 1926; he was b. JAN 15, 1901;
    Their Children:
    1. Marjorie Leigh Nuckolls; b. JUL 23, 1927 at Fairbury, NE; m. Dale D. Mooberry on JUN 22, 1948;
        Their Children:
        1. Debra Leigh Mooberry; b. SEP 26, 1950.
        2. Mark Mooberry; b. MAY 18, 1952.
    2. William Cramb Nuckolls; b. DEC 17, 1929 at Fairbury, NE.; m. Wynn Smithberger on SEP 20, 1959;
        Their Children:
        1. Nancy Elaine Nuckolls; b. MAY 4, 1961.
        2. David William Nuckolls; b. MAY 28, 1963.

Frank Morris CRAMB (1873-1876)
[152411796]

Frank was born DEC 20, 1873 at Morris, IL, and died JAN 2, 1876 (or 1878) of scarlet fever.

Edgar Myron CRAMB (1876-1947)
[152411797]

Edgar was born JUN 16, 1876 at Polo, IL., and died OCT 16, 1947. He married Iona CUYKENDALL on JUL 16, 1901. She was born OCT 17, 1976, and died NOV 19, 1949. No children.

Lewis Oliver CRAMB (1878-1906)
[152411798]

Lewis was born SEP 8, 1878 at Polo, IL., and died DEC 2, 1906, unmarried.

Mary Emma CRAMB (1880-1961)
[152411799]

Mary was born OCT 2, 1880 at Galena, IL., and died SEP 28, 1961. She married Dr. Byron Frank McALLISTER on JUN 27, 1901 at Kirksville, MO. He was born in Millersburg, IA. on MAR 1, 1870, and died JUL 18, 1943 at Fayetteville, Arkansas.
 Their Children:
  1. Ila Mildred McAllister; b. JUN 21, 1902 at Fayetteville; m. Marvin Eugene Newborn, Jr., on SEP 21, 1927; he was b. at Newport, AR. on SEP 16, 1904;
   Their Child:
    1. Marvin Eugene Newborn III; b. APR 14, 1930 at Memphis, TN.
  2. Max Franklin McAllister; b. MAY 2, 1904 at Fayetteville, AR.; m. FEB 12, 1932 to Bess Meiser at Little Rock; she was b. at Paragould, AR on DEC 5, 1907;
   Their Children:
    1. Max Franklin McAllister, Jr.; b. JAN 22, 1935 at Nashville, TN.
    2. John Garrison McAllister; b. FEB 23, 1938 at Nashville.
  3. Donald Byron McAllister; b. JUL 23, 1908 at Fayetteville, AR.; d. APR 18, 1952; m. Helen Hail on MAY 21, 1939 at Tulsa, OK.; she was b. at Springdale, AR. on APR 29, 1913;
   Their Children:
    1. Donald B. McAllister, Jr.; b. JAN 17, 1946.
    2. Mary Margaret McAllister; b. MAY 25, 1948.

Levi Kelsey CRAMB (1882-)
[15241179A]

Levi was born DEC 8, 1882 near Fairbury, NE. He married Carrie Halford ASHLOCK, daughter of William Jesse and Virginia (Fleming) Ashlock, on FEB 2, 1904. She was born FEB 4, 1872, and died MAR 26, 1948.
 Their Child.
  1. Virginia Lee Cramb [15241179A1] b. FEB 3, 1910 at Kirksville, MO.; m. Earle Dutton HALLOCK on MAY 18, 1933 at Dalles, Oregon; they resided at Butte, Montana;
   Their Child:
    1. William Lee Hallock; b. MAR 12, 1934 at Bend, Oregon; m. Lynn Garrett on JUL 23, 1965.

Arthur Benjamin CRAMB (1885-1960)
[15241179B]

Arthur was born JAN 5, 1885 near Fairbury, NE. , and died OCT 1, 1960 in Lakeland, Florida. He married
Lurah LOOMIS, daughter of George Webster and Marita (Clark) Loomis, on SEP 8, 1909 at Kirksville, MO.
Their Children:
1. Jean Kelsey Cramb [15241179B1] b. DEC 19, 1912; m. MAY 27, 1936 to Lester H.
   LOVELL, s/o Edgar & Melissa (Gould) Lovell.
   Their Children:
   1. Jo Jean Lovell; b. FEB 4, 1941.
   2. David Lovell; b. OCT 5, 1942; died young.
   3. Lester Michael Lovell; b. AUG 3, 1943.
   4. Mary Tamaria Lovell; b. JUL 21, 1947.
2. Helen May Cramb [15241179B2] b. DEC 14, 1914; m. AUG 2, 1937 to Bryce H.
   BONDURANT, s/o James & Lydia (Porter) Bondurant;
   Their Children:
   1. Stephan Bryce Bondurant; b. JAN 27, 1945.
   2. Brent Loomis Bondurant; b. JUL 20, 1949.

Myra Alphonsine CRAMB (1887-1936)
[15241179C]

Myra was born DEC 14, 1887 and died MAY 25, 1936. She never married.

References:

Ancestry of James Oliver Cramb & His Wife Lydia Alphonsine Kelsey
Letter to Ralph W. Cram from Dr. John L. Cramb (dtd. SEP 6, 1926)
Unpublished manuscript of Elmer Cram (file 167)

family of LEVI CRAM [15243321]

Levi CRAM [15243321]
b. OCT 3, 1806
d. JAN 18, 1892

m. JAN, 1826

Lovey BUNKER
B. SEP 29, 1804
D. SEP 20, 1875

1. Rufus [152433211] b. JUL 4, 1826
2. **Samuel Norris [152433212]** JUL 17, 1829
3. **Sylvester [152433213]** b. JUN 24, 1832
4. Mary [152433214] b. APR 17, 1834

Rufus Frederick CRAM (1826-1911)
[152433211]

Rufus was born JUL 4, 1826 in Newmarket, and died MAR 12, 1911 in Lawrence, MA. He married first Susan P. COLBEATH, daughter of William E. and Susan (Pinkham) Colbeath of Dover, NH. on APR 8, 1855. She was born MAY 10, 1824, in Dover, NH., and died MAR 20, 1892 in Lawrence, MA. He married second Emily C. STACKPOLE on JAN 15, 1893.

   His Children:
1. William Franklin [1524332111] b. SEP 21, 1857 in Newmarket; d. NOV 27, 1905 in Lawrence, MA; m. Mahala H. SMITH on DEC 29, 1877, a native of Blue Hills, ME. No children.
2. Emma Belle [1524332112] b. OCT, 1859 in Lawrence, MA; d. JUL 22, 1864 in Lawrence, MA.

Samuel Norris CRAM (1829-1905)*
[152433212]

Samuel Norris was born JUL 17, 1829 in Newmarket. He died APR 22, 1905 in Boston, MA. He married first Dolly C. LANGLEY, daughter of John and Mary (Willey) Langley of Durham Point, NH., in East Boston in MAY, 1854. She was born NOV 12, 1832 and died NOV 10, 1854. He married second Dorothy Jane WINSLOW, daughter of Samuel Winslow. She died in JAN, 1864.

   Their Children:
1. Georgianna [1524332121]
2. George Albert [1524332122] b. SEP 10, 1861.
3. Hattie Augusta [1524332123] b. MAR 9, 1863.

Sylvester CRAM (1832-1890)*
[152433213]

Sylvester was born JUN 24, 1832 in Newmarket, NH., and died DEC 22, 1890 in Exeter, NH. He was first married on JUL 11, 1860 in Dorchester, MA. to Sarah MOULTON, the daughter of William and Sarah (Chase) Moulton. She was born FEB 21, 1835 in Dorchester, MA. and died there DEC 29, 1863. He was married for the second time to Mary Wiggin JONES, daughter of Theophilous and Dolly (Thurston) Jones of Exeter, NH. on FEB 6, 1865 at Neponset, MA. She was born SEP 20, 1831 at Exeter, NH. and died JAN 19, 1914 in Greenwood, MA. There were children by both wives.

   Children by Sarah Moulton:
1. Sarah Lillias [1524332131] b. APR 2, 1861.
2. Emily Frances [1524332132] b. MAY 4, 1863.
   Children by Mary Jones:
3. **Elmer Herbert [1524332133]** b. SEP 25, 1865.
4. William Eugene [1524332134] b. JUL 13, 1867.

Mary Frances CRAM (1834-1922)
[152433214]

Mary was born APR 17, 1834 in Newmarket, NH. She died JUL 8, 1922 in Lowell, MA. She married Hiram KNOWLES, son of Simon and Abigail Knowles, on FEB 6, 1860. He was born NOV 28, 1819 in Campton, NH. and died there JAN 29, 1885. They resided in Campton, NH.

> Their Children:
> 1. William Knowles; b. FEB 15, 1864; m. Alice G. Emerson on SEP 27, 1888; dau. of Erastus and Mary D. (Goodhue) Emerson who was b. in 1866 in Peacham, VT.; they lived in Lowell, MA.; no children.
> 2. Edwin Knowles; b. NOV 26, 1865; m Sarah E. Greenwood on AUG 24, 1887 in Lowell, MA.; d/o William H. and Sarah Ann (Ridley) Greenwood of North Billerica, MA.
>> Their Children (tenth generation)
>> 1. Chester Knowles; b. OCT 24, 1890; d. APR 2, 1935 in Lowell, MA.
>> 2. Robert Knowles; b. NOV 8, 1893 in Lowell, MA.; m.1. Marion Oxton; m.2. Helen ----.

References

History of Newfields, NH.
History of Sandwich, NH.
Unpublished Manuscript by Elmer H. Cram (file 215)

family of Joseph Carr CRAM [15243324]

Joseph Carr CRAM [15243324]
b. JUL 12, 1819
d. MAY 14, 1885

1. Newell Augustus [152433241] b. AUG 25, 1840
2. Helen Frances [152433242] b. SEP 10, 1847

m.1. AUG 20, 1840

3. Emma Frances [152433243] b. DEC 23, 1849
4. Frank Herbert [152433244] b. DEC 22, 1850
5. Marianna [152433245] b. MAY 22, 1855

Sarah Hill SMITH
b. JUL 11, 1819
d. MAY 16, 1870

6. Ella Flora [152433246] b. DEC 24, 1861

m.2. JAN 31, 1871

7. George Henry [152433247] b. MAY 15, 1873
8. Cora Ann [152433248] b. JAN 27, 1875
9. Arthur Joseph [152433249] b. DEC 13, 1877

Clara E. SMITH
b. JUL 12, 1819
d. MAY 14, 1885 (?)

Newell Augustus CRAM (1840-1907)
[152433241]

Newell Augustus was born AUG 25, 1840 at Newmarket, NH. and died APR 20, 1907 at Lowell, MA. He married first Nancy Dean KEMPTON, who died in NOV, 1888. He married second Alice ROLLINS on JUN 2, 1889. She was the daughter of Joshua and Amanda (Clark) Rollins. She was born OCT 28, 1858 in Grantham, NH.

Helen Frances CRAM (1847-1848)
[15243324 2]

Helen Frances was born SEP 10, 1847 and died JAN 3, 1848 in Lowell, MA.

Emma Frances CRAM (1849-1857)
[152433243]

Emma Frances was born DEC 23, 1849 and died FEB 5, 1857.

Frank Herbert CRAM (1850-1926)
[152433244]

Frank Herbert was born DEC 22, 1850 and died APR 7, 1926. He married Jenny C. CHASE on DEC 23, 1879 in Pelham, NH. She was born SEP 5, 1854 and died JUL 30, 1931.

Marianna CRAM (1855- 1934)
[152433245]

Marianna was born MAY 22, 1855 and died JAN 31, 1934, not married. She was buried at Lowell, MA.

Ella Flora CRAM (1861-)
[152433246]

Ella Flora was born DEC 24, 1861. She married William P. COLBY on JUN 7, 1899. They had no children.

George Henry CRAM (1873)
[152433247]

George Henry was born MAY 15, 1873, and died AUG 6, 1873 in Dracut.

Cora Ann CRAM (1875-1934)
[152433248]

Cora Ann was born JAN 27, 1875, and died OCT 22, 1934 at Lowell, MA. She married Joseph ROCK on AUG 18, 1898 in Lowell.

Arthur Joseph CRAM (1877-)
[152433249]

Arthur Joseph was born DEC 13, 1877. He died unmarried.

Reference:

Unpublished manuscript of Elmer Cram (File 144)

family of Latinas Morse CRAM [15243413]

Latinas Morse CRAM [15243413]
b. OCT 31, 1810
d. APR 9, 1842

m. AUG 13, 1836

Ann HART
b. JUL 19, 1811
d. DEC 27, 1893

1. Susan F. [152434131] b. MAY 26, 1837
2. Mary Elizabeth [152434132] b. MAY 30, 1839
3. Amelia Ann [152434133] b. FEB 10, 1842 (twin)
4. Emily Ann [152434134] b. FEB 10, 1842 (twin)

Susan F. CRAM (1837-1863)
[152434131]

Susan F. was born MAY 26, 1837 on a farm south of Hillsboro, Illinois. She died APR 4, 1863 at Gillespie, IL. and is buried with her husband at Oak Grove Cemetery, Hillsboro. Susan married Charles F. VAN DORN on MAY 10, 1860. He was born APR 7, 1835, and died FEB 13, 1866.
   Their Child:
       1. Norman Phordice Van Dorn; b. FEB 9, 1862; d. AUG 11, 1862.

Mary Elizabeth CRAM (1839-)
[152434132]

Mary Elizabeth was born MAY 30, 1839 at South Hillsboro, IL. She married Oliver Spurr DALE, son of Archelaus and Jemima (Spurr) Dale, on DEC 15, 1864. Oliver was born MAY 10, 1839 at Otisfield, ME., and Died NOV 10, 1907 at Butler, IL. The Dale family moved from Maine to Illinois on MAR 24, 1856. Oliver enlisted in Company E, First Regiment, Illinois Volunteers, Cavalry on JUL 23, 1861.
   Their Children:
       1. a daughter born and died APR 14, 1866 at Hillsboro.
       2. Amelia Cram Dale; b. APR 4, 1868 at Pana, IL.; m. Thomas Knowlton Wescott
          on NOV 3, 1891; he was b. at Scituate, RI. on SEP 20, 1862 and d.
          SEP 7, 1912 at Butler, IL.
              Their Children (eleventh generation):
                  1. Nathan Hart Wescott
                  2. Faith Iola Wescott
                  3. Charles M. Wescott
                  4. Warren Dale Wescott
                  5. Mary Joyce Wescott
                  6. Lucy Gertrude Wescott

Amelia Ann CRAM (1842-1908)
[152434133]

Amelia Ann was born FEB 10, 1842 on a farm south of Hillsboro and died FEB 27, 1908 at North Hillsboro, IL. She was a twin of Emily Ann, below. She never married.

Emily Ann CRAM (1842-1865)
[152434134]

Emily Ann was born FEB 10, 1842 on a farm south of Hillsboro, and died OCT 1, 1865 at Hillsboro. She married James M. ARTHURS on JAN 24, 1864. He was born MAY 17, 1838 at Hillsboro and died JAN 4, 1903 at Hutchinson, Kansas. He married second Mollie Gunning of Hillsboro, who was born MAR 19, 1847 and died in 1935/6.
   Children by Emily:
       1. Walter Clifford Arthurs; b. NOV 29, 1864 at Hillsboro; d. SEP 16, 1928 at
          Mt. Vernon, IL.; m. Iola E. Settlemire of Litchfield, IL on NOV 28, 1888.

She was b. DEC 13, 1863 at Gillespie, IL., and d. APR 9, 1938 at St. Petersburg, FL. Walter was president of Mount Vernon Car Shop; they had no children, but adopted two; both were buried in private mausoleums at Mt. Vernon, IL.

Their Adopted Children:
1. David Clifford Arthurs
2. Emma Jane Arthurs

References:

Unpublished Manuscript of Elmer Cram (file 242)

family of Nathaniel Octavus CRAM [15243414]

Nathaniel Octavus CRAM [15243414]
b. MAR 9, 1813
d. MAR 10, 1894

m.1. JUL 6, 1837

Rebecca Ball KITTREDGE
b. MAY 10, 1815
d. MAY 12, 1861

m.2. JUN 30, 1863

Julia Abbie HODGKINS
b. MAR 28, 1834
d. MAR 11, 1915

1. George Octavus Kittredge [152434141] b. 1844
2. Nathaniel Gorton [152434142] b. 1845
3. Octavia Kittredge [152434143] b. 1852
4. Harry Kittredge [152434144] b. 1854
5. Grace May Kittredge [152434145] b. 1855

6. Octavia Lombard [152434146] b. 1864
7. Julia Hodgkins [152434147] b. 1866
8. Margaret Hodgkins [152434148] b. 1868

George Octavus Kittredge CRAM (1844-)
[152434141]

George was born JAN 2, 1844 at Portland, ME. Upon graduation from high school he took a clerical position with Chase Brothers and Co., importers of West India goods, remaining for a period of six years. He then became an office salesman for the Forest City Sugar Refining Co., and in 1867 was promoted to the office of treasurer. In 1887 the company was merged into the trust known as the American Sugar Refineries Company, and at this time he and George S. Hunt formed the firm of George S. Hunt & Cram, sugar brokers and agents in Portland for the American Sugar Refineries Co. This relationship continued until 1896, when Mr. Hunt died and was succeeded in business by his son, Arthur K. Hunt.

For three decades George owned and lived in the square brick house at 92 Spring Street. He was a member of St. Luke's Cathedral, in which he served as vestryman for a quarter of a century. He was a thirty-second degree Mason, and a member of the Ancient Landmark Lodge, Greenleaf Royal Arch Chapter, Portland Council, Portland Commandery, and all the bodies of the Scottish Rite.

He married first Ellen Hopkins SMITH, daughter of St. John and Susan (Hopkins) Smith, on SEP 13, 1871. She was born APR 2, 1848, at Portland, ME., and died there on NOV 29, 1899. He married second Etta ESTABROOK of Lexington, MA., on JUL 3, 1901 at St. Lukes Cathedral. She was the daughter of Joseph and Mary Estabrook, born at Acton, on APR 4, 1865, and died at Portland on AUG 26, 1939. Etta was the granddaughter of the Rev. Joseph Estabrook, pastor of the Congregational Church of Acton, MA., during the Revolutionary War. His name is carved on the Revolutionary Soldiers' Monument at Acton.
  Children:
1. Susan Hopkins [1524341411] b. JUN 30, 1872; m. JUN 3, 1903 to Dr.
    William Pearce COUES of Boston;
        Their Child:
            1. William Pearce Coues, Jr.
            2. Ursula Carne Coues; b. MAY 11, 914 in Boston
            3. Robert Wheaton Coues; b. in Portland about 1916 (twin)
            4. Mary Balch Coues; b. Portland ME. about 1916 (twin)
                d. one week later.

2. Elinor Kittredge [1524341412] b. JAN 22, 1875; m. MAY 27, 1903 to
    Harold Everett SANDERSON of Chicago;
        Their Children:
            1. George Kittredge Sanderson
            2. Edward Cram Sanderson

Nathaniel Gorton CRAM (1845-)
[152434142]

Nathaniel was born MAY 25, 1845 at Portland, ME. He married Sarah CHOAT on AUG 19, 1871. Records indicate he died at Berlin, NH.
> Their Child:
>> 1. Mary [1524341421] d. unmarried

Octavia Kittredge CRAM (1851-1852)
[152434143]

Octavia was born AUG 16, 1851 at Portland, ME., and died AUG 7, 1852 at Portland, age 11 months.

Harry Kittredge CRAM (1853-1854)
[152434144]

Harry Kittredge was born JUL 2, 1853 at Portland, ME., and died APR 22 (or 23), 1854 at Portland.

Grace May Kittredge CRAM (1855-1903)
[152434145]

Grace was born OCT 5, 1855 at Portland, ME. and died MAR 27, 1903 at Roxbury, MA.. She married Harry Augustus SMITH on DEC 26, 1876. He was born JUN 28, 1850 at Roxbury, MA. He married second Harriet H. (Fuller) Griggs of Brookline, MA.
> Children of Grace and Harry (tenth generation):
>> 1. Hammand Sargent Smith; b. FEB 25, 1878 at Roxbury; d. OCT 1913, unmarried.
>> 2. Eleanor Cram Smith; b. JUN 10, 1882 at Roxbury; m. David Pierce Settlemire on OCT 8, 1906; he was b. NOV 8, 1880 at Litchfield, IL. He married second Mrs. Geneva Lewis of Los Angeles, CA. on OCT 2, 1940 at Marshall, MN.
>>> Children of Eleanor & David (eleventh generation):
>>>> 1. Elizabeth Kittredge Settlemire; b. AUG 19, 1907 at Mt. Vernon, IL.; m.1. OCT 10, 1931, Arthur J. Zuber; they resided in Detroit, MI; divorced; m.2. Joseph Dunn of Brainerd, MN.
>>>> 2. Walter Lynn Settlemire; b. APR 8, 1911 at Mt. Vernon; m. Jeanette Faulkner on JUL 22, 1939.

Octavia Lombard CRAM (1864-1930)
[152434146]
Octavia was born JUL 9, 1864 in Portland, ME. She died MAR 15, 1930 in Brookline, MA, not married.

Julia Hodgkins CRAM (1866-1940)
[152434147)

Julia was born FEB 2, 1866 in Portland, ME. and died JUL 13, 1940 in Brookline, MA., not married.

Margaret Hodgkins CRAM (1868-1959)
[152434148]

Margaret was born APR 26, 1868 in Portland, ME. She died FEB 14, 1959, unmarried.

References:

Genealogical Dictionary of the State of Maine (p. 674)
Letter to the author from William Coues (dtd. JUN, 1990)
Unpublished Manuscript of Elmer Cram (file 242)

family of Calvin Hidden CRAM [15243416]

Calvin Hidden CRAM [15243416]
b. MAY 8, 1816
d. APR 5, 1893

m. SEP 10, 1839

Mary Insley WARREN
b. NOV 2, 1819
d. OCT 29, 1908

1. Charles Warren [152434161] b. SEP 3, 1840
2. Susan Maria [152434162] b. JUN 20, 1842
3. Mary Sophia [152434163] b. NOV 14, 1843
4. Calvin Morse [152434164] b. OCT 1, 1845
5. Pamelia [152434165] b. NOV 1 1855
6. Agnes Storer [152434166] b. FEB 1, 1859
7. Susan [152434167] b. JUN, 1862

Charles Warren CRAM (1840-1891)
[152434161]

Charles Warren was born SEP 3, 1840, in Portland, ME., and died in New York on JUN 6, 1891. He married Ella Brooks CARTER on APR 29, 1869. She was born MAY 1, 1849 in New York and died NOV 20, 1896.
    Their Children:
        1. Ethel [1524341611] b; FEB 25, 1869, in Paris, France; d. OCT 20, 1920, at New
            York City; m. her cousin, Edward Calvin MOEN on JUN 26, 1898; he was b.
            OCT 12, 1870 in New York City, and d. there OCT 20, 1920.
        2. Harward [1524341612] b. AUG 1, 1875, in Paris, France; m. his cousin, Kittie
            Lyall (Moen) Smith on MAY 25, 1919; he was her second husband; she was
            b. JUL 31, 1876.

Susan Maria CRAM (1842-1843)
[152434162]

Susan Maria was born JUN 20, 1842, and died SEP 3, 1843.

Mary Sophia CRAM (1843-1901)
[152434163]

Mary Sophia was born NOV 14, 1843, in Portland and died MAR 17, 1901, at New York City. She married Edwin Arthur MOEN of Worcester, MA. on AUG 11, 1864. He was born MAY 25, 1841, in Brooklyn, NY., and died DEC 2, 1903, at New York City.
    Their Children (in the 10th generation):
        1. Agnes Cram Moen; b. JUL 23, 1865, at Brooklyn; d. OCT 1, 1940, at
            Huntington, Long Island; m. Daniel Lawrence Shaw of New York City on
            JAN 30, 1890; he was b. JAN 30, 1854 and d. SEP 17, 1905.
        2. Rene Moen; b. NOV 29, 1867, at New York City; d. MAY 20, 1936, at New York
            City; m.1. Mary Miller Peabody (a widow - divorced); m.2. ----
            APR 13, 1934, a widow.
        3. Edward Calvin Moen; b. OCT 12, 1870 at New York City; d. OCT 20, 1920 at
            New York; m. Ethel Cram [1524341611] (his cousin) on JUN 26, 1898, the
            daughter of Charles Warren Cram;
                two daughters:
                        1. Yvonne; b. FEB 17, 1900; m. Frederick T.
                            Cunnerford on OCT 6, 1934; no children
                        2. Renee Moen; b. DEC 3, 1903, unmarried
        4. Kate Lyall Moen; b. JUL 31, 1876, at New York City; m.1. Howard Caswell Smith
            on OCT 26, 1898 - divorced; m.2. Harward Cram [1524341612] (her cousin) on
            MAY 25, 1919 - he was the son of Charles Warren Cram.

Their Children:
1. Caswell Moen Smith; b. JUL 10, 1899 in New York;
    m. Ellen Florence Marquick on OCT 6, 1926;
    she was b. SEP 4, 1898.
2. Howard Caswell Smith; b. MAR 2, 1901
3. Rene Moen Smith; b. AUG 15, 1903
5. Leclanche Moen; b. MAR 4, 1881, at New York City (appears in the files of Elmer
    Cram, but not the typescript of Hank Cram)
6. Mary Warren Moen; b. NOV 14, 1882, at New York City.

Calvin Morse CRAM (1845-1919)
[152434164]

Calvin Morse was born OCT 1, 1845, at Portland, and died SEP 12, 1919, in Bangor, ME. He married
Fannie DENNISON at Mechanic Falls, ME., on OCT 3, 1866. She was born JAN 15, 1847, at Norway,
ME. and died APR 21, 1931, at Bangor ME. They were both buried at Evergreen Cemetery at Portland,
ME.
Their Children:
1. Agnes Dennison [1524341641] b. SEP 3, 1870, at Mechanic Falls, ME.; m.
    George Thoreau THATCHER on DEC 7, 1892, at New York City; he was b.
    NOV 14, 1867, at Bangor, ME.
    Their Children:
    1. Hilda Ella Thatcher; b. SEP 27, 1893; m. Henry Jeffardo
        Wheelwright on JUL 26, 1919, at Bangor; he was b.
        JUN 28, 1892 at Bangor.
        Their Children:
        1. Hilda Thoreau Wheelwright;
            b. SEP 25, 1920.
        2. Henry Jeffardo Wheelwright, Jr.;
            b. MAR 14, 1922.
    2. Barbara Thatcher; b. JUL 29, 1895, at Bangor; m.
        Charles F. Guild at Bangor on APR 16, 1919; they
        later divorced;
        Their Children:
        1. Barbara Guild; b. SEP 4, 1920 at Boston
        2. Charles F. Guild, Jr.; b. JAN 25, 1922,
            at Boston.
2. Fannie Warren [1524341642] b. OCT 24, 1872, at Mechanic Falls, ME.; m.
    Alden Palmer Webster on MAY 6, 1896; he was b. at Orono, ME. on
    JUL 26, 1870, and d. MAY 23, 1935;
    Their Children:
    1. Prudence Webster; b. APR 7, 1897, at Orono; m.
        Clarence Alden Whitney on DEC 8, 1918;
        Their Child (in the 12th generation):
        1. Alden Webster Whitney;
            b. APR 25, 1919, at Orono, ME.
    2. Priscilla Webster; b. FEB 18, 1898, at Orono; m. Francis
        Menton Munroe in JUN, 1920 at Orono in a double
        wedding with her sister Frances; he was b. at Boston
        Their Children:
        1. Virginia Munroe; b. MAR 8, 1922 at
            Boston, MA.
        2. Priscilla Munroe; b. OCT 16, 1926, at
            Boston, MA.
    3. Frances Annie Webster; b. JUN 13, 1901 at Orono; m.
        James Price Brisco in JUN, 1920 at Orono in a double
        wedding (see above); he was b. in Detroit, MI.

Their Children:
1. Patricia Brisco; b. MAR 17, 1921,
   at Detroit, MI.; d. in 1924,
   at Santa Fe, NM.
2. Jane Price Brisco; b. DEC 14, 1925
   at Bangor, ME.
3. Polly Ann Brisco; b. JUL 8, 1928 at
   Bangor, ME.
4. Alden Eben Webster; b. OCT 12, 1907; not married.
3. Calvin E. [1524341643] b. OCT 14, 1878; d. OCT 24, 1878.

Permelia CRAM (1855-)
[152434165]

Permelia was called "Mellie." She was born NOV 1, 1855, at Portland, ME., and died APR 28, 1937 at Brookline, MA. She married George AGRY on SEP 8, 1880. He was born at Hallowell, ME. and died at Newton, MA. in 1927. They were buried at Evergreen Cemetery at Portland, ME.
Their Children:
1. George Agry, Jr.; b. APR 20, 1883 at Newton, MA.; m. Mercedes Smith on APR
   20, 1912 at New Orleans, LA.; she was b. SEP 7, 1883, at Columbus Texas.
   Their Child:
   1. Nancy Smith Agry; b. APR 1, 1919, at Newton.
2. Warren Cram Agry; b. NOV 17, 1889, at Newton, MA.; m. Marion Stetson of
   Newton on DEC 29, 1914; she was b. MAR 29, 1889.
   Their Children:
   1. Marion Fairbanks Agry; b. DEC 22, 1916, at Evanston,
      IL.; m. Dr. Robert Berson on APR 13, 1940 at
      Nashville, TN.
   2. Ann Agry; b. JUN 11, 1918, at Winnetka, IL
   3. Warren Agry, Jr.; b. JUN 9, 1923 at Winnetka, IL.

Agnes Storer CRAM (1859-1860)
[152434166]

Agnes was born FEB 1, 1859 (or NOV, 1858, according to Elmer Cram), and died JAN 24, 1860. She was buried at Evergreen Cemetery, Portland, ME.

Susan CRAM (1862-1863)
[152434167]

Susan was born JUN, 1862, and died SEP 21, 1863.

Reference:

Notes on the Cram Family and Some Related Families by Hank Cram
Unpublished manuscript of Elmer Cram (file 52)

family of William Clough CRAM [15251624]

William Clough CRAM [15251624]
b. NOV 4, 1830
d. DEC 15, 1899

1. Everett Fuller [152516241] b. APR 20, 1859
m.1. JUN 15, 1856
2. Rev. Elmer E. [152516242] b. JAN 10, 1862
3. William A. [152516243] b. AUG 18, 1869

Serena M. FULLER
b. NOV 27, 1836
d. MAY 1, 1880

4. Earl [152516244] b. AUG 27, 1881
m.2. OCT 29, 1880
5. Rushford Sayre [152516245] b. JAN 8, 1883
6. Arizona Victoria [152516246] b. JUL 25, 1884
Amelia A. ST. JOHN
7. Alonzo [152516247] b. SEP 19, 1888
b. APR 14, 1841
d.

Everett Fuller CRAM (1859-1946)
[152516241]

Everett Fuller was born APR 20, 1859 at the old family homestead at Hartland, (Freeborn County) MN. He died JAN 26, 1946, and was buried at Freeborn, MN. Everett married Sarah Maria MALLERY, daughter of Garrick Bolton & Susan (Essington) Mallery of Ohio. The marriage took place OCT 1, 1882 in Eurecka, MN. She was born FEB 26, 1855 in Noblesville, IN. and died MAY 4, 1942 at Blue Earth, MN.

Their Children:
1. Susanna Serena [1525162411] b. SEP 17, 1885 in Hartland, MN; m. Dave CHRISTIE, s/o Robert Bruce & Mary Jane (Johnson) Christie on JUN 20, 1917 at Blue Earth, MN.; he was b. FEB 25, 1880 at Goodell, (Boone County) IA.
2. Eva Maria [1525162412] b. JUL 29, 1889, in Hartland, MN.; m. Arthur Lee BASSETT on OCT 1, 1919; he was b. DEC 13, 1884, in Delawan, MN., and d. SEP 23, 1938.

Rev. Elmer Elsworth CRAM (1862-1935)
[152516242]

Elmer was born JAN 10, 1862 on the old homestead in Hartland, MN. and died JUN 5, 1935, in Minot, ND. He graduated from Carlton College in 1885, and was ordained at Gray Eagle, MN. on JUL 17, 1900, shortly after his first marriage. He taught school in MN. and ND. from 1890 to 1900. From 1900 to 1902 he served as pastor at Gray Eagle, Burtrum, MN., and Wimbledon, ND. In 1903 he filed a deed for land in Bottineau County, and for the next three years he was a farmer, serving as pastor as needed. He devoted his entire time to farming until 1918, when he began teaching school, a vocation he pursued for several years in Sherman and Mt. Rose Township, also at Deering, Dwight, Clyde, and Willow City. In 1925 he took a pastorate in McIntosh, MN. He retired in 1927, to live at Minot, ND.

Elmer married first Sarah FISK, daughter of Rev. William and Angeline S. (Drew) Fisk. They were married on MAY 1, 1890 in New Richland, MN., with Sarah's father performing the ceremony. She was born SEP 10, 1867 at Genever, KS., and died MAY 25, 1923 at Clyde, ND. She was buried at Renville, ND. Sarah's father, Rev. Fisk, came from VT., and was pastor of the Congregation Church of Freeborn, MN. He served in the Civil War, and after the war became a farmer (1865-1875) in KS. He died MAR 12, 1914 in Geneva, KS. His wife, Angeline Drew, died MAY 20, 1898. Both she and her husband were buried in Freeborn, MN.

Elmer married second Mrs. Dianna Blanch SHADDUCK in MacIntosh, MN. on MLAY 2, 1926. She was born NOV 11, 1871, and died MAY 25, 1923. There were no children by the second marriage.

Children of Elmer & Sarah Fisk (in the 10th generation):
1. Edith Maybelle [1525162421]
2. Kenneth Everett [1525162422]
3. Clifford Harlan [1525162423]
4. Elmer Elsworth [1525162424]
5. Wilber Fisk [1525162425]
6. William Arthur [1525162426]
7. Stephen Fuller [1525162427]
8. Serena Mae [1525162428]
9. Harold Franklin [1525162429]
10. Howard Lucine [152516242A]

William Arthur CRAM (1869-)
[152516243]

William was born on the old homestead in Hartland, MN. on AUG 16, 1869. He was educated in the public school of Hartland, attending high school at Fairbault, MN., and Carlton College in Northfield. He later graduated with honors from a school of telegraphy in WI. He received his first job on a branch line of the Illinois Central Railroad in MN. about 1890. He remained with the same railroad until his death on JUN 18, 1938 of acute indigestion at McComb. MS., at the age of 54 years. He was buried at Amite, LA.

William married Minnie E. GOAR, daughter of Levi Van Buren and Deliah B. (Fisher) Goar. They were married on JUL 6, 1893 at Ogden, IA. She was born SEP 1, 1866 in Tipton, IN. In 1904 the family moved to Cruger, MS, and later to Crystal Springs. In 1916 they moved to Amite, LA, and in 1921 their residence was Gulletts, LA. In 1933, Mr. Cram was transferred to McComb, MS. They were members of the Baptist Church, where Mr. Cram taught Sunday School.

Their Children (in the 10th generation):
1. Alma Beatrice [1525162431] b. AUG 2, 1894, in Hartland, MN.;
d. AUG 28, 1897, in Ogden, IA; buried in Freeborn, MN.
2. Lilah Lucille [1525162432] b. JUN 22, 1897, in Albert Lee, MN.; m.
Emmett E. HOUEY; he served in WWI; she was a teacher of home economics;
Their Children:
1, Miles William Houey; b. JUL 20, 1925 at Amite, LA.;
joined the Marines and served in WWII with the
Sixth Division at Okinawa.
2. Edwin E. Houey; b. JAN 1, 1927 at Amite, LA.;
attended University of Louisiana.
3. Leah Beth Houey; b. SEP 26, 1928 at Amite, LA.;
represented the Baptist Bible School
at Baton Rouge, LA.
3. Marion Leota [1525162433] b. AUG 3, 1900 in Albert Lee, MN.; d. OCT 26,
1906 in Tehula, MS.; buried at Lexington, MS.
4. Helen Estelle [1525162434] b. MAR 2, 1902, in Albert Lee, MN.;
m. Harry D. JOYNTON;
Their Children:
1. Harry Dudley Joynton, Jr.; b. SEP 21, 1925 in Macon,
GA.; was a student at University of Los Angeles in
1943, later attended Notre Dame University in IN.
2. Marion Altine Joynton; b. APR 7, 1929 in Amite, LA.;
was a teacher in the Daily Vacation Bible School.

Earl St. John CRAM (1881-)
[152516244]

Earl was born AUG 27, 1881, at the old homestead in Hartland, MN. He married Dora Henrietta WOLF on SEP 26, 1906 at Everett, WA. She was born AUG 23, 1884 in Hartland and died in APR, 1934 at Hartland, at her mother's home.

Their Children:
1. Dora Eunice [1525162441] b. JUN 8, 1908.
2. Irene Lorine [1525162442] b. FEB 14, 1914 (twin)
3. George Wolf [1525162443] b. FEB 14, 1914 (twin)

Rushford Syre CRAM (1883-1943)
[152516245]

Rushford was born JAN 8, 1883, at Albert Lee, MN., and died MAR 22, 1943 at Vancouver, WA. He was married SEP 23, 1912, wife unknown.
Their Children:
1. Rose Mary [1525162451] b. JUL 16, 1929; resided at St. Paul, MN.
2. John [1525162452] b. JAN 31, 1931.

Arizona Victoria CRAM (1884-)
[152516246]

Arizona was born JUL 25, 1884. She resided in Toronto, Canada. Nothing further is known about her.

Alonzo Wilson CRAM (1888-)
[152516247]

Alonzo was born SEP 19, 1888 in Alden, MN. He married Esther LONGSHORE. She was born JAN 10, 1891.
Their Children (in the 10th generation):
1. Raymond Alonzo [1525162471] b. NOV 26, 1909; m. Esther ANDERSON on JAN 12, 1934;
    Their Children (in the 11th generation):
    1. Lonne Ann [15251624711] b. OCT 11, 1936.
    2. Jack Owen [15251624712] b. JUN 30, 1938.
2. Alma Beatrice [1525162472] b. JAN 4, 1911; m. Manley OLSON in 1929;
    Their Children (all born at Albert Lee, MN.):
    1. Darienne Valdel Olson; b. SEP 8, 1930.
    2. Delane Richard Olson; b. AUG 26, 1931.
    3. Orland Craig Olson; b. AUG 26, 1936.
3. William (Bill) Earl [1525162473] b. DEC 15, 1916; m. Hazel TORGESON on SEP 28, 1934;
    Their Child:
    1. Lonna Byll [15251624731] b. MAY 28, 1937.
4. Cleo Amy [1525162474] b. JUN 11, 1922; d. FEB 9, 1926.
5. Marlene Kee [1525162475] b. JUL 7, 1935.

References:

Records of Mrs. Everett Fuller Cram
Unpublished manuscript of Elmer Cram (file 307)

family of Frank Edward CRAM [15251887]

Frank Edward CRAM [15251887]
b. JAN 5, 1847
d. JUL 1, 1924

m. NOV 24, 1870

Ida A. YOUNG
b. APR 10, 1850
d.

1. Natt Allen [152518871] b. OCT 26, 1871.
2. Frank Guy [152518872] b. MAR 13, 1876.
3. Alroy Blake [152518873] b. OCT 8, 1881.

Natt Allen CRAM (1871-1929)*
[152518871]

The files of Elmer Cram relate to this man as both as Natt and Nathaniel. The Genealogical and Family History of the State of New Hampshire (p. 1391) lists his name only in the abbreviated form. A letter from Ruth (Mrs. Clifton) Cram clears up the confusion. She relates that at his birth, he was "officially" named Natt A. Cram. Natt was his full given name and the A. was simply an initial, signifying no middle name. When he was married, Natt decided the A. should stand for something and adopted "Allen."

Natt was born in Pittsfield on OCT 21, 1871 and died there FEB 23, 1929. He was educated in the public schools and graduated from Pittsfield High School. After leaving school he was a bookkeeper, and later read law two years with Pattee & George, attorneys, in Manchester, NH. On APR 1, 1899, he was appointed postmaster of Pittsfield, and after serving four years was appointed for a second term. He was a member of Corinthian Lodge, Knights of Pythias of Pittsfield and Ancient Free and Accepted Masons.

He married Edith Elizabeth SWETT of Pittsfield, daughter of David Knowlton and Elizabeth (Lane) Swett, on JUN 3, 1893 (Elmer Cramsays 1903). She was born JUL 24, 1873, and living in Pittsfield in 1947.
    Their Children:
        1. Clifton Swett [1525188711] b. APR 1, 1905 in Pittsfield.
        2. Ruth Elizabeth [1525188712] b. AUG 1, 1912 at Pittsfield.

Frank Guy CRAM (1876-1921)
[152518872]

Frank Guy was born MAR 13, 1876 and died in OCT, 1921 in Birmingham, Alabama, unmarried.

Alroy Blake CRAM (1882-1940)
[152518873]

Alroy Blake was born on OCT 8, 1882 at Pittsfield and died FEB 2, 1940 in St. Petersburg, Florida. The Genealogical and Family History of The State of New Hampshire incorrectly spells his name, "Alvoy." Ruth Cram verifies the spelling of his name through an old family Bible. Alroy married Aretta CROWELL. Nothing is known of where they lived, but it is reported that there were no children. Alroy was cremated and his ashes buried at West Dennis, MA.

References:

Genealogical & Family History of The State of New Hampshire (p.1391)
Letters to the Author from Ruth (Staniels) Cram (dtd. JAN 8, 1994 & JAN 21, 1994)
Unpublished Manuscript of Elmer Cram (files 113 & 235)
Who's Who of America's Crams

family of Rev. William Augustine CRAM [15253273]

William Augustine CRAM [15253273]
b. JUL 10, 1837
d. AUG 28, 1908

1. **Ralph Adams** [152532731] b. DEC 16, 1863
m. NOV 15, 1862   2. William Everett [152532732] b. JUN 22, 1871
3. Marion Blake [152532733] b. FEB 15, 1876

Sarah Elizabeth BLAKE
b. SEP 28, 1840
d. MAY 2, 1927

Ralph Adams CRAM (1863-1942)*
[152532731]

Ralph Adams was born DEC 16, 1863 in Hampton Falls, and died SEP 22, 1942 in Peter Bent Brigham Hospital in Boston from complications of pneumonia after an illness of several weeks.

The best description of his life may be found in Current Biography - 1942. It has been edited somewhat to reduce its volume:

"In his youth he had no formal religious training. His father was a retired Unitarian clergyman who had become a 'mystical philosopher,' and his mother was a woman of 'keen rationalistic convictions (albiet a poet).' He attended the Exeter High School and showed some talent in drawing. He was also interested in houses and city planning at an early age, and when at 15 he received C. J. Richardson's House Building his 'amorphous' impulses were 'crystallized into an architectural sense.'

"At seventeen, after he was graduated from high school, Ralph was taken by his father to Boston and placed in an architect's office to learn the business. He lived on Dwight Street in a boarding house inhabited by students of music, elocution, and architecture, 'a fuzzy youth fresh from the precincts of a Unitarian parsonage in a little New Hampshire town.' He remained in the architect's office for five years and received the only professional education he ever had. It was a large office with ten draftsmen, but it had no blueprints, typewriters, or telephones; all the drawings were traced by hand, and the letters were written in longhand.

" Cram's first appearance in print was a passionate appeal to the Boston Transcript urging the city to preserve Trinity Church from the 'vandals' who wanted to build a four-story triangular apartment house in front of it.

"In 1886 Cram made the first of his many trips abroad to study the architecture of Europe and to attend the Wagner festival at Bayreuth. On his return his second literary venture was a letter extolling a pre-Raphaelite exhibition. This brought him an offer of the position of art critic for The Transcript, and after some hesitation Cram accepted it. He held it for two years, until he clashed with the editors over his unwillingness to praise pictures in the galleries of good advertisers.

"When Cram left The Transcript he set about looking for some means to make a living. For a time he 'eked out a precarious existence' by doing various odd jobs: designing wallpapers, writing and illustrating articles for the Decorator and Furnisher . . . and 'helping kind ladies with other designs for such decorating and furnishing as they might need.' He started a project for a magazine that would encompass all the arts, but the venture collapsed and Cram accepted an offer to go to Europe as tutor to a friend's stepson.

"Cram did not find his new position very congenial and in Rome, with the agreement of his patron, he went off with some friends to study the mosaics in Rome, Palermo and

Monreale. At a midnight mass on Christmas Eve, in the Church of San Luigi dei Francesi at Rome, Cram was inspired with the desire to become a Catholic. As soon as he returned to Boston he went to the Church of St. John the Evangelist and placed himself in the hands of Father Hall for instruction. Shortly afterward he was baptized and in due course he received the Sacrament of Confirmation (at St. John the Evangelist Episcopal Church).

"Back in the United States, Cram decided to open an office with a partner, and in 1890 the firm of Cram and Wentworth was established. . . Two years later the firm's name was changed to Cram, Wentworth and Goodhue to accommodate a new associate with whom it was easier to share the profits than to promise a steady salary. (In 1913, after Wentworth died, and Goodhue opened an office for himself, the firm became Cram and Ferguson)

"Early in his career Cram decided that if his young firm was to achieve anything in the realm of architecture it must pick some undeveloped field and make it its own. After a careful survey, and after consulting his personal interests, Cram decided to concentrate on church building, which at the time was in a bad state. He decided to draw together the threads of Gothic development where it had been broken by other influences and 'take up the English Gothic at a point where it was cut off during the reign of Henry VIII and go on from that point, developing the style England had made her own and along what might be assumed to be logical lines, with due regard to the changing conditions of contemporary culture.'

"In the following years Cram's firm became more and more noted for its churches, although Cram did not confine himself to churches alone. His most famous church is the still uncompleted Cathedral of St. John the Divine in New York City. The original plans for this Cathedral were made by Heins and La Farge and were for a Romanesque style with Byzantine details. The cornerstone had been laid in 1892. When Christopher Grant La Farge died in 1911, Cram was called in to continue the work. He redesigned the entire plan and changed the style to 'thirteenth century French Gothic with a strong final accent of English Gothic. Under Cram's planning the Cathedral became 601 feet long, second only to St. Peter's in Rome in length and area. 'My idea of a cathedral,' Cram explained, ' is that it will be a great showing forth of the basic fact that religion is of the very essence of human life and that any community that disregards it will disintegrate, and any civilization that follows the same course will perish.'

"Among the other churches in whose design Cram has participated are St. Thomas' Protestant Episcopal Church at Fifth Avenue and Fifty-Third Street and Christ Church at Park and Sixtieth Street, both in New York City. He designed also the four million dollar East Liberty Presbyterian Church in Pittsburgh. Cram's designs for institutions other than churches also won considerable national interest and acclaim. He designed the graduate school buildings, several dormitories, and the chapel at Princeton University, and with Goodhue he designed the chapel, riding hall, post headquarters and other buildings of the United States Military Academy at West Point.

"Cram did not stop his literary career when he left the Transcript. Among his early work is some verse and the beginning of an Arthurian epic, Excalibur, which Cram still thinks one of the best things he has ever written. He was cofounder of the magazine Commonweal, and the author of a number of books on architecture and miscellaneous subjects, among them Church Building (1901); The Gothic Quest (1907); The Substance of Gothic (1917); Walled Towns (1919); The Catholic Church and Art (1929); Convictions and Controversies (1935); My Life in Architecture (1936) and The End of Democracy (1937).

"Ralph Adams Cram is a fellow of the American Academy of Arts and Sciences, the Royal Society of Arts, the Medieval Academy of America, the Boston Society of Architects (past president), and many other professional art and architectural organizations.a He was head of the department of Architecture of the Massachusetts

Institute of Technology and chairman of the Boston City Planning Board for seven years (1914-21). Although he attended no institutions of higher learning he has several honorary Litt. D.'s from Princeton, Williams, Notre Dame and Rollins College. He has an honorary LL.D. from Yale and was elected to honorary membership in the Harvard University chapter of Phi Beta Kappa.

"Cram is five feet seven inches tall and weighs 150 pounds. He is fond of chess and gardening and has a talent for amateur acting."

He married Elizabeth Carrington READ, daughter of Cap. Clement Carrington Read, C.S.A. of Virginia, in New Bedford, Massachusetts on SEP 20, 1900. She was born JUN 10, 1873 and died SEP 30, 1943.
Their Children:
1. Mary Carrington [1525327311]
2. **Ralph Wentworth [1525327312]** b. SEP 18, 1904
3. Elizabeth Strudwick [1525327313]

William Everett CRAM (1871-1947)
[152532732]

William was born in Hampton Falls on JUN 27, 1871 and died JUL 8, 1947. He was a farmer and an author, with his most notable works being: Little Beasts of Field and Wood (1900), American Animals (with Witmer Stone, 1902), More Little Beasts of Field and Wood (1912), and Time and Change. He was also a contributor to scientific and literary magazines.

He married Esther Lakin SANBORN of West Roxbury, MA. on JUN 30, 1909. He lived out his life in Hampton Falls.
Their Children:
1. Margaret Lakin [1525327321] m. Everett W. CLARK of Newburyport; four children.
2. Joseph Leavitt Sanborn [1525327322] wife unknown; five children.

Marion Blake CRAM (1876-1974)
[152532733]

Marion was born FEB 15, 1876 and died in 1974 at the age of 98 years. She married J. Edward BROWN in DEC, 1900 and that they resided in Hampton Falls, NH. He was a farmer. After her husband's death in 1921 Marion supported herself by teaching piano in the community.
Their Children:
1. Elizabeth Graham Brown; b. NOV 29, 1901; d. MAR 18, 1991; m. on Holy
    Saturday, 1924 to Ernest Follis Wall.
2. Dorothy Blake Brown; b. 1904; d. 1930; unmarried.

References:

Current Biography 1942 (pp. 163-5)
Exeter NH. News-Letter Newspaper (AUG 28, 1908 issue)
Letter to the author from Edward Wall (dtd. SEP 1, 1993)
Letter to the author from Ralph A. Cram II (dtd. AUG 4, 1993)
Who's Who In New England- 1938 (p.284)

family of Charles Sanborn CRAM [15257312]

Charles Sanborn CRAM [15257312]
b. SEP 10, 1823
d. NOV 10, 1904

m.1. APR 10, 1849

Eliza Jane PRESCOTT
b. MAY 16, 1826
d. AUG 10, 1881

m.2. JAN 18, 1868

Margaret SMITH
b. JUN 4, 1850
d. DEC 18, 1929

1. Angelo Prescott [152573121] b. NOV 6, 1850.
2. Angelina Prescott [152573122] b. NOV 22, 1853.
3. **Victor Prescott [152573123]** b. 1857.
4. Victoria [152573124] b. SEP 19, 1858.
5. Charlesetta Prescott [152573125] b. FEB, 1861.
6. Georgetta Prescott [152573126] b. MAY 8, 1864.
7. Charles Sanborn [152573127] b. APR 3, 1866.
8. Heber [152573128] b. JUL 13, 1869.

9. Clara Smith [152573129] b. DEC 2, 1868.
10. Alexander Smith [15257312A] b. OCT 2, 1873.
11. John Smith [15257312B] b. OCT 18, 1875.
12. George Smith [15257312C] b. NOV 18, 1877.

Angelo Prescott CRAM (1850-1897)
[152573121]

Angelo was born NOV 6, 1850 at Meredith, NH. and died JUL 12, 1897 in Chicago. He first married Joanna DOFFORD, daughter of Joseph Foster and Charlotte (Lord) Dofford, on OCT 12, 1874. She was born NOV 11, 1856 at Durham County, England, and died JAN 5, 1943 at San Bernardino County, CA.; They divorced and she married second Charles Shorts. He married second Mary WALLACE.
>   Children by Joanna Dofford:
>> 1. Joseph William Dofford [1525731211] b. FEB 27, 1876 in Munroe, Sevier County, UT.; d. SEP 20, 1931 in Boise, Ada County, ID.; m. Elizabeth HENDERSON.
>> 2. Violet Charlotte Dofford [1525731212] b. APR 3, 1878 in Munroe, Sevier County, UT.; m. Joseph HENDRICKSON on NOV 17, 1897.
>   Child by Mary Wallace:
>> 3. Charles Wallace [1525731213] b. APR 9, 1889 at Rock Springs, Sweetwater County, WY; m.1. Olive GEORGE; they were divorced with no children; m.2. Ethel May THOMPSON on AUG 18, 1918 at Cheyenne, WY.; she was b. OCT 4, 1898 at Salt Lake City, UT., the d/o Joseph Albert & Mary Adeline (Evans) Thompson; she d. MAY 24, 1942 at San Bernardino, CA.; he m.3. Myrtle May MACK on NOV 13, 1944 at Las Vegas, NV; she was b. JUN 11, 1908 in Cosmopolis, Grays Harbor County, WA., the d/o Joseph and Addie Ellen (Polly) Mack; Charles was her second husband, her first - George Charles Murbarger.
>>>   Children by Ethel (in the eleventh generation):
>>>> 1. Charles Wallace [15257312131] b. NOV 16, 1919 at Garfield, Salt Lake City, UT.
>>>> 2. Albert Angelo [15257312132] b. AUG 14, 1921; d. AUG 14, 1921.
>>>> 3. Ethel Marie [15257312133] b. FEB 4, 1923.
>>>> 4. Mary Jane [15257312134] b. DEC 13, 1924.
>>>> 5. Helen Lorraine [15257312135] b. OCT 15, 1926; d. 1927.
>>>> 6. LeRoy Elwood [15257312136] b. APR 8, 1931.
>>>> 7. Joan Margarite [15257312137] b. OCT 5, 1932.
>>>> 8. Eva Lou [15257312138] b. APR 22, 1936 at Loma Linda, CA.; d. MAY 15, 1937 at San Bernardino, CA.
>>>> 9. Michael Allen [15257312139] b. JUL 6, 1946 at San Bernardino.

Angelina Prescott CRAM (1853-1946)
[152573122]

Angelina was born NOV 22, 1853 at Brooklyn, NY. and died FEB 24, 1946. She married Fareman Jack BRADLEY of Owyhee, Malheur County, OR. on FEB 3, 1893. He was born AUG 31, 1831 at

Cambridge, Guernsey County, Ohio, the son of James and Mary (Laurence) Bradley, and died MAY 10, 1922 at Nyssa, OR.   She died at Nampa Canyon, ID. on FEB 24, 1946.   They were both buried at Owyhee, OR. Fareman was a cattleman and a member of the Baptist church.

Their Children:

1. Maude Eliza Bradley; b. DEC 29, 1873 at Minerville, Beaver County, UT; m. Isaiah N. Clark; she d. MAY 10, 1903 at Owyhee, OR.
2. Mary Bradley; b. AUG 21, 1874 at Round Valley, Beaver County, UT; d. AUG 21, 1874.
3. Jane Bradley; b. at Round Valley, UT.
4. Martha M. Bradley; b. DEC 4, 1877 at Round Valley; m. N. B. Matthiessen.
5. Charles C. Bradley; b. NOV 25, 1882 at Mesa, Maricopa County, AZ; m. Belle Aldredge; they resided at Nyssa, OR.
6. Margaret Bradley; b. at Bisbee, AZ.; m.1. Harry T. Pratt; m.2. Paul Besly.

Victor Prescott CRAM (1857-1927)*
[152573123]

Victor was born MAR 21, 1857 in Montgomery, Alabama and died APR 19, 1927 at Salt Lake City, Utah. He married Esther Almyra JOHNSON, daughter of William Derly and Jane C. (Brown) Johnson, on DEC 17, 1879. She was born MAY 2, 1860 at Florence, Douglas County, Nebraska;

Their Children:

1. Victor Dee [1525731231] b. OCT 6, 1880.
2. Mark William [1525731232] b. MAR 18, 1882.
3. Vivian Etta [1525731233] b. DEC 13, 1883.
4. Paul Rufus [1525731234] b. 1885 at Huntington, Emory County; d. aged two weeks.
5. Ada Bertha [1525731235] b. JAN 3, 1887.
6. Lulu Prescott [1525731236] b. JAN 4, 1890.
7. Charles Chester [1525731237] b. in 1892; d. at the age of two weeks in Huntington.
8. Eliza [1525731238] b. 1893; d. at the age of four months.
9. Alberta [1525731239] b. NOV 28, 1894.
10. Woodruff Bryan [152573123A] b. AUG 11, 1897.
11. Owen Prescott [152573123B] b. JUL 17, 1900.
12. Thelma [152573123C] b. MAY, 1903 at Provo, UT.; d. in 1903 in Provo.
13. Alton Brooks [152573123D] b. MAR 21, 1905; d. MAY 2, 1905 in Provo.

Victoria CRAM (1858-1907)
[152573124]

Victoria was born SEP 19, 1858 at Moline, Rock Island, Illinois and died APR 12, 1907 at Owyhee, Malheur County, Oregon. She married Joseph JUDD.

Charlesetta Prescott CRAM (1861-1917)
[152573125]

Charlesetta was born FEB 10, 1861 at St. Louis, Missouri, and died FEB 14, 1917. She married William Derby JOHNSON on MAY 29, 1879.

Their Children:

1. Leonard Charles Johnson; b. DEC 7, 1880 at Kanab, UT.; d. there d. SEP 19, 1882.
2. Moneta Johnson; b. JAN 29, 1882 at Kanab, UT.; in 1946 she was living in Los Angeles, CA.; m. Charles Richard Fillerup, s/o Anders Peter & Caroline (Rasmussen) Fillerup, on JUN 1, 1898, at Salt Lake City; he was b. at Provo, UT. on NOV 11, 1873 and d. at Flagstaff, UT.; he was buried at Snowflake, AZ.; he was a member of the staff at the University of Arizona as Agricultural Commissioner for the U.S. Dept. of Agriculture from 1913 to 1936; prior to that time he taught school in Mexico;

Their Children:
1. Wilma Caroline Fillerup; b. MAR 8, 1900 at Colonia Diaz, Mexico; m. JUN 1, 1920 to Frederick Andrew Turley; he was a cattle man and dude ranch owner at Airpine, AZ.
2. Kathe Moneta Fillerup; b. JUL 22, 1901 at Colonia Diaz; m. DEC 23, 1921 to James Robert Freeman, s/o James & Mary Ellen (Rowe) Freeman; he was b. NOV 5, 1899 at Snowflake, AZ. family moved to Los Angeles in 1923 and James was employed by a Gunite construction firm there;
    Their Child:
    1. James Robert Freeman; b. OCT 17, 1922 at Cottonwood, AZ; BS degree from California Institute of Technology; commissioned as Ensign in U.S. Navy MAR 8, 1945; served as communication officer on U.S.S. Montauk.
3. Charles Richard Fillerup; b. MAR 5, 1903 at Colonia Diaz; m. JAN 16, 1925 to Dorothylou Jones; he was an instructor at the National Automotive School at Los Angeles (in 1946).
4. Leonard Atmone Fillerup; b. NOV 7, 1904 at Colonia Diaz; m. APR 30, 1930 to Bessy Laverne Kirkham; he was a certified public accountant in Los Angeles.
5. Linnie Charlesetta Fillerup; b. SEP 22, 1908 at Colonia Diaz; m. DEC 21, 1928 to Herbert Ray Montieth a real estate dealer in Mesa, AZ.
6. Helen Mae Fillerup; b. JUN 14, 1908 at Colonia Diaz; m. MAY 1, 1934 to Kermit Davidson, who was in medical school in Los Angeles in 1946.
7. Genevieve Fillerup; b. NOV 25, 1909 at Colonia Diaz; m. MAY 3, 1930 to Hugh Pettingill Taylor, a certified public account in Los Angeles.
8. Vilda Fillerup; b. SEP 27, 1911 at Colonia Diaz; m. MAR 9, 1937 to Walter Bennett Sayner, who was an engineer in Rye, NY. in 1946.
9. Fernith Fillerup; b. DEC 3, 1913 at Cochise, AZ.; m. DEC 10, 1931 to Otto Wayne Palmer, a farmer in Taylor, Navajo County, AZ.
10. Derby Andrew Fillerup; b. OCT 20, 1915 at Cochise, AZ.; m.1. on FEB 2, 1934 to Vera Jeanette Laney; m.2. Margarette McNeil on DEC 4, 1940; died in service with the U.S. Navy on FEB 25, 1945; buried at the Naval Memorial Cemetery at Halawa, Oahu, Hawaiian Islands.
11. Otho Wilfred Fillerup; b. AUG 7, 1918 in Snowflake, AZ.; m. JUN , 1941 to Maudie Alice Pyle; served during W.W.II with the U.S. Army; after discharge was employed with Federal Farm Security Administration in Riverside, CA. (in 1946).
12. Phyllis Fillerup; b. FEB 22, 1922 (a twin) at Snowflake, AZ.; private secretary for a physician; not married as of 1946.
13. Ruby Fillerup; b. FEB 22, 1922 (a twin) at Snowflake, AZ.; secretary in a commercial firm; not married as of 1946.
3. Ivan Clare Johnson; b. MAR 24, 1884 at Knab; m. Anna Elisa Frederickson on OCT 11, 1906; she d. MAR 6, 1937 at Phoenix, AZ.
4. Lucy Ann Johnson; b. AUG 23, 1885 at Colonia Diaz, Chihuahua, Mexico; m. Bernard Russell Darwin on FEB 23, 1918.
5. Elmer Otho Johnson; b. AUG 17, 1887 at Colonia Diaz; m. Kathlyn Viola Tarwater on FEB 21, 1918.
6. Winnie Johnson; b. MAY 4, 1888 at Colonia Diaz; m. Francis Marion Whiting on JUN 8, 1910; she d. at Albuquerque, NM. on OCT 7, 1920.

7. Beryl Johnson; b. AUG 28, 1891 at Colonia Diaz; m. Ernest J. Whiting on SEP 30, 1913.
8. Roy Prescott Johnson; b. JUN 14, 1893 at Colonia Diaz; m. Eliza Anderson on JUL 22, 1916.
9. Beatrice Johnson; b. MAR 29, 1897 at Colonia Diaz, and d. there SEP 13, 1904.
10. Zenona Johnson; b. APR 16, 1901; m. John Valentine Barrett on SEP 10, 1922.
11. Una Johnson; b. FEB 13, 1903 at Colonia Diaz and d. there on FEB 28, 1903.
12. Beulah Eliza Johnson; b. AUG 2, 1904; m. Albert Moon on JUL 3, 1923; she d. AUG 17, 1945 at Tucson, Pima County, AZ.

Georgetta Prescott CRAM (1864-1870)
[152573126]

Georgetta was born MAY 8, 1864, and died APR 6, 1870 at Salt Lake City.

Charles Sanborn CRAM (1866-1930)
[152573127]

Charles was born APR 13, 1866 at Salt Lake City, and died JAN 24, 1930 at Kanab, Utah. He married Ruth Elizabeth GREENHALGH, daughter of Thomas and Mary (Moorcroft) Greenhalgh. She was born JUN 19, 1866 at Albany County, New York.

Heber CRAM (1869-1931)
[152573128]

Heber was born JUL 13, 1869 in Salt Lake City and died APR 5, 1931 at Flagstaff, Arizona. He married Bertha HALLIDAY, daughter of George Franklin and Rachel Marinda (Holman) Halliday. She was born JUN 2, 1878 at Pleasant Grove, UT. and died DEC 23, 1915 at Kanab, UT.
    Their Children:

1. Don Prescott [1525731281] b. AUG 17, 1900 at Kanab, UT.; m. Chloris HAMBLIN on APR 6, 1920.
    Their Children (eleventh generation):
    1. Helen [15257312811] b. FEB 26, 1921 at Kanab. UT.; m. James Edward STARR, s/o Carlton A. & Audree (Wilder) Starr, on AUG 16, 1941 at Santa Anna, Orange County, CA.; he was b. FEB 9, 1922 in Hawaii; James served in W.W.II.;
        Their Children:
        1. James Edward Starr; b. OCT 15, 1942 at Fullerton, Orange County, CA.
        2. Carole Jean Starr; b. MAR 21, 1944 at Anaheim, Orange, County, CA.
    2. Don Prescott [15257312812] b. OCT 3, 1922 in Kanab, UT.
    3. Ora Fae [15257312813] b. DEC 11, 1924 in Delta, UT.; d. MAR 15, 1931 in Anaheim, Orange County, CA., buried in Kanab, UT.
    4. Bertha Gae [15257312814] b. JUL 12, 1926 in Delta, UT.; d. DEC 15, 1926 in Delta; buried in Kanab, UT.
    5. Walter Ray [15257312815] b. JAN 28, 1928 in Delta, UT.
2. Ora Merinda [1525731282] b. AUG 2, 1903 in Kanab; d. JAN 1, 1904 in Kanab.
3. Carl [1525731283] b. DEC 2, 1910 in Kanab, and d. there on DEC 23, 1910.
4. Georgia [1525731284] b. AUG 21, 1915 in Kanab; d. AUG 211, 1915 in Kanab.

Clara Smith CRAM (1868-1904)
[152573129]

Clara was born DEC 21, 1868 in Salt Lake City. She married David BULLOCK. He died OCT 22, 1904.

Alexander Smith CRAM (1868-1904)
[15257312A]

Alexander was born OCT 21, 1873 in Salt Lake City. he married Margaret SWAPP.

John Smith CRAM (1875-1933)
[15257312B]

John was born OCT 18, 1875 at Johnson, Kane County, Utah. He died JAN 15, 1933 at Orderville, Utah. John married Fannie BUNTING, daughter of James Lovett and Harriet (Dye) Bunting, on JUL 21, 1898. He was born MAY 26, 1881 in Kanab, UT.
> Their Children:
> 1. Eldred John [15257312B1] b. FEB 19, 1899 at Kanab and d. there the same day.
> 2. Margaret [15257312B2] b. JUL 26, 1900; m. Lester Findlay LITTLE on
>   JUN 25, 1920.
> 3. Donald Bunting [15257312B3] b. NOV, 1903 at Kanab, UT.; m. NOV 3, 1930
>   Marva WHIPPLE, d/o Charles & Annie Catherine (Hansen) Whipple; she was b.
>   FEB 4, 1909 in Colonia Juarez, Chihuahua, Mexico;
>   > Their Children (eleventh generation):
>   > 1. Kathlene [15257312B31] b. MAY 8, 1931 in Kanab;
>   >   d. the same day.
>   > 2. Marleen [15257312B32] b. JAN 20, 1933 at Kanab.
>   > 3. Marva Don [15257312B33] b. MAY 23, 1935 at Kanab.
>   > 4. Valden [15257312B34] b. JAN 23, 1940 at Kanab.
> 4. La Von [15257312B4] b. NOV 18, 1905; m. Easton BLACKBURN on AUG 22, 1929.
> 5. Milton Bunting [15257312B5] b. SEP 3, 1907; m. Evelyn JENSEN on FEB 2, 1933.
> 6. Theo James [15257312B6] b. SEP 2, 1909; d. OCT 7, 1912 at Kanab, UT.
> 7. Clara [15257312B7] b. OCT 24, 1911; m. La Mar Orson PRATT on SEP 8, 1930.
> 8. Locklon Bunting [15257312B8] b. SEP 6, 1913; m. Afton Mar JOHNSON
>   in MAY, 1933.
> 9. Claude Bunting [15257312B9] b. APR 23, 1916 at Kanab; d. the same day.
> 10. Smith Bunting [15257312BA] b. JUN 24, 1917; m. Reva OLSEN in JAN, 1939.
> 11. Owen Bunting [15257312BB] b. JAN 10, 1921; m. Doris SHELTON.
> 12. Norman Bunting [15257312BC] b. MAR 8, 1923; not married in 1946.

George Smith CRAM (1877-)
[15257312C]

George was born NOV 18, 1877 at Kanab, Utah. He married Amarilla RIGGS, daughter of Albert Ensign and Margaret Ann (Stewart) Riggs, on JUN 11, 1900. She was b. FEB 28, 1878 in Kenab.
> Their Children (tenth generation):
> 1. Anna [15257312C1] b. FEB 17, 1909 in Kanab; m. Harold B. FOWTS.
>   > Their Children:
>   > 1. Gwen (?) Fowts; b. AUG 2, ---- (Elmer Cram's file 57
>   >   lists her birthdate as 1909, but that cannot be correct
>   >   if her mother's birthdate is accurate)
>   > 2. Hal Bert Fowts; b. MAR 5, 1927 at Ogden, UT.
> 2. George Riggs [15257312C2] b. JUL 20, 1902 at Kenab; m. Ruth MANNING, d/o
>   William and Lettie (Farr) Manning, on JUL 2, 1927;
>   > Their Children:
>   > 1. George William [15257312C21] b. MAR 3, 1929 in
>   >   Ogden, UT.
>   > 2. Brian [15257312C22] b. APR 25, 1938 in Caliente, NV.
> 3. Leroy Riggs [15257312C3] b. NOV 26, 1904 at Kenab; m. Adella LINK, d/o
>   William Henry and Minnie Ann (Rushton) Link on JUN 20, 1926; she was b.
>   JAN 14, 1904 at Salt Lake City, UT.;

Their Children:
1. Marilyn [15257312C31] b. OCT 23, 1926,
    at Salt Lake City, UT.
2. Roland Link [15257312C32] b. JAN 2, 1928,
    at Salt Lake City, UT.
3. Clara L. [15257312C33] b. MAR 13, 1929 at Alamo, NV.
4. Deryl Leroy [15257312C34] b. FEB 21, 1931 at Alamo,
    NV.
5. Deanna [15257312C35] b. DEC 3, 1937 at Las Vegas,
    NV.
4. Albert Riggs [15257312C4] b. MAR 17, 1907 at Los Angeles, CA.; m. Norma
    FREEMAN, d/o Elijah Norman & Mary Ann (Taylor) Freeman, on
    OCT 5, 1927; she was b. JUL 1, 1908 in Ogden, UT.;
        Their Children:
        1. Marianne [15257312C41] b. SEP 23, 1928.
        2. Del Bert [15257312C42] b. JAN 9, 1931 at Ogden, UT.
        3. Carma [15257312C43] b. AUG 21, 1934 at Alamo, NV.

References:

Records of Mrs. Angus Allred of Delta, UT.
Records of Mr. Victor D. Cram of Salt Lake City, UT.
Records of Mrs. W. B. Cram of Detroit, MI.
Records of Mrs. J. R. Freeman of Los Angeles, CA.
Records of Mrs. Milton H. Knudsen of Provo, UT.
Records of Mrs. James Nisbet of Salt Lake City, UT.
Unpublished Manuscript of Elmer Cram (files 57, 82, 294, & 295)

family of John Porter CRAM [15259321]

John Porter CRAM [15259321]
b. NOV 21, 1848
d.

m. AUG 21, 1872 _____1. William Waldron [152593211] b. APR 9, 1877

Albertina A. WALDRON
b. SEP 18, 1840
d. DEC 6, 1916

William Waldron CRAM (1877-)
[152593211]

William Waldron was born APR 9, 1877. He married Annie L. ----, who was born in Hollis, ME., and died MAY 8, 1941, at South Lebanon, ME.

    Their Children:

        1. Keith Porter [1525932111] b. in South Lebanon, ME. on MAY 25, 1908; m. Genevive Frances PARSONS, d/o Frederick Bradley & Maybell (Moody) Parsons of North Lebanon, ME. on JAN 11, 1929; She was b. JAN 14, 1909, in East Rochester, NH.

        Their Children:

            1. Jean Portia [15259321111] b. DEC 8, 1934, in Rochester, NH.

            2. John Porter [15259321112] b. MAY 31, 1938, in Rochester, NH.

            3. Judith Parsons [15259321113] b. JUL 15, 1940, in Rochester, NH.

Reference:

Unpublished manuscript of Elmer Cram (file 221)

family of John Wesley CRAM [15259381]

John Wesley CRAM [15259381]
b. OCT 28, 1858
d. 1935

1. Ralph Holton [152593811] b. MAR 16, 1890
m. _JUN 20, 1889_   2. Katherine Louise [152593812] b. JUN 6, 1896
3. Eleanor May [152593813] b. AUG 30, 1899

Katherine Mary HOLTON
b. MAY 4, 1865
d.

Ralph Holton CRAM (1890-)
[152593811]

Ralph Holton was born MAR 16, 1890. He was educated at Arms Academy and Albany Business College. Ralph served as a Lieutenant during WWI, and after the war continued as a Captain in the U.S. Reserves. On APR 12, 1918, he married Grace M. BAVIER of New Rochelle, NY.
  Their Children:
    1. Beverly Bavier [1525938111] b. JAN 23, 1919.
    2. Stephen Batchelder [1525938112] b. JAN 22, 1922.

Katherine Louise CRAM (1896-)
[152593812]

Katherine Louise was born JUN 6, 1896. She graduated from Technical High School in Springfield, MA., and later Keene, NH. Normal School. On NOV 29, 1917, she married Paul E. HITCHCOCK, son of Walter B. and Rose (Andrews) Hitchcock of Springfield, MA. He was born NOV 27, 1894, in Springfield. Katherine married second Elwin W. AVERY, son of Frank and Neva (Nason) Avery, on JUN 25, 1932, at Barre, MA. He was born AUG 5, 1908, in Haverhill, MA. They resided in East Kingston, NH.
  Child by Paul Hitchcock:
    1. Katherine Chase Hitchcock; b. SEP 24, 1922.
  Child by Elwin Avery:
    2. Elinor Mary Avery; b. MAY 19, 1934, in Boston.

Elinor Mary CRAM (1899-)
[152593813]

Elinor Mary was born JUL 30, 1899. She was a graduate of Northfield Seminary, and of the Connecticut Training School for Nurses. On JUL 9, 1930 she married Dr. Eugene F. JEFFERY of Los Angeles, CA. She later worked with hydrogalvanic therapy, described as: "The current medical vogue for low-voltage treatments. . . for total galvanization of the body surface." It was a therapeutic bath combined with low voltage stimulation alleging to treat arthritis, rheumatism, neuritis, sciatica, and chronic pelvic inflammations. Like many electro-medical devices of the time, its validity was never proven. They had no children.

References:

Cram Genealogy (privately published pamphlet)
Records of Michael A. Cram
Unpublished manuscript of Elmer Cram (file 24)

family of Ralph Warren CRAM [152593A1]

Ralph Warren CRAM [152593A1]
b. JUN 19, 1869
d. MAY 8, 1952

m. DEC 27, 1892

Mabel LAVENTURE
b.
d. JAN 9, 1948

1. Herbert Mason [152593A11] b. 1893
2. Eloise Blaine [152593A12] b. 1896
3. Margaret Mason [152593A13] b. JUL 17, 1900
4. Mary Deming [152593A14] b. MAY 21, 1903
5. **Ralph LaVenture [152593A15]** b. 1906

Herbert Mason CRAM (1893-1899)
[152593A11]

Herbert Mason was born OCT 16, 1893, and died APR 30, 1899, in Davenport, IA., succumbing to meningitis.

Eloise Blaine CRAM (1896-1957)
[152593A12]

Eloise Blaine was born JUN 11, 1896, in Davenport, IA., and died FEB 9, 1957, in San Diego, CA., unmarried. Eloise graduated from Davenport High School, class of 1914. She attended the University of Chicago, being elected to Phi Beta Kappa in her junior year, and receiving her BS. degree in 1918. Her first job was as a chemist and bacteriologist in Armour laboratories in Chicago. Her father remembers, "Now came one of her most characteristic acts: Her mother several months later being taken seriously ill, Eloise at once resigned her position and returned to be with her and run the home for the next several months."

Next she was appointed a research zoologist under the Department of Agriculture. She went to Washington, DC. and studied at George Washington University contemporaneously with her work. She was awarded her MS. degree in 1923, and her PhD. degree in 1925. Her thesis, a book of 465 pages on bird parasites, was published by the Smithsonian Institute. She was sent to Oregon to study excessive mortality among wild ducks, to Maine for ruffed grouse and to the Chesapeake bay region to observe turkeys. She subsequently went on furlough for several months to study quail in Georgia and write a chapter on parasites in Stoddard's monumental work on bob white quail.

Eloise was elected director of the Washington, D.C. Museum of Science in 1929. She was next sent to Puerto Rico to make studies of poultry raising possibilities as a means of raising the level of life among the poorer classes there. When she was listed in Who's Who in America (sometime prior to 1938) her credits included membership in the Washington Academy of Science, Helminthological Society, Association for the Advancement of Science, American Ornithological Union, American Society of Tropical Medicine, American Society of Parasitology, and the American Association of University Women.

Her early work was done in the Zoological Division of the Bureau of Animal Husbandry, Department of Agriculture. Her father writes, "When it was decided, a year or so ago (in 1938), to open the National Institute of Health for similar research in human ailments, and her chief, the brilliant Dr. Maurice C. Hall, was chosen to head it, he accepted on condition that he might bring with him half a dozen of his aides from the Agricultural Department. This transferred Dr. Cram to a wider field of important and even more interesting work, which she is now carrying on."

Eloise was employed as a parasitologist and zoologist with the National Institutes of Health in Washington, DC. at the time of her death. Her ashes were interred in Davenport, IA. in the summer of 1957.

Margaret Mason CRAM (1900-)
[152593A13]

Margaret Mason was born JUL 17, 1900. Her father said, "(she) preferred to help her mother and neighbors raise the babies -- liked it better than baking or housekeeping. She just naturally became a kindergartner after her course at the University of Chicago, until she had a home of her own." She married Frank W. SIEMAN on DEC 27, 1922. They resided in Oklahoma City, OK.

Their Children (in the tenth generation):

 1. Ralph LaVenture Sieman; b. DEC 10, 1923;
  Children:
   1. Tamara Sue Sieman; b. NOV 14, 1956.
   2. Teri Lee Sieman; b. DEC 4, 1957.
 2. Mary Belle Sieman; b. NOV 11, 1936; m. ---- Kumaran, a veterinarian from India;
  Children:
   1. Jennifer Rene Kumaran; b. MAY 1, 1955
   2. Kiran Margaret Anna Kumaran; b. DEC 28, 1968.

Mary Deming CRAM (1903-)
[152593A1]

Mary Deming was born MAY 21, 1903. "To Mary, home keeping always appealed, so she took the training for it in home economics at Iowa State, and passed on to her scholars what she learned . . . (She) taught domestic science and English at Delmar and then sewing in the Davenport schools until she married Miles Max MILLER also an Ames graduate and then head of the science department of the Amsterdam, NH. high school," noted her father. They lived for a number of years in New York, both being active in school and civic activities. They later resided in Bristol, VA.

Their Children:

 1. John Miller; m. Donna ---- in JUN, 1969.
 2. Eloise Miller; m. Daniel Orr; He received a Master's Degree in Community
  Development from the University of Missouri;
  Their Child:
   1. Sarah Deming Orr; b. JUN 16, 1971.

Ralph LaVenture CRAM (1906-1939)*
[152593A15]

Ralph LaVenture was born NOV 6, 1906 and died MAR 18, 1939. After high school he graduated from Iowa State University majoring in mechanical engineering. He helped build Monocoupes during two summer vacations, and from that experience decided that aeronautical engineering held the greatest appeal for him. Switching to the Guggenheim School of Aeronautics at the University of New York for his senior year, Ralph finished there under the noted Dr. Alexander Klemin. In 1929, when he graduated, a good job was awaiting him with Boeing in Seattle.

He rose steadily within the company. His father remembers him stopping at Davenport on several flights from Seattle to the east coast. "On one he represented the engineering staff with company officers when then went to New York and returned with a contract for six super-clippers to fly the Atlantic for Pan-American. Soon afterward he was flying to Langley field, on the Virginia coast, to conduct wind-tunnel and tank tests of models of these big ships-to-be. And when the first of the lot was taken into the air off the Sound near the Seattle factory and landed on Lake Washington (its test base for further flights) he was in it with the crew, observing and figuring performance of the biggest airplane ever built in America. How far all that seems from the two-place Jennie in which I had my first flight, 19 years ago (in 1938), to the 72-passenger, 33,000 pound Clipper in which Ralph, Jr. had a place on its first flight."

Justifiably proud, his father recalled, "A few months ago, after he had shown me through the Boeing plant and I had seen this plane in an early stage of construction, and he had remarked that he would have an office of his own in the new office-building extension then under way, I asked him if he had any title that went with the office. 'Chief of the Aerodynamic Section,' he responded. And he'd never even written home about that." Ralph was killed MAR 18, 1939 in a plane crash near Seattle. He was testing an aircraft for the Boeing Co., under contract to the U.S. Government.

He married Doris ARCHIBALD, daughter of Thomas Archibald, on JAN 22, 1930.
        Their Child :
                1. Ralph Archibald [152593A151] b. NOV 6, 1930.

References:

Cram Family (privately published pamphlet) p. 3
Cram, Ralph W. "Dad Tells About Rearing Children." Davenport Democrat Leader (dtd. AUG 7, 1938)
Letter to the author from Margaret Sieman (dtd. NOV 12, 1971)

family of Charles Edwin CRAM [152593A2]

Charles E. CRAM [152593A2]
b. DEC 11, 1871
d. JAN 29, 1936

1. **Maynard Urlin [152593A21]** b. 1897
m. AUG 15, 1895 _____ 2. **Ramon Shoup [152593A22]** b. 1902
3. Donald Deming [152593A23] b. 1909

Blanche SHOUP
b. FEB 1, 1876
d. JUL 20, 1956

Maynard Urlin CRAM (1897-1957)*
[152593A21]

Maynard was born AUG 17, 1897 just west of Carey near Vanlue, OH. and died JAN 6, 1957 in Charlotte, NC. The family moved to Carey from Vanlue, and Maynard graduated from Carey High School in 1915. After high school he worked for the Carey Times until joining the U. S. Army in AUG, 1918. His tour of duty, cut short early in 1919 by the armistice, was spent playing the clarinet in the Army Band at Camp Jackson, near Columbia, SC.

Returning to civilian life Maynard worked first for the Crowell (or Crowell-Collier) Publishing Company in Springfield, OH. In 1920 he was employed for a short time by a weekly newspaper in Forest, OH., before accepting a position with the Fostoria Review (OH.). About 1923 a better offer took him to Mansfield, Oh. and the Mansfield News. He remained there about ten years until the non-union News was purchased by the unionized Journal, and the non-union employees lost out.

Shortly thereafter he received a phone call from his sister-in-law telling him of the death of an employee of the Upper Sandusky Daily Union, and the resulting job opening. He was hired as a Linotypist and job setter, but when the Daily Union and the Daily Chief became the Chief-Union newspaper in 1937, he took over as head of the mechanical shop. While residing in Upper Sandusky (from 1933-1942) Maynard was an active member of the American Legion.

During World War II Maynard worked at a government supply depot at Marion, OH. As the war came to an end he transferred to a similar governmental agency near Charlotte, NC. After the war he joined Goodwill Press, a publishing house in Gastonia, NC. where he worked until his death.

His son John reports that most of the time during his career he would have a printing press in the basement, the garage, or a detached building in the back yard to do job shop printing. From 1919 to 1931 Maynard published a monthly magazine titled The Swapper's Friend. From 1936 to 1939 he wrote and printed a similar publication called The Trading Post. "These weren't what you could call money making enterprises since much of the advertising was paid for in trade. He loved printing and swapping which was pay enough I guess," John relates.

He married first Dorothy KEMMERLY at Carey on JUN 20, 1918. They were divorced. He married second Edna WARWICK in 1945. Maynard was employed by Goodwill Publishing Company in Charlotte, NC. for the last 10 years of his life. He is buried there. Dorothy died JAN 2, 1993 and was buried in Upper Sandusky next to her daughter Louise.
Children by Dorothy:
1. **John Charles [152593A211]** b. FEB 13, 1919.
2. Margaret Elizabeth (Betty) [152593A212] b. DEC 4, 1920.
3. Louise Mae [152593A213] b. AUG 7, 1926.

Ramon Shoup CRAM (1902-1961)*
[152593A22]

Ramon was born NOV 14, 1902 in Carey, OH. and died JAN 13, 1961, in Birmingham, Alabama. After graduating from high school in Carey, Ramon completed an apprenticeship course in mechanical engineering and graduated from draftsman to tool engineer position with the Defiance Machine Works, Defiance, Ohio. The company manufactured machine tools and special machinery for the automobile industry. From 1922 to 1926 he was employed by the Marion Steam Shovel Company, Marion, OH., as draftsman, later as assistant service manager and assistant advertising manager. In 1926, Ramon was featured in an article in the Marion Star announcing his invention of four-wheel brakes for automobiles to control skidding. While the article mentioned application for patent had been made, a search of U.S. Patent files could not substantiate that statement. He was employed by the Marion Steel Body Company from 1926 to 1930 as sales manager, and from 1930 to 1935 by the Wyandot Vault Company, Upper Sandusky, OH., where he was vice president and general manager.

In 1935, Ramon began his career in advertising and public relations when he was appointed promotion manager and director of public relations for the Columbus Dispatch newspaper in Columbus, OH. In that position he wrote three house publications, coordinated market research for newspaper advertisers including annual consumer analysis and development of business statistics. Public relations duties included coordination of newspaper cooking schools, gardening and decorating schools. Promotion projects included golf tournaments, baseball and basketball games, speaker's bureau, tourist bureau, Christmas toy campaign, and directing newspaper sponsorship of the construction of model homes at the state fair, home shows, bicycle meets, food shows music jubilees, carnivals and wild west shows. For a several years just prior to and following World War II he conducted newspaper sponsored tours to Washington, D.C. and New York City.

Ramon was quite active in civic affairs in Columbus. He was a member of the official board of North Broadway Methodist Church, founder and president of the Columbus Junior Police; member of the board of trustees of the Volunteers of America, and president of the Exchange Club of Columbus. He served as secretary of the Columbus Zoological Society, and the society in gratitude named one of the zoo's bears after him. He was also recognized for his contributions to his profession, serving as president of the National Newspaper Promotion Association for two terms (1942-1944).

In 1950 the family moved to Birmingham, AL., when Ramon became advertising manager and director of public relations for the Ingalls companies - Ingalls Iron Works Co., Ingalls Steel Construction Co., Ingalls Shipbuilding Corp., Birmingham Tank Co., and the Longfellow House. He wrote advertising pieces for each company including direct mail pieces, sales letters and advertising layout for professional journals. His public relations duties included coordinating ship launchings and commissionings, news releases and technical articles. During this time he also acted as advertising counsel for Gregs Cookie Company, Five Points Bank (later known as Exchange Security Bank) and Moulton, Allen & Williams Insurance agency.

For a year, 1955-1956, he served as editor of Mansfield News-Journal, Mansfield, OH. He returned to Birmingham and founded his own public relations firm in 1956. Ramon was an active member of the First Methodist Church in Birmingham at the time of his death (from a heart attack), and a 33rd degree Scottish Rite Mason. He was founder and president of the Bentley Pines Garden Club in Birmingham.

Ramon married Helen Fern HOLLAND, daughter of Lewis and Pearl (McCombs) Holland of Marion, OH. on JUN 25, 1927. She was born AUG 22, 1902 in Marion, and died MAR 5, 1971 in Lima, Ohio. Helen graduated from Harding High School, Marion, OH., and attended Miami University and Marion County Normal School. Before her marriage she was employed as an instructor at Vernon Heights Junior High School, Marion, OH. Following their marriage, she remained a homemaker while her husband was alive. After his death, she accepted a position as receptionist and file clerk for Gregs Cookie Company in Birmingham, until her health declined. In 1969 Helen was diagnosed with cancer. She received both radiation and chemotherapy to shrink the size of the tumor, but the measure offered only temporary relief. While on a visit to her sister, Hilda (Holland) Sortman, in Lima, Ohio, in the fall of 1970 she fell and broke her hip, and was confined to bed at Lima Memorial Hospital. She died there from heart failure resulting from complications of her other physical ailments. Both she and Ramon were buried in Elmwood Cemetery in Birmingham.

Their Child:

1. **Michael Alan** [152593A221] b. NOV 8, 1938.

Donald Deming CRAM (1909-1960)
[152593A23]

Donald (known as Bud) was born NOV 4, 1909 in Carey, OH., and died FEB 5, 1960, in Mansfield, OH. He graduated from Harding High School in Marion, OH. Donald was always active in sports. He was once awarded a medal for high jumping by Warren G. Harding (later president of the United States), and pedaled a bicycle for 24 1/2 hours to win a National Marathon Race.

He joined the Marion Star newspaper as reporter and stereotyper. Later, his father purchased the Putnam County Gazette, a weekly newspaper in Ottawa, Ohio. Donald, his father and one Linotype operator comprised the staff that published the paper. In 1932 he left the newspaper and returned to Marion. For a time he coached the Marion Business College athletic teams, and in 1934 was named physical director of the Marion YMCA, coaching the basketball team to a state YMCA championship. In 1936 he accepted the post of physical director of the Mansfield, YMCA, and shortly thereafter was named district softball commissioner and district A.A.U. boxing commissioner. His outstanding ability to promote and successfully direct activities brought a number of athletic awards to Mansfield.

In 1942 Donald entered the U.S. Army and spent two years as a military psychologist with a special training unit at Ft. Knox, KY. and in special service at Camp Polk, LA., where he was director of athletic and entertainment events for the servicemen.

Donald returned to the Mansfield YMCA after World War II, and three years later joined the Mansfield News-Journal newspaper's advertising staff. He later served as general advertising manager. Ironically, his promotion from that position to the newly-created post of manager of special services of the newspaper was announced just three days before he suffered the heart attack which ultimately caused his death.

He was an active member of the Holy Trinity Lutheran Church, of which he was a charter member and a member of the church organization committee. He was a charter member of the Buckeye Hobby Club and a longtime member of the Richland County Fair Board.

He married first Naomi DOYLE. They were divorced. He married second Mrs. Melba (Hall) ALBERS. She was born OCT 8, 1907, and died FEB 2, 1980. Melba had one child, Henry Albers, from her former marriage. They had no children of their own. Donald was buried at Carey, OH., and Melba's final resting place was the Mansfield, OH. Cemetery.

Author's Note: It is interesting to note that all three brothers worked for the same newspaper company in Mansfield, OH. at various times during their lives. All three also died before the age of 60 from heart attacks.

References:

Birmingham News (JAN 15, 1961)
Birmingham News (MAR 8, 1971)
Cram Genealogy (privately printed pamphlet)
Letter to the Author from Betty (Cram) Welch (dtd. APR 25, 1994
Letter to the Author from John C. Cram (dtd. MAY 10, 1991)
Mansfield News Journal (FEB 6, 1960)
Mansfield News Journal (FEB 8, 1960)
Records of Michael Cram
Unpublished manuscript of Elmer Cram (file 221)
Who's Who Monthly Supplement, SEP, 1943 (p.179)

family of Franklin Lewis CRAM [15263194]

Franklin Lewis CRAM [15263194]
b. DEC 27, 1872
d.

                                  1. Frederick Laurence [152631941] b. JUL 1, 1896
m. OCT 31, 1895   2. Mary Elizabeth [152631942] b. MAY 27, 1900

Kathryn LONGMIRE
b. DEC 3, 1874
d.

Frederick Laurence CRAM (1896-1935)
[152631941]

Fred L. was born JUL 1, 1896 and died JAN 18, 1935 in Highland, CA. He married Nellie CARTER, daughter of Thomas Osland and Birdie (Roberts) Carter of England, on NOV 15, 1919. She was born MAY 23, 1900 at San Bernardino, CA.
> Their Children:
> > 1. Lucile E. [1526319411] b. DEC 29, 1920 at Highland, CA.; m. JUN 21, 1945 to Henry Jay WHITECOTTON, Jr. of Uvalde, TX.
> > > Their Child:
> > > > 1. Frederick Jay Whitecotton; b. MAY 25, 1946 in Highland, CA.
> > 2. Marilyn Ann [1526319412] b. MAR 4, 1932.

Mary E. CRAM (1900-)
[152631942]

Mary was born MAY 27, 1900 in Highland, CA. She married Orlyn ROBERTSON, son of James G. and Margaret (Nelson) Robertson of Claremont, CA., on APR 25, 1925.
> Their child:
> > 1. Mary Jane Robertson; b. APR 8, 1928.

References:

History of San Bernardino & Riverside County (pp. 1345-1346, 1484-1485)
Records of the Families of California Pioneers (Vol XXI, pp. 27, 29)
Unpublished manuscript of Elmer Cram (files 117 & 216)

family of Ransom CRAM [15263614]

Ransom CRAM [15263614]
b. DEC 25, 1833
d. JUL 15, 1915

m.1. JUN 27, 1859

Frances Isadore ROSEMEYER
b. FEB 4, 1845
d. NOV 27, 1900

m.2. NOV 18, 1901

Julia Bedford CAMPBELL
b. DEC 15, 1855
d. SEP 18, 1943

1. Maurice [152636141] b. NOV 22, 1861.
2. **Rinaldo Orland** [152636142] b. JAN 1, 1864.
3. Lillian May [152636143] b. APR 27, 1867.
4. Alta May [152636144] b. NOV 28, 1872.
5. LeRoy Milton [152636145] b. JUL 25, 1874.
6. Edith Julia [152636146] b. SEP 8, 1877.
7. Una Fern [152636147] b. APR 24, 1882.
8. Eva Gilberta [152636148] b. JUN 23, 1890.

Maurice CRAM (1861-)
[152636141]

Maurice was born NOV 22, 1861 at Richland County, Wisconsin, and died at Bellingham, Washington. He was an expert with machinery, making his own saws while working in the family sawmill in South Charlevoix, MI. He later moved to Washington state and started a shingle mill near Bellingham. He married Winifred (Minnie) WHITFORD.

Rinaldo Orland CRAM (1864-1940)*
[152636142]

Rinaldo was born JAN 1, 1863/64 at Muscoda, Wisconsin and died JUL 11, 1940 at Charlevoix, Michigan. He was called "Nally" by family members throughout his life. While still a young man, he drove a stage out of Madison, WI. on a corduroy road. He worked at the family sawmill in Wisconsin and later at Undine and Charlevoix. He also worked for Booth Fisheries in Charlevoix. Those who knew him remember him as a very even-tempered man.

He married Lena "Granny Cram" JENKINS, daughter of Willard and Elizabeth Jenkins, on DEC 31, 1890 at Petoskey, MI. She was born SEP 11, 1873 at Pinckney, MI. and died JUN 14, 1954 at Port Huron, MI. Lena was a renowned baker and cook, as evidenced by the fact that she cooked for lumberjacks. She loved autos and couldn't understand how anyone could tire of "riding." She taught each of her grandchildren how to drive emphasizing the necessity of watching for road signs and Burma Shave signs. Her special instructions concerning traffic signals were: "Green means GO; red means STOP; and yellow means GO LIKE HELL TO BEAT THE LIGHT."
Their Children:
1. Verl Orland [1526361421] b. NOV 3, 1891.
2. **Leland Leslie [1526361422]** b. OCT 13, 1893.

Lillian May CRAM (1867-)
[152636143]

Lillian was born APR 27, 1867. She married George BACOT. Nothing more is known about her.
Their Children:
1. Ralph Bacot.
2. Ronald Bacot.
3. Hazel Bacot.

Alta May CRAM (1872-1960)
[152636144]

Alta was born NOV 28, 1872 and died in MAR, 1960 at Bellingham, WA. She married Charles HALE.
Their Children (birth order not known):
1. Vern Hale.
2. Alvin Hale.
3. Florence Hale.
4. Roy Hale.
5. Harry Hale.

LeRoy Milton CRAM (1874-1900)
[152636145]

LeRoy was born JUL 25, 1874 and died JUN 22, 1900 in a sawmill accident at South Charlevoix, MI.
LeRoy was working in the family sawmill in 1900, when he suffered a severe injury to his arm that became
badly infected, leading to his death. He married Nora COOPER on DEC 6, 1896 at Charlevoix. She was
born DEC 25, 1873 and died MAY 2, 1949.
Their Child:
1. Rena [1526361451] b. APR 30, 1899 at Charlevoix.

Edith Julia CRAM (1877-1915)
[152636146]

Edith was born SEP 8, 1877 and died MAY 3, 1915 at Charlevoix. She married Amos WEBSTER, son of
Isaac and Mary (Crisley) Webster, on NOV 4, 1894 at Petoskey, MI. Amos' father was a native of New
York, and his mother was born in Ohio.

Una Fern CRAM (1882-1920)
[152636147]

Una was born APR 24, 1882 and died in 1920. She married William CAMPBELL, son of Lanson "Lance"
and Julia (Bedford) Campbell, on APR 15, 1899 at Charlevoix, MI.
Their Children:
1. Albin Campbell; b. FEB 18, 1900.
2. Winifred Campbell; b. JAN 26, 1903.

Eva Gilberta CRAM (1890-1956)
[152636148]

Eva was born JUN 23, 1890 and d. in NOV, 1956 at the VA Hospital at Sawtelle, CA. She was a nurse,
and saw action in World War I. She married first ---- DONNELL, and married second Frank NAGLE.

Reference:

Letter to the author from Anna Ruth Cram (dtd. JUN 7, 1991)

family of David CRAM [15263672]

David Cram [15263672]
b.
d. 1884

m. OCT 29, 1874

Mary (Cheeseman) McCLURE
b. FEB 20, 1844
d. JUN 8, 1927

1. Alfred [152636721] b. JUL 18, 1876.
2. Elmer E. [152636722] b. SEP 22, 1877.
3. Daniel W. [152636723] b. MAR 2, 1879.
4. Mildred [152636724] b. FEB 17, 1881.
5. Walter [152636725] b. APR 18, 1883.

Alfred CRAM (1876-1947)
[152636721]

Alfred was born JUL 18, 1876 at Shannon, IL. and died JUN 4, 1947 at Lanark, IL. He married Matilda MILLER on DEC 20, 1905 at Britt, Iowa. She was born AUG 4, 1882 at Freeport, IL.
    Their Children (In the tenth generation):
        1. Florence [1526367211] b. SEP 13, 1906 at Lanark, IL.; m. P. J. WOLFE on JUN 5, 1930 at Chicago, IL.; he was b. MAR 1, 1904 at South Range, MI.; they resided at Granite City, IL.
            Their Children:
                1. Catherine Joan Wolfe; b. AUG 13, 1932 at Hanibal, MO.
                2. Edwin Phyllis Wolfe; b. JAN 27, 1934 at Mansfield, IL.
                3. David J. Wolfe; b. AUG 16, 1936 at San Barrildo, CA.
                4. James Alfred Wolfe; b. MAR 5, 1939 at Canton, IL.
                5. Joseph Paul Wolfe; b. APR 7, 1940 at Canton, IL.
                6. John Frederick Wolfe; b. SEP 2, 1945.
        2. Lewis H. [1526367212] b. JUL 1, 1909 at Madison, SD.; m. Elsie MILLER on MAR 18, 1932; she was b. JUN 13, 1908 at Dorothy, IA.
            Their Child:
                1. Paul Lewis [15263672121] b. APR 9, 1942 at Lanark, IL.

Elmer E. CRAM (1877-)
[152636722]

Elmer was born SEP 2, 1877 at Shannon, IL. He married Claire RHODES on JUN 27, 1900 at Maquoketa, IA. She was born APR 8, 1878 at Maquoketa, IA. They were later divorced at Clinton, IA.
    Their Children:
        1. Mildred [1526367221] b. JUL 16, 1901 at Clinton, IA.; m. Guy WASSENAAR on NOV 25, 1922 at Fulton, IL.; he was b. at Dronnype, Holland on JAN 23, 1892; they resided at Clinton, IA.
            Their Child:
                1. Marilyn Wassenaar; b. FEB 9, 1930 at Clinton, IA.
        2. Harold E. [1526367222] b. DEC 4, 1902 at Maquoketa, IA.; m.1. Clara HANSON on MAR 3, 1923 at Clinton, IA.; she was b. APR 1, 1906 at Clinton, IA.; they divorced in JAN, 1938; he m.2. Ruby SAUNDERS on MAR 1, 1938 at Minneapolis, MN.; she was b. at Minneapolis on JUN 4, 1909;
            Children by Clara Hanson (born at Clinton, IA.):
                1. Martin H. [15263672221] b. APR 23, 1923.
                2. Eugene [15263672222] b. SEP 13, 1924; m. Lois Ann MARTINSEN on JUN 5, 1943 at Clinton, IA.;
                    Their Children (Born at Clinton, IA.):
                        1. Gerald Gene [152636722221] b. DEC 16, 1944.
                        2. Warren Carl [152636722222] b. FEB 10, 1947.
                3. Claire L. [15263672223] b. DEC 1, 1925; m. Henry E. OBERMILLER on APR 27, 1944 at Clemson, SC.;
                    Their Child (born at Clinton, IA.):
                        1. John William Obermiller; b. SEP 26, 1945

    4. Robert C. [15263672224] b. MAR 20, 1928.

    5. Helen Doris [15263672225] b. NOV 6, 1929; m. James
        SKEFFINGTON on AUG 12, 1945 at Dewitt, IA.;
            Their Child: Linda Jean Skeffington; b. JUL 2, 1946.

    6. Sheila Ann [15263672226] b. OCT 1, 1935.

Children by Ruby Saunders (all born in Minneapolis, MN.):

    7. Ronald Terry [15263672227] b. DEC 11, 1938.

    8. Donald Gene [15263672228] b. OCT 28, 1943.

    9. Henry Wayne [15263672229] b. JUL 17, 1945.

3. Bruce R. [1526367223] b. MAR 21, 1905 at Maquoketa, IA.; m. Lily GRAY on
JAN 24, 1923 at Clinton, IA.; she was b. DEC 3, 1904 at Savanna, IL.;
   Their Children (all born at Clinton, IA.):

    1. Bruce R., Jr. [15263672231] b. MAR 21, 1923; m. Betty
      HOWARD on JAN 25, 1943 at Clinton, IA.;
        Their Children (born at Clinton, IA.):

          1. Bruce Rhodes, III [152636722311]
            b. AUG 3, 1943.

          2. Barbara Jean [152636722312] b. MAY 28, 1946.

    2. Betty Mae [15263672232] b. JUN 11, 1926; m. Edward E. JESS
      on JUN 30, 1945 at Oakland, CA.;
        Their Child:

          1. Betty Lou Jess; b. MAY 8, 1946 at Clinton, IA.

    3. Richard M. [15263672233] b. MAY 13, 1927.

    4. Dorothy Dale [15263672234] b. JUN 26, 1929; m. Vernon
      GUIMOND on OCT 16, 1946 at Iowa City, IA.;
        Their Child:

          1. Vernon Guimond, Jr.; b. JUN 9, 1947
            at Davenport, IA.

    5. Donald E. [15263672235] b. JUN 23, 1931.

    6. Doris E. [15263672236] b. AUG 23, 1933.

    7. Darlene [15263672237] b. SEP 23, 1935.

    8. Bernice Ann [15263672238] b. MAR 12, 1937.

    9. Nancy Fay [15263672239] b. FEB 15, 1939.

4. Ralph [1526367224] b. MAR 16, 1907 at Maquoketa, IA.; m. Genevieve MANNING
on OCT 4, 1927 at Clinton, IA.; she was b. MAR 3, 1909; lived in Clinton;
   Their Children (All born in Clinton, IA.):

    1. Lois Mae [15263672241] b. JUN 27, 1928; m. James BIRELY on
      FEB 22, 1947 at Camanche, IA.

    2. Ralph M. [15263672242] b. NOV 22, 1930.

    3. Ardelle J. [15263672243] b. JUL 22, 1932.

    4. Marjorie Ann [15263672244] b. JAN 23, 1935.

    5. Allen James [15263672245] b. DEC 6, 1939.

    6. Dennis Gary [15263672246] b. JAN 24, 1942.

    7. Stephan Warren [15263672247] b. NOV 2, 1944.

5. Frank A. [1526367225] b. APR 2, 1908 at Clinton, IA.; m. Loretta KIRSHNER on
OCT 26, 1927 at Clinton, IA.; she was b. OCT 7, 1911 at New York;
   Their Child:

    1. Patricia Joan [15263672251] b. FEB 17, 1935 at Clinton, IA.

6. Carl R. [1526367226] b. JAN 9, 1910 at Clinton, IA.; m. Evelyn LARSON on
FEB 24, 1938 at Dubuque, IA.; she was b. SEP 29, 1917 at DeWitt, IA.;
   Their Child:

    1. Roger R. [15263672261] b. FEB 19, 1937 at Clinton, IA.

7. Roy Eugene [1526367227] b. JAN 1, 1912 at Clinton, IA.; he was adopted by
his aunt, Mildred (Cram) Andorfer, and changed his name to Donald Edwin.

Daniel W. CRAM (1879-)
[152636723]

Daniel was born MAR 2, 1879 at Shannon, IL.   He married Delia Ellis GILBERT at Canton, IL. on JAN 6, 1904. She was born JUL 20, 1878 at Afton, IA. They resided at Freeport, IL.

Their Children:
1. Ellis Gilbert [1526367231] b. JUL 20, 1905 at Shannon, IL.; m. Phyllis Faye CAUL on NOV 3, 1928 at Iowa City, IA.; she was b. at Manchester, IA. on AUG 3, 1904; they resided at Oak Park, IL.;

    Their Children:
    1. Richard Allen [15263672311] b. JUL 15, 1934 at Galesburg, IL.
    2. Roger Lane [15263672312] b. NOV 16, 1936 at Freeport, IL.
2. Raymond Edgar [1526367232] b. SEP 1, 1907 at Shannon, IL.; m. Dora E. FAHRNEY on MAR 16, 1936 at Chicago, IL.; she was b. at Monticello, WI. on SEP 16, 1911; they resided at Chicago, IL.
3. Helen Louise [1526367233] b. SEP 4, 1910 at Shannon, IL.; m. Donald R. BOLENDER on OCT 31, 1930 at Dixon, IL.; he was b. JUN 15, 1910 at McConnell, IL.; they resided at Cedarville, IL.;

    Their Children:
    1. Carol Jean Bolender; b. NOV 6, 1931 at Freeport, IL.
    2. Joan Louise Bolender; b. MAR 21, 1936 at Freeport, IL.
4. Gladis Cordelia [1526367234] b. MAY 7, 1914 at Whitewater, WI.; m. Irvin Eugene RUNTE on APR 8, 1938 at Freeport, IL.; he was b. OCT 1, 1913 at Freeport. Their Children (all born at Freeport, IL.): Gerald Paul Runte; b. FEB 5, 1940; David Eugene Runte; b. MAR 6, 1942; Lee Allen Runte; b. APR 18, 1946.
5. Margaret Edith [1526367235] b. SEP 15, 1917 at Freeport, IL.
6. Katherine Virginia [1526367236] b. FEB 21, 1920 at Freeport, IL.

Mildred CRAM (1881-)
[152636724]

Mildred was born FEB 17, 1881. She married Arthur ANDORFER on DEC 20, 1906 at Shannon, IL. He was born at Bolton, IL. on DEC 8, 1883. They resided at Morrestown, Michigan.

Their Child:
1. Donald Edwin Andorfer - born Roy Eugene Cram [1526367227]; he was the nephew of Mildred (the son of Elmer E. Cram) adopted by Mildred and her husband; he changed his name subsequent to his adoption; he m. Loretta KUHNKE on JAN 24, 1935 at Rockford, IL; she was b. at Clintonville, WI.;

    Their Children (born at Ft. Atkinson, WI.): Donald Arthur Andorfer; b. SEP 19, 1936; Sylvia Mildred Andorfer; b. MAR 12, 1938.

Walter CRAM (1883-)
[152636725]

Walter was born APR 18, 1883 at Shannon, IL. He married Ella May BURNER on NOV 29, 1906 at Forreston, IL. She was born JUN 19, 1888 at Beatrice, NE.; they resided at Milwaukee, WI.

Their Child:
1. Glenn Burner [1526367251] b. AUG 23, 1908 at Lake Wilson, MN.; m. Leona BORGANHAGEN on NOV 14, 1931 at Oregon, IL.; she was b. SEP 15, 1906 at Milwaukee, WI.; they resided at Shorewood, WI.

    Their Child:
    1. Beverly Burner [15263672511] b. AUG 19, 1933 at Wilkes Barre, PA.

References:

Biographical Record of Webster County, Iowa (pp. 668-671)
Family records of Ilene Johnson

family of Heman CRAM [15263674]

Heman CRAM [15263674]
b. DEC 13, 1833
d. APR 4, 1922

1. Willie [152636741]

m. FEB 14, 1866

2. **Adelbert [152636742]** b. NOV 6, 1875.
3. Lee [152636743]
4. Susie [152636744]

Mary Frances SHOOK
b. OCT 27, 1843
d. MAY 4, 1917

Willie CRAM
[152636741]

Willie was the eldest of the Cram children to survive the diphtheria epidemic. Nothing is known of his life. He is buried with four of his brothers and sisters in Lot #81 in the Dresden Cemetery. No stone or other identification marks their graves except a base for a stone that was placed on this gravesite in 1971.

Adelbert CRAM (1875-1960)*
[152636742]

Adelbert, who was known as Bert, was born NOV 6, 1875 in Powshiek County, IA. and died on SEP 23, 1960 at North English, IA. He married Enness MINER at Springdale Church, near Thornburg, IA on MAR 31, 1897. She was born DEC 18, 1871 and died in Iowa County, IA. on MAY 19, 1926. Ennes was the daughter of William A. and Jeanette (Findlay) Miner.

Bert was mostly a tenant farmer, which his son Harold admits, "meant that we were always very poor." He tried other vocations at various times, including a dray line business in Deep River, IA. Harold recalls:
> "This was long before the days of good roads, truck lines or even automobiles. All freight in those days moved by railroad. Father's job was to pick up the boxes of freight at the depot and deliver them to the various retail stores in town. Equipment consisted of a team of draft horses and a large dray wagon. The team of horses were as fine as could be found in those days, two steel grey geldings, perfectly matched in coloring and size. The gentle team survived the dray line days and were used in later farming ventures until they became too old for work and were put away by the chloroform method. The day the old horses were put to sleep will never leave my memory, nor will I forget the sadness that I felt when they were led away to the field far back of the house and there put to sleep by chloroform administered by a local medical doctor, not a veterinarian. They were buried on that same spot and I have since thought how in this day and age they would have doubtless ended up as food on some mink farm. My sadness at seeing the old team go was somewhat soothed by my mother who took considerable pains to explain to me that they had lost most of their teeth and that they would soon have died of old age anyway."

When World War I began families throughout the midwest faced many hardships in addition to young men being drafted. In his book, Tall Corn, Harold remembers another family business venture:
> "Foods became very scarce, especially white flour and sugar along with butter which were the staples in the family diet. Sugar was especially difficult to get and the price rose to many times its original price. Because of the shortages people began to search for substitutes. It was the search for a sugar substitute that put my father into one of the most prosperous periods of his life, albeit ever so short. Father bought a sorghum mill and set up a molasses factory on our little rented farm. He not only planted his few acres of land to sorghum, but he also made sorghum for other families from many miles around. Sorghum time was late fall lasting from September into October or later. Father's reputation for making sorghum was excellent and he turned out many hundreds of gallons of the thick golden stuff each fall. Payment for making the syrup was either on a cash basis of so much per gallon or on a share basis which could be turned into quick cash as the demand exceeded the supply during those sugar short years."

Ennes also did her share to supplement the family income. Harold recalls,

> "She developed an excellent flock of red rock chickens which brought in a steady income from the eggs that were sold, and also from the young roosters which brought a good price on the market. Red rock chickens are a large breed and are excellent as roasting and frying chickens and were a ready source of meat for the family. She also raised a large flock of grey geese. These were slaughtered and dressed, packed in wooden barrels and shipped off to the Chicago market in time for the holiday trade. A by-product of the geese was the fine goose feathers and down that they yielded at plucking time. During those years mother was able to get enough feathers to make a feather tick for each of her six sons. Although feather ticks and the need for them has passed in most areas of the world, the feathers have not and in the case of those made by mother, these have been converted into goose down pillows and I am sure are still in use by many of the children and grandchildren of the Cram family."

Their Children:
1. Cecil Marion [1526367421] b. FEB 7, 1898.
2. Donald Adelbert [1526367422] b. SEP 1, 1901.
3. William Miner [1526367423] b. DEC 22, 1903.
4. Clarence Findlay [1526367424] b. APR 5, 1905.
5. **Harold Raymond** [1526367425] b. JUN 19, 1909.
6. Randall Maurice [1526367426] b. APR 19, 1914.

Lee CRAM
[152636743]

Nothing is known of the life of Lee.

Susie CRAM
[152636744]

The life of Susie is unrecorded. It is only known that she married Charles McWILLIAMS.

References:

Tall Corn by Harold R. Cram
Letter to the author from Harold R. Cram (dtd. DEC 11, 1993)

family of Richard J. CRAM [15269216]

Richard J. CRAM [15269216]
b. DEC 23, 1846
d. JUL 22, 1912

m. JAN 1, 1874

Nancy J. ROWELL
b. 1850
d. SEP 7, 1913

1. Leonora E. [152692161] b. AUG 15, 1875
2. Hattie [152692162] b. about 1877
3. Inez F. [152692163] b. MAR 7, 1906
4. Thomas [152692164} b. about 1879

Leonora E. CRAM (1875-1902)
[152672161]

Leonora was born in Bradley, ME. on AUG 15, 1875 and died there on FEB 11, 1902. She was buried in Knapp Cemetery. She married Henry Warren KNOWLTON.
> Their Children:
>> 1. Forrest Greenleaf Knowlton; d. in 1918 during World War I; unmarried.
>> 2. Merle George Knowlton; b. 1898; m. Cora Emily Rand; d. after 1975; were said to have had a large family.
>> 3. Hazel Julia Knowlton; b. AUG 17, 1899; m.1. Morris Wilbur in 1915 and divorced him in 1922; m.2. in 1923 to George Collins; she was still living in 1990;
>>> Children by Morris (in the 11th generation):
>>>> 1. Elizabeth Ada Wilbur (listed on marriage certificate as Collins); b. in 1922 at Litchfield, ME.; m. Oscar Clinton Bragg on MAR 24, 1939; he was b. JUN 15, 1918;
>>>>> Their Children (in the 12th generation):
>>>>>> 1. Jeffrey Lloyd Bragg; b. AUG 5, 1949 in Bradley, ME.; m.1. SEP 11, 1970 to Joyce Marie Rogers; divorced FEB, 1975; she was b. JAN 25, 1953 at Brewer ME.; he m.2. Marie Littlefield; she m.2. Galen R. Sanborn on JUL 10, 1975;
>>>>>>> Child by first wife:
>>>>>>>> 1. Marie Lynn Bragg; b. MAR 15, 1971 at Bradley, ME.; she changed her last name to Sanborn on her 18th birthday
>>>>>> 2. Mildred Bragg; m. Donald Hanson; 2 children - Timothy; Paula.
>>>>>> 3. Althea Bragg; m. Lloyd Libby; 3 children - Lloyd, Jr.; Sharon; Edward.
>>>>>> 4. Dwight Oscar Bragg; d. young.
>>>>>> 5. Judy Bragg; m. Robert Smith; 5 children - Robert, Jr.; Michael; Michelle; Shane; Tammie.
>>>>>> 6. Bruce Bragg; m. twice with five children - unlisted.
>>>>>> 7. Dale Bragg; m. twice; 3 children: Lisa (by 1st wife); Dale, Jr. and an unknown child by 2nd.
>>>>>> 8. Kathy Bragg; married; 1 child.
>>>>>> 9. Patty Bragg; married; 2 children.
>>>> 2. Gertrude Wilber
>>>> 3. Josephine Wilber
>>>> 4. Mertie Wilber
>>> Children by George (11th generation):
>>>> 5. Virginia Collins; m. Charles Emerson;

Their Children:
1. Forrest Emerson
2. Glenys Emerson
3. Nathan Emerson
6. Dorothy Collins; m. David Brissette;
Their Children:
1. David Brissette
2. Dorene Brissette
3. Debra Brissette
7. George Collins; m. Betty Haskell;
Their Children:
1. Jamie Collins
2. George Collins, Jr.
3. Alice Collins

4. Lenora Julia Knowlton; b. 1902; d. 1964; unmarried.

Hattie CRAM (1877-)
[152692162]

Hattie was born about 1877. She married a Mr. BOYNTON. Nothing more is known of her life.

Inez F. CRAM (-1906)
[152692163]

Inez was born in Bradley, ME. She died of acute tuberculosis following a case of measles at Bradley on MAR 7, 1906 at the age of 19 years, 11 months and 11 days. She married William LANSIL, but because of her death at such an early age, the length of their marriage is not known.

Thomas CRAM (1879-)
[152692164]

Thomas was born about 1879. Nothing more is known of him.

References:

Letters to the author from Joyce Sanborn (dtd. MAR 16, 1990 and APR 17, 1990)
Unpublished manuscript of Elmer Cram (file 289)

family of George W. CRAM [1526B813]

George W. CRAM [1526B813]
b. FEB 14, 1862
d. JAN 20, 1917

m. JUL 15, 1885

Blanche E. MITCHELL
b. JAN 27, 1868
d. MAY 31, 1932

1. Stella Mabel [1526B8131] (1886-1973)
2. Geneva M. [1526B8132] (1889-1970)
3. **Sherman M. [1526B8133]** (1891-1938)

Stella Mabel CRAM (1886-1973)
[1526B8131]

Stella was born JUL 4, 1886 in Liberty, ME. and died OCT 12, 1973. She married Earl Francis MALONEY on JUN 20, 1911, the Elder Pentecost officiating. They resided in Collingswood, NJ.
    Their Children:
        1. Betty Maloney; b. MAR 30, 1912.
        2. Phyllis Maloney; b. MAY 11, 1913.
        3. Earl Francis Maloney, Jr.; b. AUG 27, 1915.
        4. Nancy Maloney; b. FEB 23, 1919.
        5. Anne Maloney; b. SEP 29, 1922.
        6. David Maloney; b. APR 3, 1925.

Geneva M. CRAM (1889-1970)
[1526B8132]

Geneva was born JUN 14, 1889 in Liberty, ME. and died AUG 20, 1970. She married Everett Howard SHERMAN on SEP 3, 1910 with the Rev. George R. Berry, pastor of the Baptist Church, officiating. They resided in Beverly, MA.
    Their Child:
        1. Blanche Marion Sherman; b. JAN 12, 1917.

Sherman Mitchell CRAM (1891-1938)*
[1526B8133]

Sherman was born JUN 14, 1891 in Liberty, ME. and died JUN 4, 1938. He married Bernice BENNETT, daughter of Frank P. and Georgia Eva (Cram) Bennett of Liberty, ME., on MAR 14, 1915. She was born MAY 9, 1893 and died JAN 23, 1990. They resided in Liberty. Sherman was a painter by trade, and according to his son Keith he died of lead poisoning. His wife Bernice was a homemaker. They attended the Baptist Church in Liberty.
    Their Children:
        1. George F. [1526B81331] b. AUG 4, 1916.
        2. Robert L. [1526B81332] b. JUN 29, 1918.
        3. **Keith B. [1526B81333]** b. JAN 18, 1920.
        4. John M. [1526B81334] b. JAN 13, 1921.
        5. Bessie E. [1526B81335] b. OCT 21, 1922.
        6. Sherman B. [1526B81336] b. OCT 4, 1924.
        7. Maude [1526B81337] died at birth in 1926.
        8. Barbara [1526B81338] b. AUG 16, 1927.

References:

Letter to the author from Keith Cram (dtd. MAR, 1991)
Records of Keith Cram
Records of Mrs. Addie B. Moore

family of Frank Eugene CRAM [15365243]

Frank Eugene CRAM [15365243]
b. SEP 9, 1862
d. FEB 24, 1913

1. Eugene Dow [153652431] b. OCT 20, 1903
m. OCT 15, 1902   2. Ruby Mabelle [153652432] b. OCT 5, 1908
3. Frank Webster [153652433] b. OCT 2, 1911

Ruby Mabel DOW
b. MAY 27, 1878
d.

Eugene Dow CRAM (1903-)
[153652431]

Eugene Dow was born OCT 20, 1903 at Fort Fairfield, ME. He married Laura Margaret HEWITT, daughter of Charles and Ethel (Robinson) Hewitt, on APR 11, 1928 at Boston, MA. She was born MAR 11, 1908 at Boston. The family has lived at North Berwick, Calais, and Sabattus, ME.

Their Children (in the tenth Generation):
1. Laura Ann [1536524311] b. JAN 7, 1927.
2. Ruby Blanche [1536524312] b. MAR 26, 1930.
3. Eugene Charles [1536524313] b. FEB 27, 1931 in N. Berwick, ME.; he retired from the Army after a twenty-year career that included assignments in Korea and Viet Nam; he currently teaches history to high school students; received his BA in education from Radford University, VA. in 1978; m. SEP 30, 1950 in Topsham, ME. to Phyllis Althea ARMES; she was b. SEP 2, 1930 in Topsham, ME.; she holds a BA degree in education from Gainesville University, FL., graduating in 1984; she teaches English and history in the middle school;
Their Children:
1. Eugene Douglass [15365243131] (adopted) b. JUL 19, 1960 in Bad Aibling, Germany; served 4 years in the U.S. Army before being discharged due to sinusitis; he lost the sight of one eye when the optic nerves were crushed due to the swelling of the face; he now attends Central Florida Community College; he m. Virginia Alyne BRYANT on AUG 8, 1981 at Colorado Springs, CO.; they were divorced AUG 6, 1984;
Their Child (in the twelfth generation):
1. JoVonna Maria [153652431311] b. OCT 24, 1982.
2. Lisa K. [15365243132] (adopted) b. DEC 11, 1961 at Bad Aibling, Germany; now attending Central Florida Community College studying interior design; m. Samuel M. LEONARD on JUN 23, 1979 at Draper, VA; they were divorced APR 19, 1993, no children; Lisa is presently (in 1994) engaged to George Luis LORENZO, Jr.
3. Marc Dexter [15365243133] b. FEB 4, 1971 at Dade, FL.; he holds an Associates Degree from FLOART in Palatka, FL., and is now attending Florida State University; Marc has talents in music in acting; he started a band called "Breez" while in high school; his acting credits include the television show, "America's Most Wanted;" he has acted with his father in the Florida State University sponsored state pageant "The Cross and The Sword," depicting the founding of St. Augustine.
4. Joyce Marie [1536524314] b. OCT 15, 1934.
5. Samuel Keith [1536524315] b. FEB 29, 1939.

Ruby Mabelle CRAM (1908-)
[153652432]

Ruby was born OCT 5, 1908. She married Dr. Charles W. STEELE in 1931. Nothing more is known of her life.

Frank Webster CRAM (1911-)
[153652433]

Frank was born OCT 2, 1911 at Fort Fairfield, ME. He married Clare Stevens FOSS, daughter of George Herbert and Grace Louise (Stevens) Foss on AUG 6, 1932 in Woodstock, NB. She was born JAN 27, 1913 at Ft. Fairfield. Frank is an osteopathic physician, a member of the Baptist Church, and a strict Republican. The family resides in Lewiston, ME.
>   Their Children:
>   1. Robert Frank [1536524331] b. NOV 28, 1937.
>   2. Nancy Claire [1536524332] b. SEP 4, 1940.

References:

Letters to the author from Lisa K. Cram (dtd. DEC 22, 1993 & FEB 7, 1994)
Records of Mrs. Ruth Henderson Roach
Unpublished manuscript of Elmer Cram (files 103 & 268)

family of John Sergeant CRAM [15382221]

John Sergeant CRAM [15382221]
b. 1851
d.

m.1. SEP 2, ----

Beatrice (Budd) CLEVELAND
b.
d. OCT 20, 1903

m.2. JAN 17, 1906

Edith Clare BRYCE
b. 1880
d. 1960

1. **Henry Sergeant   [153822211]** b. 1907
2. Edith Bryce [153822212] b. 1908
3. John Sergeant, Jr. [153822213] b. 1910

Henry Sergeant CRAM (1907-)*
[153822211]

Henry (known as Harry) was born JAN 21 (or 22), 1907 in New York City. He married first Edith Kingdon DREXEL on MAY 5, 1931, in New York City. She was born NOV 18, 1911 in New York, and died there in 1934. He married second Ruthven VAUX in Ridgeland, SC. She was born in 1911 and died in Beaufort, SC. in 198-. No issue. Third, he married (Emma) Elouise FORREN, daughter of Owen Benjamin & Odessa (Gilkeson) Forren at Ridgeland, SC. on SEP 26, 1945. She was born JUN 16, 1923 near Lawn, WV. and died in Atlanta, GA., on NOV 5, 1949.

Fourth, he married Lucy Catherine (Ladd) GUEST, widow of William Leroy Guest, on APR 20, 1950. She was born AUG 12, 1916, at Dawkins, SC. and died in NOV, 1993 at Bluffton, SC. Lucy had two children from her previous marriage. Harry credits Lucy for saving him from an early death by encouraging him to give up liquor. Harry was a bon vivant in his younger days. He traveled widely throughout the world, and has long been listed in the New York Social Register.

An article in the SEP, 1993 issue of Esquire magazine describes Harry today, and tells of the eccentric behavior of his youth (some of which Harry denies):
> "At eighty-five, Harry Cram is the epitome of the gentleman hunter, having spent a lifetime shooting grouse in Scotland, duck on Long Island, and quail in South Carolina. A superb marksman, Harry is a fanatic about gun safety, but he's not above having a little fun now and then. People still talk about how, back in the 1930s, Harry would invite guests for Sunday lunch at noon and tell them to be sure to be on time. At the stroke of 12:00, he would climb a tree with a drink and a rifle and shoot the hood ornaments off the cars of latecomers. He could plink the three-pointed star off a Mercedes without disturbing the ring around it."

Author's Note: Harry claims he never did that, although he adds he could have if he had wanted to.

A scrapbook of local newspaper clippings details many escapades, some of which are undeniably true. One story relates that Harry's car quit running late one night several miles from his house. While looking for a way home he spied a white mule in a nearby pasture. Harry ran over and caught the mule. In order to keep his dinner jacket from smelling like mule sweat, he stripped to the buff, hung his clothes on a nearby tree, climbed on the mule and set off for home. When he got there he decided the mule deserved a treat so he mixed up a shaker of martinis, poured it in a silver champagne bucket and invited the mule to drink his fill. He was chagrined to find out that the entire episode had been witnessed by a neighbor who dutifully reported it to the local newspaper the next day.

In Bluffton, Harry was a gentleman farmer breeding and raising cattle on his Victoria Bluff Plantation. He later retired to an island he owns named Devil's Elbow offshore from Bluffton.

Perhaps his most frightening experience occurred in 1976 when two Marines from nearby Parris Island donned wet suits and swam to Harry's island, Devil's Elbow, with the intention of robbing him. "(They) broke into his house in the dead of night, grabbed his son (Peter) at knife point, took him down the hall to Harry's locked bedroom door, and demanded money. When Harry swung the door open, his son ducked, knowing what was about to happen. Harry fired two quick shots, dropping each of the Marines with a .38 slug between the eyes." (Esquire SEP 1993, p. 39) A third Marine conspirator was later sentenced to 45 years in prison for masterminding the crime.

> Children by Edith (in the tenth generation):
> 1. John Sergeant, III [1538222111] b. MAY 31, 1932; called "Jackie"
> 2. a daughter who died at birth or shortly thereafter; buried in the Cram plot of the Bluffton, SC. cemetery.

> Children by Elouise:
> 3. Henry Sergeant, Jr. [1538222112] b. JUN 12, 1945, New York City.

> Children by Lucy:
> 4. Edith Clare Cooper [1538222113] b. FEB 5, 1954, in Savannah, GA.
> 5. Peter Cooper [1538222114] b. MAR 15, 1956, in Savannah, GA.

Edith Bryce CRAM (1908-1972)
[153822212]

Edith was born in New York City in 1908, and died at St. Joseph's Hospital in Savannah, GA., in 1972. She is buried at Bluffton, SC. Edith attended Spence School in New York City. She married Arthur Howell GERHARD, Jr., son of Dr. Arthur Howell and Mary Rebecca Drifton (Coxe) Gerhard of Overbrook, Philadelphia, PA. Arthur was born NOV 7, 1909 and died at Hilton Head Hospital on SEP 16, 1990.

Hank Cram states that he believes that Arthur's grandfather was a Sergeant, meaning Edith married a cousin. He relates, " My brother Jackie . . . told a funny (and sad) tale of how whenever Edie brought a beau home for her mother's approval Granny said the guy wasn't good enough for her. When Granny said this of Uncle Arthur, Edie replied, ' But he's a cousin. He has to be good enough for me.' Jakie called them 'Ardith and Ethur.'"

John Sergeant CRAM, Jr. (1910-)
[153822213]

John was born at home in New York City, in 1910. He graduated from Princeton and Oxford Universities. He lives in New York City, and is unmarried. He has had several brushes with local police because of his association with and benevolence to the homeless and addicted

References:

Coxe Family (pp. 37-38)
Letter to the author from Hank Cram (dtd. NOV 23, 1990)
Notes on the Cram Family and Some Related Families (pp. 20-21)

family of Chauncey CRAM [16113413]

Chauncey CRAM [16113413]
b. FEB 22, 1823
d. MAY 7, 1907

m. AUG 22, 1844

Sarah M. KEISER
b.
d.

1. William Henry [161134131] b. AlPR 7, 1848.
2. Chalres O. [161134132] b. MAY 4, 1853.
3. May A. [161134133]
4. Clara E. [161134134]
5. Alton C. [161134135]
6. Etta M. [161134136]
7. J. B. [161134137] b. JUN 10, 1865.
8. Lucious L. [161134138]
9. Chauncey J. [161134139]
10. Charley P. [16113413A]
11. Kate A. [16113413B]

William Henry CRAM (1848-1902)
[161134131]

William was born APR 7, 1848 in Springfield, IL. and died in OCT, 1902. He married Bessie M. DICKENSON on JAN 24, 1875. William owned and operated a wheat farm and fruit orchard in Almota, WA. All of their children were born in Pennawawa, WA.

Their Children:
1. Unnamed Girl; b. 1870; d. at birth.
2. Ennis Chauncey [1611341311] b. JAN 4, 1877; d. JUL 21, 1942; m. Lois KINGSLEY on SEP 15, 1900.
3. Pearl Etta [1611341312] b. JUN 7, 1879; d. JUL 25, 1925; m. William Henry LEE on SEP 15, 1898.
4. Alice [1611341313] b. OCT 15, 1880; d. OCT 1, 1891.
5. Minnie E. [1611341314] b. APR 25, 1882; d. MAR 24, 1916; m. Edward SWIFT.
6. Grace Roxey [1611341315] b. FEB 11, 1884; d. MAY 29, 1969; m. John STEVIG on NOV 12, 1902.
7. Nellie [1611341316] b. DEC 28, 1885; d. FEB, 1993; m. Carlton SAXON on JUN 8, 1904.
8. Jessie M. [1611341317] b. FEB 27, 1887; d. SEP 24, 1958; m. Clyde STEVICK on OCT 11, 1905.
9. Cora A. [1611341318] b. AUG 20, 1888; d. APR 7, 1984; m. George PIERCE on MAR 19, 1908.
10. Willie [1611341319] b. APR 9, 1890; d. 1891.
11. Leroy Leslie [161134131A] b. AUG 5, 1892; d. OCT 14, 1980 at Moscow, Idaho; he was a farmer most of his life, in later years owned three apartment complexes; he m. Pearl Leona LAMB on MAY 4, 1918;

Their Children (eleventh generation):
1. Ervin Leslie [161134131A1] b. MAY 9, 1919 at Pennawawa, WA; d. FEB 3, 1986 in New Mexico; he was a welder and supervisor of large construction projects; according to his LDS family group record he was married a number of times; the dates of the ceremonies are not recorded; he was m. to Sri SUMARSI, Sylvia HAYES, Elsie CECIL, Rita SEVERIA, Betty RUST, and Elva PLANT (on DEC 24, 1938);

His Child (mother unknown):
1. Betty [161134131A11]
Children by Elva Plant Cram:
2. Richard [161134131A12] b. MAR 18, 1940; he is a welder and operates a heating and air conditioning business in Longview, WA.
3. Margaret [161134131A13] b. FEB 20, 1941.
4. Ervin John leroy [161134131A14] b. NOV 7, 1944 at Kelso, WA.; he is an auto engine machinist and lives in CA.

Children by Rita Severia Cram:
5. Daryle [161134131A15] b. MAY 11, 1948 at
Spokane, WA.; he is a welder, lives in NM.
6. Lucille [161134131A16] b. JUL 24, 1949 at
Spokane.
7. Donna [161134131A17] b. OCT 6, 1950 at
Spokane.
8. Glenda [161134131A18] b. SEP 27, 1952 at
Spokane.
9. Dana [161134131A19] he was b. NOV 12, 1951.
10. Gloria [161134131A1A] b. MAY 7, 1961 at
Spokane.
Children by Sri Sumarsi Cram:
11. Juli [161134131A1B] she was adopted by Ervin L.
Cram [161134131a14] (?); she lives in
Indonesia.
12. Tyson Lee [161134131A1C] b. JUN 16, 1983 in
Farmington, NM.
2. Ralph Leroy [161134131A2] b. MAY 28, 1922 at Stites, Idaho;
m. Mavis Louise HALL, d/o Harry Hall, on SEP 6, 1942; she
was b. MAY 12, 1924, and d. in 1992; he is in the auto
salvage business in Spokane, WA.;
Their Children:
1. Clyde Allen [161134131A21] b. JUL 6, 1944 at
Douglas, AZ.; m. Helen GARCIA on OCT
1, 1966; he was a truck driver, but now
works with his father in the auto salvage
business in Spokane; four children.
2. Ralph Wesley [161134131A22] b. OCT 5, 1945
in Lewiston, ID; m. Verena CIPA on DEC
6, 1965; he works as a policeman and in
police security; they have one daughter and
live in Seattle, WA.
3. Bruce Victor [161134131A23] b. JAN 1, 1947 at
Spokane; m. Linda ANDERSON; he has
worked for Kaiser Aluminum for about 20
years; they live in Spokane and have two
boys; a third, Benjamin, died in 1990.
3. Archie Glen [161134131A3] b. JAN 23, 1926; at Almota, WA.; m.
Viola Margurite McINROY on JUN 5, 1946; she was b.
FEB 21, 1927 at Kimberly, British Columbia, Canada, the d/o
Arthur & Mary Ellen (Wilson) McInroy; Archie is in the auto
salvage business in Missoula, MT.
Their Children:
1. Gary Glen [161134131A31] b. AUG 2, 1947 at
Moscow, ID; m. Louise THOMPSON on
SEP 20, 1971.
2. Gayle Lynn [161134131A32] b. FEB 28, 1950 at
Lewiston, ID.; m.1. Dennis STEADMAN
on MAR 28, 1968; they divorced NOV 30,
1970; m.2. Wayne SCHWARTZ on MAY
25, 1974; Gayle is bookkeeper at her father's
business;
Children:
1. Keven Schwartz; auto mechanic
2. Jason Schwartz; high school Sr.
12. Perry W. [161134131B] b. JUL 4, 1894; d. SEP 4, 1982; m. Pearl MORGON
on AUG 25, 1936.

13. Harold Zenos [161134131C] b. SEP 25, 1895; d. NOV 20, 1985; m. Edna Leona MAY on DEC 13, 1921; they lived in California where he worked in the post office; their first-born son played in the Harry James Band for some time and then established his own band; he was later murdered, a crime which has never been solved; another son was also a musician, but gave the profession up to be a Greyhound bus driver.
14. Charley [161134131D] b. FEB 28, 1897; d. APR, 1898.
15. Ellery Maynard [161134131F] b. AUG 20, 1900; he was a school teacher at Gig Harbor, WA. m. Ethel KETCHAM on AUG 25, 1928.

Charles O. CRAM (1853-)
[161134132]

Charles was born MAY 14, 1853. He married Ella DICKENSON on FEB 9, 1875. Nothing more is known of him.

May A. CRAM
[161134133]

May married S. K. REED. There are no extant vital statistics for her.

Clara E. CRAM
[161134134]

The LDS Family Group Record notes only that Clara married Wesley J. CANTOMINE.

Alton C. CRAM
[161134135]

There is no information about the life of Alton.

Etta M. CRAM
[161134136]

Etta married Edward KELLOGG. Nothing more is known of her.

J. B. CRAM (1865-)
[161134137]

J. B. was a male born into the family on JUNE 0, 1865. It is not known what his initials stood for. He married Ida M. SEVER on NOV 6, 1891.

There is no information on the final four members of the family:

Lucious L. CRAM
[161134138]

Chauncey J. CRAM
[161134139]

Charley P. CRAM
[16113413A]

Kate A. CRAM
[16113413B]

References:

Letter to the author from Archie Cram (dtd. DEC 7, 1993)
LDS Family Group Records collected by Archie Cram

family of Loren David CRAM [16113422]

Loren David CRAM [16113422]
b. FEB 14, 1824
d.

1. Loren Monroe Franklin [161134221] b. 1853
m._____   2. Wesley Orlando [161134222] b. 1859

Sarah E. RICHARDSON
b. FEB 6, 1829
d. MAR 19, 1915

Loren Monroe Franklin CRAM (1853-1943)
[161134222]

Loren was born MAY 12, 1853 at Roxbury, VT. and died MAR 28, 1943 at Loma Linda, CA. He was a farmer and bee keeper, voted Republican, and was a member of the Seventh Day Adventist Church.

On JAN 17, 1882 he married Anna Gertrude DUTTON, daughter of Albert C. and Carrie (Corey) Dutton. She was born MAY 22, 1863 in Lincoln, VT. and died APR 18, 1927 at Rutland, VT.
     Their Children (in the tenth generation):
     1. Jennie Gertrude [1611342211] b. SEP 4, 1891; m. Allen Guy CASSADY, s/o
          Alexander and Flora (Vermouth) Cassady, on OCT 26, 1913; she was a nurse and
          a member of the Seventh Day Adventist church; they resided in Melrose, MA.
          and Washington, DC. before moving to Loma Linda, CA.
               One Adopted Daughter - Juanito Thelma Cassady; b. FEB 22, 1922;
               m. Elmer GRAY on APR 14, 1938.
     2. Albert Monroe [1611342212] b. DEC 1, 1882 in Roxbury, VT.; d. MAY 9, 1957
          in Bridgewater, VT.; received his M.D. degree from George Washington U. in
          1912 and after interning became a general practitioner in Bridgewater and
          Woodstock, VT. for the remainder of his life; his son characterizes him as the
          "last of the old country doctors"; he also served as Bridgewater town clerk and
          treasurer from 1922 to 1957, as as president of the Vermont Medical Society
          1940-41; he was Republican and enjoyed travel, map collecting and reading for
          relaxation; he was a Congregationalist; m. Winifred Belle YOUNG, d/o Lewis
          Frank Young of Rutland, on JUL 3, 1912;

          Their Children (eleventh generation):
          1. Earle Albert [16113422121]
          2. Wendall Robert [16113422122] b. JAN 15, 1920 at Bridgewater,
               VT.; he is a ski instructor.
          3. Vernon Monroe [16113422123] b. MAY 26, 1924 at Rutland; m.
               Therese Helen PECOR, d/o Richard Stephan & Margarete
               Pecor, she was b. FEB 1, 1930; they are retired and reside in
               Black Mountain, NC.
               Their Children:
               1. Paula Winifred [161134221231] b. APR 26, 1951;
                    m. a Mr. ARRIAGA.
               2. Vicki Monroe [161134221232] b. SEP 23, 1952;
                    m. a Mr. EDWARDS.
               3. Heidi Theresa [161134221233] b. MAR 16, 1954.
               4. Christopher Vernon [161134221234]
                    b. JUN 23, 1958.
               5. Lisa Dominic [161134221235] b. JUN 20, 1959;
                    m. a Mr. HUTCHINS.

Wesley Orlando CRAM (1859-)
[161134222]

Wesley was born SEP 3, 1859. He married first Della LOCKWOOD on DEC 24, 1885. She died on NOV 23, 1902. He married second Hester KNAPP on JUN 26, 1902.

Children (mother not specified):
1. Leon Wesley [1611342221] m. Katherine ELPHENSTONE
2. Elmer Lockwood [1611342222] m. Mary JOBBS

References:

History of Roxbury, VT. (p. 450)
National Cyclopaedia (p. 260)
Unpublished Manuscript of Elmer Cram (files 211, 28, 218, and 250)

Family of Abram CRAM [16113423]

Abram CRAM [16113423]
b. NOV 30, 1830
d. MAR 22, 1914

m.1._____1. James Edwin [161134231] b. OCT 6, 1858.
                                2. A son; b. JUL 8, 1860; d. very young.
Sarah JUDD (?)   3. A daughter; b. JUl 7, 1861; d. three days later
b.   4. A son; AUG 27, 1862; d. three days later of diphtheria.
d.   5. Mary Abigail [161134232] b. APR 25, 1868.

m.2. NOV 17, 1878_____6. Fred Danford [161134233] b. MAR 17, 1880.
                                7. George A. [161134234] b. FEB 25, 1881.
Lucy Clay SIPE
b. FEB 28, 1841
w. AUG 12, 1893

James Edwin CRAM (1858-1920)*
[161134231]

James was born NOV 6, 1858 in Barre, VT. he married Ida FORREY, d/o Joseph & Ellen (Buck) Forrey, on MAY 10, 1885. She was b. MAY 16, 1863 in State Center, IA. James was a blacksmith, fireman and engineer for the railroad. He lost his job in Emporia, KS. due to the great strike of 1894. In 1897 they moved to Abram's (James' father's) farm because he was getting up in years and needed some help. He deeded the farm to James and Ida in exchange for letting him live with them, along with his two teenage sons, Fred and George. James and Ida lived on the farm until 1911 when they moved into town in St. Francis. James died on APR 15, 1920 from kidney disease. His wife survived him and lived out her later years with their daughter Hazel in Cheyenne, Wyoming.

 Their Children (in the 10th generation):
  1. Ole Robert [1611342311] b. MAR 22, 1887.
  2. George Edwin [1611342312] b. OCT 5, 1889.
  3. Hazel Eva [1611342313] b. MAR 27, 1892

Mary Abigail CRAM (1868-1914)
[161134232]

Mary was born APR 25, 1868. She died about 1914. Mary married William RAINEY, and died without issue. According to Gary Keeter she lived in California, and her mother lived with her for several years before Mary died.

Fred Danford CRAM (1880-)
[161134233]

Fred Danford was born MAR 17, 1880 in Marshall County, IA. On JAN 15, 1903 he married Myra SELLERSON, the daughter of Charles F. & Emily (Moler) Sellerson. She was born FEB 18, 1883. He was a college professor and moderator of the Congregational Christian Conference of Iowa, with offices in Cedar Falls.

 Their Child (in the tenth generation):
  1. Edwin Clay [1611342331] b. JUN 6, 1913, in Mason City, LA.; m. Helen
   CROSSWAIT, d/o Glen & Belva Crosswait, on DEC 30, 1936; she was
   b. JAN 2, 1916; he was a field representative for the Red Cross;
    Their Child (eleventh genertion):
     1. Susan Dale [16113423311] b. APR 6, 1940, in Des Moines, IA.

George A. CRAM (1881-1922)
[161134234]

George was born FEB 25, 1881 and died in an auto accident in Lakeland, Florida in the summer of 1922. He served in the U. S. Navy around the turn of the century. George married first Timmy ---- . They divorced. He married second Minnie ----. George left three children by two marriages.

Children by Timmy Cram:
1. Thelma [1611342341]
2. Muriel [1611342342] d. young.

Children by Minnie Cram:
3. Cuba [1611342343] b. APR 12, 1922 in Lake Wales, FL.; married O. F. DOWNUM; they resided in Tampa, FL.

References:

Cram Family History (p. 6)
Letter from Fred D. Cram to Ralph W. Cram (dtd. JAN 1, 1938)
Letter to the author from Dr. E. R. Cram (dtd. NOV 30, 1993)
Letter to the author from Dr. Ole Robert Cram, Jr. (dtd. DEC 20, 1993)
Records of Myra Cram (wife of Fred D. Crlam) of Des Moines, IA. and Cedar Falls, IA.
Unpublished manuscript of Elmer Cram (files 21, 28, and 250)

family of Orin CRAM [16113454]

Orin CRAM [16113454]
b. JAN 25, 1836
d. FEB 4, 1893

m._____

Caroline M. SHEDD
b. AUG 5, 1837'
d. APR 11, 1887

1. Nelson S. [161134541] b. 1866
2. Charles [161134542] b. 1865
3. George W. [161134543] b. 1867
4. Richard Ward [161134544] b. 1869
5. Carrie E. [161134545] b. 1872

Nelson S. CRAM (1863-1904)
[161134541]

Nelson was born SEP 26, 1863 and died OCT 16, 1904 at Goffstown, NH. Nothing more is known about him.

Charles CRAM (1865-1940)
[161134542]

Charles was born JUL 27, 1865. He died NOV 15, 1940 at Hartford, CT.

George W. CRAM (1867-1868)
[161134543]

George was born AUG 20, 1867 and died SEP 10, 1868.

Richard Ward CRAM (1869-1941)
[161134544]

Richard was born DEC 6, 1869 at Lyndeborough, NH., and died JAN 28, 1941 at Lynn, MA. The History of Lyndeborough, NH. erroneously recorded the name as "Rebecca." According to Barbara Ballard, "Richard was a kind and loving family man, husky of frame, (who) worked in bronze and brass foundries in Bridgeport, CT. and Peoria, IL." Many name plaques in the old Boston financial district are the result of his work along with numerous church bells, for which he had his own bronze formula. In the later years of his life he developed angina and could no longer work. He and his wife got by on her meager earnings as a stitcher at Spindell's Surgical Appliance Co. in Lynn, MA. The name "Richard" has been carried forward in the family through four generations to the present day.

On SEP 1, 1890 he married Ida Jane WINN, daughter of George E. and Cynthia Jane (Smith) Winn. She was born AUG 13, 18-- in Wilton, NH., and died JUL 28, 1961 in Lynn, MA. Both she and Richard were buried in the Pine Grove Cemetery in Lynn, MA. Barbara Ballard comments that Ida was a petite, hardworking person, agile and keen of mind until her last days. She was in her 90's when she died.
    Their Children:
    1. Elmer Frank [1611345441] d. at 9 months of age and was buried on APR 25, 1892.
    2. Richard [1611345442] b. MAY 2, 1893; he was a carrier for the Fitchburg, MA. Post Office;
          m.1. Eva MASON; d. APR 28, 1959 in Fitchburg, MA.; after her death he married
          again; no issue from either marriage; in the later years of his life he became legally blind.
    3. Carrie Ida [1611345443] b. DEC 13, 1897 in Lynn, MA.; d. MAR 19, 1969 in
          Framingham, MA.; m. Welton Baylies BALLARD, s/o Frank & Frances
          (Currie) Ballard on JUN 19, 1922; he was b. NOV 19, 1890 in Lynn, MA., and
          d. there on JUN 9, 1966; the couple were burdened with having Welton's mother move
          in with them soon after being married and later Carrie's mother came to live with them;
          they had only a few years together in their later life without either a parent or child
          present in the house; Carrie was a housewife who liked to maintain her own schedule and
          became slightly upset if anything disturbed her routine; she enjoyed needle work and

sewing, but devoted her Saturdays to baking bread, pies and cookies for the following week; she suffered from hay fever and allergies, and had chronic high blood pressure most of her adult life; both of her children were born at home; both she and her husband were buried in Pine Grove Cemetery in Lynn;

Their Children:

1. Mildred May Ballard; b. JUN 25, 1923 in Lynn, MA.; she is blonde, with blue eyes, stands 5'10" tall and wears glasses; Mildred was a member of the Girls Drum & Bugle Corps at Lynn English High School, and later worked as a secretary for a Lynn insurance agent until her marriage; m. Richard G. Whitney, s/o Clarence E. O. & Mabelle Lucille (Patterson) Whitney, on AUG 27, 1949 in Lynn, MA.; he was b. APR 16, 1924 in Framingham, MA.;

    Their Children (all born at Framingham, MA.):

    1. Bruce Richard Whitney; b. JUN 2, 1950; m. Leslie Dennis on SEP 2, 1972 at Framingham;

        Their Children (born in Framingham):

        1. Brian Whitney; b. AUG 12, 1972.
        2. Barbara Renee Whitney; b. FEB 15, 1984.

    2. David Ballard Whitney; b. APR 23, 1953; m. Janice Huling on MAY 24, 1980 in Natick, MA.; David was a lance corporal in the Marines who was wounded in Viet Nam;

        Their Children (born in Framingham):

        1. Kristen Leah Whitney; b. OCT 29, 1982
        2. Shannon Marie Whitney; b. JUL 9, 1986

    3. Karen Louise Whitney; b. MAY 15, 1955; m.1. Billy Chesser; m.2. David Keenan;

        Children (both by first marriage):

        1. William Chesser; b. MAR 16, 1975.
        2. Diana Chesser; b. NOV 3, 1979.

    4. Janet Lynn Whitney; b. AUG 16, 1957; m.1. Dan ----; m.2. Edward Riley;

        Children (both by second marriage);

        1. Edward Riley
        2. Richard Whitney Riley

    5. Craig Patterson Whitney; b. JAN 11, 1965.

2. Welton Richard Ballard; b. DEC 30, 1925 in Lynn, MA.; he was the only person in the family with red hair; being tall, like his father, he played basketball and tennis and spent a great deal of time at the beach in the summer; he entered the Y-12 Naval Officer's Training Program in 1943 and completed the two-year program in 18 months; he did not receive a commission because of program cuts; he continued in Naval specialist schools until OCT, 1945 when be became part of the ship's company of a new "baby flat-top" aircraft carrier, the U.S.S. Point Cruz; after discharge from the Navy in MAY, 1946, he re-entered college, enrolling in the University of Massachusetts, graduating in JAN, 1950 with a B.S. degree in Electrical Engineering; he worked at Cornell-Dubilier Electric Co. in New Bedford, MA. for six years, and then moved to Rockford, IL. to accept a position with Sundstrand Corp., from which he retired after 32 years; in his spare time he enjoys woodworking and photography; since retirement he has maintained two homes, one in Rockford, IL, and another in Sun Lakes, AR.; he is active in church affairs being a charter member of the Spring Creek Congregational Church in Rockford, and serving as deacon, president, and a member in the church choir for over 30 years; m. Barbara Turner, d/o William Percy & Lillian Mae (Smith) (St. Onge) Turner, on JUL 3, 1950 at Framingham, MA.; she was b. DEC 9, 1925 at Fairhaven, MA.

Their Children:
1. Richard Scott Ballard; b. DEC 12, 1951 in Fairhaven,
MA.; he is blonde, with blue eyes, and stands 6'6"
tall; received his BS degree in chemistry from
Elmhurst College and took additional coursework in
management and computer technology; he is
employee by Sundstrand and in his spare time enjoys
flying, and singing in the church choir with his
father; m. Sandra Stewart on OCT 10, 1987.
2. Robert Turner Ballard; b. JAN 30, 1954 in Fairhaven,
MA.; he is the shortest male in the family at 6'2";
after graduating from Rockford public schools he
attended the University of Madison and Rockford
College; he helped organized and coordinated the first
Walk for Development in Rockford, established his
own decorating business and now does extensive
restoration work for Rockford Museum Center; m.
Valerie Nofsinger, d/o James Jensen & Alice Driscoll
who was adopted by Eldon Nofsinger; she was b.
SEP 14, 1957 in WI.; the family resides in Rockford,
IL. (in 1991);
Their Children (all born in Rockford, IL.):
1. Robert Sean Ballard; b. JUN 28, 1981
2. Phillip William Ballard; b. APR 16,
1984.
3. Stuart Richard Ballard; b. MAR 5, 1990.
3. Cynthia Ballard; b. APR 15, 1962 in Rockford, IL.; she
was educated in Rockford, and afterward worked in the
retail industry, in restaurants, and as a fashion model;
m. Eric David Johnson, s/o Lloyd A. W. & Mary
Lillian (Mosher) Johnson, on AUG 22, 1987; he was
b. APR 9, 1962; he is a physician who is currently
(in 1991) serving a three year enlistment in the U.S.
Navy; she has been active in local singing groups.
Their Child:
1. Daniel Tristan Johnson; b. JAN 12, 1990
at Pensacola, FL.
2. Andrew Ballard Johnson;
b. NOV 23, 1993.

Carrie E. CRAM (1872-1872)
[161134525]

Carrie was born FEB 18, 1872 and died eight months later on OCT 11, 1872.

References:

History of Lyndeborough, NH.
Letter to the author from Barbara Ballard (dtd. MAR 25, 1991)
Unpublished manuscript of Elmer Cram (file 75)

family of Clinton Warren CRAM [16113919]

Clinton Warren CRAM [16113919]
b. AUG 20, 1855
d. NOV 25, 1929

1. Winfred Clinton [161139191] b. AUG 31, 1881
m. MAR 19, 1876   2. Forrest Allen [161139192] b. SEP 6, 1883
3. Archie Rice [161139193] b. FEB 28, 1887

Maria RICE
b. JAN 10, 1852
d. DEC 29, 1919

Winfred Clinton CRAM (1881-1946/47)
[161139191]

Winfred was born in Williamstown on AUG 31, 1881. She married a Mr. MAO, no issue. Winfred died in 1946/47 in Newark, NJ.

Forrest Allen CRAM (1883-1958/59)
[161139192]

Forrest was born SEP 6, 1883, and died in MAR, 1958/59. He married first Christine MACAULEY and married second Anna ARMINGTON.
Child by Anna:
1. Esther [1611391921]

Archie Rice CRAM (1887-1937)*
[161139193]

Archie was born FEB 28, 1887 in Williamstown and died OCT 3, 1937, in Brookline, MA. He married Beatrice Mae CLEVELAND on MAR 12, 1913. She was born FEB 10, 1896.
Their Child:
1. Reginald Maurice [1611391931] b. APR 29, 1914.

References:

Letter to the author from Reginald Cram (dtd. SEP 16, 1990)
Records of Reginald Cram
Unpublished manuscript of Elmer Cram (file 192)

family of Horace Russell CRAM [16162353]

Horace Russell CRAM [16162353]
b. SEP 30, 1832
d. JAN 2, 1904

m._____ 1. William Archer [161623531] b. JAN 12, 1859
                                              2. Sarah Elizabeth [161623532] b. NOV 28, 1860
Agnes DUFFIELD
b.
d.

William Archer CRAM (1859-)
[161623531]

William Archer was born JAN 12, 1859. He resided with his parents until his marriage in 1883, and continued to assist his father in his farm operations until 1896. In that year he purchased a general mercantile establishment at Johnson Center, OH. which he conducted three years. He then disposed of the business and purchased a cheese manufactory, which, under his management, turned out 200,000 pounds per annum. He also owned a farm in Johnson Township of 104 acres, as well as a home at Johnson Center, located on four acres of well improved ground.

For many years William was a leading Republican of Trumbull County, serving as township trustee, township treasurer (five terms) and as postmaster of Johnson for a period of eight years. He took a great interest in fraternal organizations, belonging to Cortland Lodge, No. 554, I.O.O.F., Ideal Grange, and Knights of the Maccabees of Johnson.

On OCT 3, 1883, he married Elizabeth MILLIKIN, daughter of Thomas and Tamar (Clark) Millikin. She was born at Johnson, Ohio. Her father was born in Ireland and her mother was a native of Homewood, PA.
    Their Children:
          1. Charles N. [1616235311] b. JUN 25, 1884; became a ticket agent on the Erie
                Railroad at Warren, Ohio.
          2. Harry H. [1616235312] b. SEP 27, 1885; d. SEP 14, 1886
          3. Alton A. [1616235313] b. MAR 5, 1894.
          4. Horace [1616235314] b. AUG 5, 1895.

Sarah Elizabeth CRAM (1860-)
[161623532]

Sarah Elizabeth was born NOV 28, 1860. She married Hendison HAIN and resided in Warren, Ohio. There is no further information concerning her life.

References:

History of Trumbull County, Ohio (pp. 374-375)
Records of J. G. Cram
Unpublished manuscript of Elmer Cram (file 13)

family of Wilbur Irvin CRAM [16163461]

Wilbur Irvin CRAM [16163461]
b. AUG 18, 1846
d. MAR 18, 1918

1. **Osceola Canel [161634611]** b. MAR, 1870
m. OCT 8, 1868   2. **Albert Irvin [161634612]** b. NOV 16, 1871
3. John Edwin [161634613] b. DEC 23, 1873
Honor Elizabeth FILBY   4. Fred Franklin [161634614] b. AUG 22, 1875
b. DEC 7, 1843
d. MAY 17, 1929

Osceola Canel CRAM (1870-1961)*
[161634611]

Osceola (Osce) Canel was born MAR 24, 1870, in Monmouth, Iowa, and died AUG 24, 1961, in Burwell, NE. He married first, Laura Edna McCLIMANS on NOV 10, 1898. She was born DEC 24, 1876, and died MAR 2, 1920, from burns in Custer County. The couple lived in Walworth, NE. when they were first married. Osceola was a livestock grower and a farmer. Osceola farmed and ranched with his father Wilbur in Loup County, near Walworth until the family moved to Burwell, NE., in the fall of 1893. After two or three years Osceola moved back to Loup County and the old homestead where he farmed for the rest of his life, prospering considerably. He married second Alice (Torrey) HUFFMAN in 1925. She was born MAY 10, 1889, and died DEC 13, 1931, at Mayo Clinic, Rochester, Minnesota. She was buried in Sargent, NE. Laura and Osceola were buried in Burwell, NE.
 Children by Laura:
  1. Richard Wilbur [1616346111] b. JUL 11, 1899.
  2. Julia Maria [1616346112] b. FEB 14, 1901.
  3. Mabel Elsie [1616346113] b. JUN 30, 1902.
  4. **John Conrad [1616346114]** b. JUN 26, 1905.
  5. Honor Lucile [1616346115] b. MAR 27, 1907.
  6. Bernice Irene [1616346116] b. MAR 5, 1913.
 Child by Alice:
  7. Fred Lee [1616346117] b. OCT 25, 1930.

Albert Irvin CRAM (1871-1957)*
[161634612]

Albert Irvin was born NOV 16, 1871 in Monmouth, IA. He was a lumberman and a banker who moved to Burwell, NE. in 1893 and lived there until his death on JUN 21, 1957. Albert, who was called "Bert," worked in and then owned a bank with others for 30 years after he settled in Burwell. He also had a lumber and coal company named: A. I. Cram Lumber & Coal Company. He married Effie Violet WILSON, daughter of Spencer and Mary Jane (Ingles) Wilson, on SEP 1, 1897. She was born DEC 14, 1876, in Dallas, Iowa and died JAN 11, 1958, in Burwell, NE. She was a teacher and owned a style and gift shop.
 Their Children:
  1. Besse Iola [1616346121] b. SEP 22, 1898.
  2. Jay Irvin [1616346122] b. JUL 23, 1900.
  3. **Roy Spencer [1616346123]** b. FEB 3, 1903.
  4. Honor Elva [1616346124] b. FEB 3, 1906.

John Edwin CRAM (1873-1954)
[161634613]

John Edwin was born DEC 23, 1873 in Maquoketa, Iowa and died APR 8, 1954, in Burwell, NE., unmarried. He worked on the railroad and was in the real estate business.

Fred Franklin CRAM (1875-1914)
[161634614]

Fred Franklin was born AUG 22, 1875 in Maquoketa, Iowa, and died FEB 9, 1914, in Sargent, NE. He was buried in Burwell, NE. He married Florence THOSTESEN on DEC 28, 1907 in Broken Bow, NE. She was born JAN 6, 1883 in Merna, NE and died JAN 10, 1934, in Bridgeport, NE. Both she and her husband were buried in Burwell, NE. He was a livestock dealer in Sargent, NE.

Their Child:
1. Wayne Porter [1616346141] b. OCT 18, 1908 in Sargent, NE.; he married Ardis Marie DOWNEY on JUN 3, 1933; she was b. MAY 5, 1908, in O'Neill, NE.
   Their Child (in the eleventh generation):
   1. Fred Wayne [16163461411] b. OCT 18, 1935 in Bridgeport, NE.; m. Aileen (Nordeen) DOUGLAS on OCT 12, 1958.

References:

Cram (pp. b-10 and b-11)
Letter to the author from John C. Cram (dtd. NOV 16, 1990)

family of Edwin Alfred CRAM [16163462]

Edwin Alfred CRAM [16163462]
b. AUG 25, 1849
d. APR 18, 1926

m. NOV 24, 1874

Hannah FRENCH
b. SEP 8, 1853
d. JAN 1, 1927

1. Jonathan Edward [161634621] b. SEP 4, 1875
2. Laura May [161634622] b. MAY 13, 1877
3. Henry Lewellyn [161634623] b. AUG 26, 1879
4. Mabel Edna [161634624] b. MAR 18, 1881
5. Matt Arthur [161634625] b. JUL 23, 1885

Jonathan Edward CRAM (1875-1876)
[161634621]

Jonathon Edward was born SEP 4, 1875 and died AUG 5, 1876.

Laura May CRAM (1877-1945)
[161634622]

Laura May was also known as Maria. She was born MAY 13, 1877 in Monmouth Iowa and died AUG, 1945 in California. She married Franklin Myers DORSEY on JUN 20, 1900.
>   Their Children:
>   1. Jonathan Edward Dorsey (deceased by 1980)
>   2. Eloise Loudon Dorsey
>   3. Francis Leigh Dorsey
>   4. Helen Lucille Dorsey
>   5. Batie (or Batey) Reid Dorsey
>   6. Alan G. Dorsey; b. AUG 4, 1910.

Henry Lewellyn CRAM (1879-1966)
[161634623]

Henry Lewellyn was born AUG 26, 1879 in Monmouth, Iowa. He Died JAN 11, 1966 in Plainview, Texas. He married Katherine Mae MENCH on NOV 16, 1912 in David City, NE. She was born AUG 2, 1888, in Bellwood, NE. and died there.

Mabel Edna CRAM (1881-1950)
[161634624]

Mabel Edna was born MAR 18, 1881 in Monmouth, IA., and died FEB 11, 1950, in Los Angeles, CA. Cram states that she was a trained nurse. She married Charles Earl McDONALD on DEC 21, 1912 in David City, NE. He was born SEP 8, 1879 and died DEC 24, 1936. All their children were born at David City, NE.
>   Their Children:
>   1. Dr. Edwin Earl McDonald; b. FEB 14, 1914.
>   2. Helen Anne McDonald; b. APR 12, 1916.
>   3. Wallace Brooks McDonald; b. MAY 30, 1918.
>   4. John Bartlett McDonald; b. NOV 15, 1919; living in Dallas, Texas in 1980.

Matt Arthur CRAM (1885-)
[161634625]

Matt Arthur was born JUL 23, 1885, in David City, NE. He married first Maude B. HARRIS on JAN 14, 1911, at Lincoln, NE. While her birth date is unknown, the date of her death was JUN 26, 1948 in Dallas, Texas. He married second Hazel F. FOSTER on DEC 23, 1955. Again the date of her birth is unknown, but the date of her death was MAY 26, 1964. He married third Alice B. ALEXANDER on DEC 24, 1968. She died in late AUG or SEP, 1978.

Children by Maude:
    1. John Marion [1616346251] b. FEB 15, 1915.
    2. Betty Claire [1616346252]; b. NOV 30, 1920.

References:

Cram (pp. b-12 and b-13)

family of Charles Hilliard CRAM [16312122]

Charles Hilliard CRAM [16312122]
b. MAR 22, 1832
d. MAR 21, 1881

m. APR 30, 1856

Harriet BLAISDELL
b. NOV 11, 1834
d.

1. Clara [163121221] b. JAN 19, 1857
2. Nathan Dow [163121222] b. AUG 2, 1863
3. Charles Hilliard [163121223] b. NOV 12, 1863
4. Harriet B. [163121224] b. AUG 26, 1864
5. Bessie [163121225] b. APR 28, 1868
6. Timothy [163121226] b. APR 26, 1870
7. Rupert [163121227] b. FEB 10, 1872
8. Walter [163121228] b. JAN 10, 1874
9. Mildred [163121229] b. AUG 11, 1876
10. Margery [16312122A] b. MAR 6, 1878

Clara CRAM (1857-1900)
[163121221]

Clara was born JAN 19, 1857 in Chicago and died there on MAR 18, 1900. She married Edward R. BACON on OCT 9, 1879.
> Their Children:
> 1. Raymond E. Bacon; b. in Pasadena, CA.
> 2. Richardson Bacon; b. in Chicago, IL.
> 3. John Bacon; b. in Hermosa Beach, CA.
> 4. Robert C. Bacon; resided in Boston

Nathan Dow CRAM (1859-)
[163121222]

Nathan Dow was born AUG 9, 1859, in Chicago and died MAR 4, 1934 (or 1935), in Natick, MA. He was a graduate of Dartmouth, class of 1881, and while in school was a baseball catcher on the school's varsity team. He married Mary QUEEN. He was a school book publisher and editor-in-chief of Silver, Burdett & Company, publishers in New York City.
> Their Child:
> 1. Mildred Cram [1631212221] b. OCT 17, 1889 in Washington, D.C.; she attended Barnard School For Girls 1905-1908; her writing career began with the publication of her first book in 1917 (Old Seaport Towns of the South); other works include: Lotus Salad, a novel, in 1920; Stranger Things (short stories) in 1923; The Tide, a novel, in 1924; Scotch Valley, 1928; Madder Music, 1930; Forever, her most famous novel, in 1935; Kingdom of Innocents, a novel, in 1940; The Promise, a novel, in 1949; Sir in 1973; she also wrote filmscripts including, "An Affair to Remember," "Beyond Tomorrow," "Love Affair" (which received an Academy Award nomination), "Wings over Honolulu," and "Loves of Pandora;" she was also a contributor of over 200 short stories and articles to Harper's Bazaar, Red Book, Cosmopolitan and other periodicals; Helmut Dantine reportedly offered Metro-Goldwyn-Mayer $250,000 for the film rights to Forever, which MGM has held for over 30 years; she m. Clyde S. McDOWELL, a naval officer in OCT, 1925; they resided in Santa Barbara, CA.; there is no report of children.

Charles Hilliard CRAM (1863-1881)
[163121223]

Charles Hilliard was born NOV 12, 1863, in Chicago. He married Ysabel del VALLE and was a merchant and a ranchman. He died MAR 21, 1881.

Harriet Blaisdell CRAM (1864-)
[163121224]

Harriet Blaisdell was born AUG 26, 1864 in Chicago. She was twice married. Her first husband was Dr. T. W. MILLER, who she married on FEB 5, 1889. Her second husband was Dr. W. W. QUINLAN. Both men were residents of Chicago. She later returned to her old home to live.

> Her Children:
> 1. Marjorie Miller; resided in Hartford, CT.
> 2. William Quinlin; b. in Chicago, IL.
> 3. Howard Quinlin; resided in Pacific Palisades, CA.

Bessie CRAM (1868-)
[163121225]

Bessie was born APR 28, 1868, in Chicago. She married W. C. RENNOLDS of that city, on JUN 2, 1892. He was in the wholesale paint business.

> Their Children:
> 1. Harriet Rennolds
> 2. William E. Rennolds; resided in Chicago.

Timothy Blaisdell CRAM (1870-)*
[163121226]

Timothy was born APR 26, 1870. He married Georgia SHORES on MAY 22, 1894. She was born MAR 11, 1872. Timothy was in the business of railroad supplies in Chicago.

> Their Children:
> 1. Kenneth Blaisdell [1631212261] b. FEB 22, 1897.
> 2. Virginia L. [1631212262] b. AUG 12, 1904.

Rupert CRAM (1872-)
[163121227]

Rupert was born FEB 10, 1872, in Chicago. He married Cora NEIDIG on MAY 22, 1894. She was born MAR 11, 1872. He was a merchant and ranchman.

> Their Children:
> 1. Caddie [1631212271] m. Mr. BISKOW of Hermosa Beach, CA.
> 2. Barbara [1631212272] resided in Los Angeles, CA.

Walter Burkhart CRAM (1874-1949)*
[163121228]

Walter was born JAN 10, 1874, in Chicago, and died in Los Angeles on DEC 23, 1949. He was a merchant and ranchman in California. Walter married Nina del VALLE on APR 13, 1898 in Carniolos, CA. She was the daughter of Javentino and Susan (Avila) del Valle, who was born FEB 16, 1873 in Carniolos.

> Their Child:
> 1. Charles Hilliard [1631212281] b. AUG 29, 1900.

Mildred CRAM (1876-)
[163121229]

Mildred was born AUG 11, 1876. She married J. V. PAULSON of Chicago, who died MAR 5, 1900. She later lived with her mother in Haverhill, NH.

Margery CRAM (1878)
[16312122A]

Margery was born MAR 6, 1878. She died in infancy.

References:

Contemporary Authors (p. 130)
Genealogical and Family History of the State of New Hampshire (Vol 2, p. 619)
History of Acworth, N.H. (p. 204)
Unpublished manuscript of Elmer Cram (file 58)

family of Ebenezer CRAM [16314213]

Ebenezer CRAM [16314213]
b. NOV 6, 1833
d. FEB 28, 1897

m.   APR 11, 1861

Susan E. WORTHLEY
b. JAN 7, 1840
d. MAR 7, 1909

1. Oren [163142131] b. AUG 22, 1862
2. Charles Albert [163142132] b. JUL 4, 1867
3. Abbie May [163142133]

Oren CRAM (1862-1921)
[163142131]

Oren was born in Goffstown on AUG 22, 1862 and died there MAR 4, 1921. He married MAY 17, 1890, Nina Annabel MANSUR of Lowell, MA., the daughter of George E. and Malina (Green) Mansur. She was born JAN 4, 1865 and died DEC 1, 1911, in Goffstown. He was a mechanic, employed in the sash and blind factory in Goffstown. Their children were all born in Goffstown.
>   Their Children:
>   1. Loretta May [1631421311] b. DEC 28, 1890; m. Eugene GAGNON
>   2. Linnie Eaton [1631421312] b. APR 27, 1893; m. FEB 10, 1910, John DANIELS of
>   New Boston, s/o Joseph and Angeline (Basha) Daniels; he was b. in 1884.
>   Their Children:
>   1. George Eben Daniels; b. SEP 1, 1911 in New Boston
>   2. Leon Rowell Daniels; b. MAR 19, 1912 in Francestown
>   3. Victor Joseph Daniels; b. JUL 28, 1913 in Francestown
>   3. Fay Ione [1631421313] b. FEB 14, 1900; m. AUG 9, 1920, to Elkie J. CLEMENT

Charles Albert CRAM (1867-)
[163142132]

Charles Albert was born in Goffstown on JUL 4, 1867. He was a mechanic, employed in the sash and blind factory in Goffstown. He owned and lived in the residence of his late father at Shirley. He married NOV 16, 1895, Caroline G. EVANS, daughter of George F. and Mary (Henry) Evans. She was born AUG 18, 1877.
>   Their Children:
>   1. Lucena Elizabeth [1631421321] b. MAR 8, 1901; m. MAY 14, 1919 to
>   Wilber A. LINEHAN.
>   2. Ardena Mae [1631421322] b. JUL 27, 1903.

Abbie May CRAM
[163142133]

There are no birth or death dates for Abbie. She married first George FRENCH on NOV 1, 1890. She married second George ORDWAY on JUL 3, 1895.

Reference:

History of Goffstown, NH. (pp. 105-106)

family of George CRAM [16393122]

George CRAM [16393122]
b. JUL 2, 1857
d. JUN 28, 1876

m. JUL 4, 1882

Annette EATLEY
b. AUG 3, 1865
d.

1. Bertha Olive [163931221] b. NOV 26, 1884
2. Mabel Etta [163931222] b. DEC 23, 1886
3. Edwin G. [163931223] b. MAR 22, 1889
4. Ernest Victor [163931224] b. MAR 12, 1892

Bertha Olive CRAM (1884-)
[163931221]

Bertha was born NOV 26, 1884 in Sanford, ME. She married first Albert CORBETT on MAR 28, 1910 in Haverhill. He died JUL 26, 1910. She married second Edward FEE on JUN 15 (or 17), 1917. Edward was born AUG 27, 1868, and died DEC 18, 1944.

Mabel Etta CRAM (1886-)
[163931222]

Mabel was born DEC 23, 1886. She married Louis J. COTY on JUN 20, 1904. He was born MAR 31, 1883 in Biddeford, ME., and died MAR 21, 1947 at a hospital for the insane in Augusta, ME.
> Their Children:
>> 1. Louis Richard Coty; b. SEP 21, 1914, at S. Sanford, ME.
>> 2. Mildred Mabel Coty; b. AUG 5, 1905, at Sanford.
>> 3. Doris Etta Coty; b. NOV 18, 1916, at Sanford.

Edwin G. CRAM (1888-)
[163931223]

Edwin was born MAR 22, 1888. He married Vera NICHOLL, daughter of Jabez & Jane (Holmes) Nicholl of Roslindale, MA., on DEC 27, 1919. She was born DEC 27, 1892 in Boston, and died in the summer of 1980. She was buried in a Long Island National Cemetery. In 1981, Edwin was living in Closter, NJ. where he was a professional commercial artist and a land and seascape artist. His wife was an artist also.
> Their Child:
>> 1. Richard [1639312231] b. New York City on JUL 1, 1923; m. Virginia MEYER on AUG 25, 1946; she was b. JAN 2, 1923, in CT.; he served in World War II, and was wounded at Okinawa; she was a physical therapist and her husband was a chemist with Lederle Laboratories; they reside in Montvale, NJ.
>> Their Children:
>>> 1. Richard Furness, Jr. [16393122311] b. FEB 20, 1948, in NJ.; m. Lee CLAUSS; at the time of this writing he is director of admissions for the Tilton School in Tilton, NH.;
>>> Their Children:
>>>> 1. Richard III [163931223111] b. about 1977.
>>>> 2. Justin [163931223112] b. about 1979.
>>> 2. Laura E. [1639312232] b. MAR 25, 1950 in NJ.; after college she became a librarian with the State of Virginia; in the 1980's moved to Australia; unmarried.

Ernest Victor CRAM (1892-1936)
[163931224]

Ernest was born MAR 12, 1892. He married Katharine BRADSTREET, daughter of J. Fuller & Jane (Teague) Bradstreet, on SEP 2, 1922. He died in JUL, 1936 in an automobile accident.
> Their Children:
> > 1. Mildred Evelyn [1639312241] b. NOV 16, 1922 at Millenockett, ME.; m. Lawrence TRAFTON on OCT 18, 1943; he was killed in action at Iwo Jima on MAR 18, 1945;
> > > Their Child:
> > > > 1. Katharine Trafton; b. JUL 25, 1944, in CA.
> > 2. Robert Dana [1639312242] b. JUL 18, 1934.

References:

Letter to the author from Laura E. Cram (dtd. OCT 6, 1981)
Records of John G. Cram
Records of Mr. George Cram of Sanford, ME., and Azro Cram
Unpublished manuscript of Elmer Cram (file 158)

Ninth American Generation

family of Henry Osbourne CRAM [152411711]

Henry Osbourne CRAM [152411711]
b. JUL 27, 1836
d.

m. APR 6, 1867

Frances Ellen VAN BIBBER
b. DEC 25, 1847
d. APR 23, 1919

1. Blanche Osbourne [1524117111] b. MAR 5, 1876
2. Paul Henry [1524117112] b. JAN 26, 1879
3. Harold Edgerly [1524117113] b. JAN 27, 1884

Blanche Osbourne CRAM (1876-1924)
[1524117111]

Blanche Osbourne was born MAR 5, 1876 in Baltimore, MD. and died in 1924. She married Arthur Henry LONGFELLOW, a lawyer in New York City. He was a nephew of the poet Henry Wadsworth Longfellow.

Paul Henry CRAM (1879-1944)
[1524117112]

Paul Henry was born JAN 26, 1879 at Portland, ME., and died in JAN 1, 1944. He was a graduate of Portland High School and Harvard College. Paul also studied at the University of Grenoble, majoring in French. He was married in France to a lady who was a native of Alsace Lorraine. For more than 20 years he served in the United States Diplomatic Service in Marseille, France. In 1932 he retired, and after a brief trip back to the United States, he and his wife took up residence in Monaco, on the Riviera between France and Italy. On AUG 11, 1944, American relatives were informed by the State Department that Paul and his wife had died JAN 1, 1944, at their home in Monaco, but gave no information regarding the cause of their deaths, nor the circumstances surrounding them.

Harold Edgerly CRAM (1884-1948)
[1524117113]

Harold was born JAN 27, 1884 in Portland, ME. and died there NOV 21, 1948. He graduated from Portland High School, and became a student at the Eric Pape School of Art in Boston. He married Berniece Nina BANKS, a newspaperwoman, on JUN 3, 1937. He was an illustrator and newspaper artist 1910-1918, and then began writing short stories, becoming a free lance writer for newspapers and magazines. He began his career with the Portland Evening Express, but in 1925 was employed by the Portland Telegram. He started as automobile editor, and was promoted to assistant editor in 1928, before being named editor in 1937. Elmer Cram lists a son, but no mention is made of him in Who Was Who in America.
       Their Child (in the eleventh generation):
            1. Harold [15241171131]

References:

Portland Evening Express (AUG 11, 1944 issue)
Who Was Who In America (Vol. 2, p. 132)
Unpublished manuscript of Elmer Cram (file 87)

family of Samuel Norris CRAM [152433212]

Samuel Norris CRAM [152433212]
b. JUL 17, 1829
d. APR 22, 1905

m.1. MAY, 1854

Dolly C. LANGLEY
b. NOV 12, 1832
d. NOV 10, 1854

m.2.

Dorothy Jane WINSLOW
b.
d. JAN, 1864

1. Georgianna [1524332121]
2. George Albert [1524332122] b. SEP 10, 1861
3. Hattie Augusta [1524332123] b. MAR 9, 1863

Georgianna CRAM
[1524332121]

No vital statistics exist for Georgianna. It is only known that she died young.

George Albert CRAM (1861-1906)
[1524332122]

George Albert was born SEP 10, 1861 in Dorchester, MA. and died in 1906 in Boston, MA. He was buried in the Cram Cemetery at Exeter, NH. George married Laurette BRAGDON in AUG, 1883. She was born MAY 20, 1851, and died SEP 18, 1904, in Cambridge, MA. One child by adoption.
>   Their adopted child:
>> 1. Eleanor [15243321221] b. APR 17, 1897.

Hattie Augusta CRAM (1863-1944)
[1524332123]

Hattie Augusta was born MAR 9, 1863 in Dorchester MA. and died JUN 11, 1944 at Worcester, MA. She married John C. BASSETT of New Haven, CT., on APR 30, 1880 in Exeter. He was born JUL 7, 1862, and died DEC 28, 1915 at Dorchester, MA. Both were buried at Woodlawn Cemetery in Everett, MA.
>   Their Children:
>> 1. Charles Bassett; b. MAR 3, 1885 in E. Boston; d. MAY 24, 1887.
>> 2. Myrtle Bassett; b. APR 4, 1888; d. JUN 28, 1912 in East Boston.

Reference:

Unpublished Manuscript of Elmer Cram (file 215)

family of Sylvester CRAM [152433213]

Sylvester CRAM [152433213]
b. JUN 24, 1832
d. DEC 22, 1890

1. Sarah Lillias [1524332131] b. APR 2, 1861
m.1. JUL 11, 1860 _____ 2. Emily Frances [1524332132] b. MAY 4, 1863

Sarah MOULTON
b. FEB 21, 1835
d. DEC 29, 1863

3. **Elmer Herbert [1524332133]** b. SEP, 1865
m.2. FEB 6, 1865 _____ 4. William Eugene [1524332134] b. JUL 13, 1867

Mary Wiggin JONES
b. SEP 20, 1831
d. JAN 19, 1914

Sarah Lillias CRAM (1861-)
[1524332131]

Sarah Lillias was born APR 2, 1861 in Dorchester, MA. She married Frank W. WILDER, son of Wilber Flint and Fidelia (Searl) Wilder of Ludlow, MA., on DEC 31, 1888. They resided in Worcester, MA.
    Their Child:
> 1. Shirley Wilder; b. APR 6, 1889; m. Gladys Angel (?) on NOV 19, 1913; she
>   was the daughter of Benjamin A. & Rose (Clark) Angel of Block Island.
>   Their Children:
>> 1. Muriel Wilder; b. JUL 12, 1915; m. William
>>   Patterson, son of Herbert H. & Mary Patterson.
>> 2. Phylis Wilder; b. JUN 11, 1918.
>> 3. Rosere Wilder; b. FEB 24, 1920; m. Stanley Thomas
>>   Burbank.
> 2. Ralph Wilder; b. AUG 6, 1891; m. Eva Hamel on SEP 26, 1916 at Worcester,
>   MA.; she was the d/o Emery and Catherine A. McLaughlin. No children.
> 3. Ray Wilder; b. NOV 23, 1894.
> 4. Mildred Wilder; b. AUG 26, 1897.
> 5. Wilber Wilder; b. JUL 26, 1904; m. Edna Parrott;
>   Their Child (twelfth generation):
>> 1. Nancy Josephine Wilder; b. FEB 25, 1937.

Emily Frances CRAM (1863-)
[1524332132]

Emily Frances was born MAY 4, 1863 in Dorchester, MA. She married Earnest A. WEBSTER, son of Robert and Caroline (Ellis) Webster, on FEB 22, 1890 in East Boston. They had one child, who was born, and died the same day. He died in 1918.

Elmer Herbert CRAM (1865-)*
[1524332133]

Elmer Herbert was born SEP 25, 1865 in Dorchester, MA. He married Abbie Louise KELLEY of Wakefield, MA., daughter of David and Emma (Blanchard) Kelley, on NOV 11, 1891. He was the author of the Unpublished Manuscript (#200) at the New England Historic Genealogical Society that is often quoted in this work.
    Their Child (eleventh generation):
> 1. Theodore Francis [15243321331] b. SEP 29, 1892.

William Eugene CRAM (1867-1941)
[1524332134]

William Eugene was born JUL 13, 1867 at Dorchester, MA. He was a representative of Pheonixville District, CT., where he lived. He was not married. He died in Manchester Hospital on JUN 7, 1941. He was buried at North Coventry (CT.) Cemetery.

William was a resident of Exeter, NH. in his early life. He was an electrician by occupation and a member of the firm of Beckford and Fuller of Boston, MA. He later bought out the other members of the firm. After he retired he moved to Eastford, CT. where he purchased the Warren Estate. The last year of his life he resided with friends, Mr. and Mrs. Arthur J. Vinton of North Coventry, CT.

References:

Unpublished manuscript of Elmer Cram (files 215 and 144)

family of Natt Allen CRAM [152518871]

Natt Allen CRAM [152518871]
b. OCT 21, 1871
d. FEB 23, 1929

m. JUN 3, 1893 _____ 1. Clifton Swett [1525188711] b. APR 1, 1905
2. Ruth Elizabeth [1525188712] b. AUG 1, 1912

Edith Elizabeth SWETT
b. JUL 24, 1873
d.

Clifton Swett CRAM (1905-1986)
[1525188711]

Clifton Swett was born APR 1, 1905 in Pittsfield, NH. and died SEP 30, 1986. He graduated from Gorham Teacher's College, majoring in Manual Arts. Clifton served as post office clerk in Pittsfield for 48 years before retiring. He also served as a volunteer sponsor for children placed on probation in the Pittsfield area.

Clifton's marriage to Ruth May STANIELS, daughter of Arthur Hubbard and Bell Marion (Healey) Staniels of Croydon, NH. and Fargo, ND. on MAR 22, 1936 in Concord, NH. was not mundane. It was the middle of the 1936 flooding of the Merrimack River, and Cpl. Clifton Cram of the National Guard was taking a break after 26 consecutive hours of duty patrolling the streets of Concord. He approached his commanding officer to request "emergency" time off to be married. The officer, misunderstanding his request replied, "Anniversaries don't count as emergencies." Clifton figuring that the officer's reply didn't apply to his situation promptly made his way to the Staniels home and proceeded with the ceremony. Some may say he went AWOL to get married, but after a short stay for the reception he returned to duty, and over the next week saw his new bride an average of 30 minutes a day.

Ruth was born DEC 12, 1915 in Hopkinton, NH. She graduated from Concord High School in 1934 and attended Concord Business College. Ruth worked at Catamount Woven Label Co. for 32 years. One summer's day in 1961, however, is a day she will never forget. Ruth came home from work to tell her husband, "If this wasn't Pittsfield, I'd say the factory was being cased." She had noticed someone sitting on the wall opposite the factory all week, but soon forgot her observation. The following Friday morning, Ruth went to the bank to collect the cash for the payroll for the company. She got into her car and had driven only a block when a young man ran into the road forcing her to stop. Immediately a second youth jumped into the passenger seat, while the first thief opened the door on the driver's side of the car and pushed her to the middle of the front seat between them. She found herself uncomfortable sitting on the black shopping bag containing the payroll. They demanded the money, assuring her they weren't interested in stealing her car. Ruth replied, "Oh you mean the payroll. Too bad, I paid off last night." (she admits today that it wasn't a complete lie as she had paid the night shift employees the day before) Thinking she had no money with her in the car the two would-be robbers drove through town, stopped the car, threw open both doors simultaneously and ran off. Although shaken, Ruth drove back to the factory and delivered the payroll to the waiting employees.

The Cram's lived on Page Street in Pittsfield. On the occasion of their golden wedding anniversary, the local newspaper detailed a bit about their lives. "The house has been home to over a dozen foster children since 1960. Some stayed overnight and others for as long as ten years. Visiting pastors, former Pittsfield residents, extended family and just plain friends have always found a full table, an evening around the piano, a turned-down bed, and a friendly smile at the Cram's . . . Their children's schoolday friends remember hula hoop contests on the front porch; amateur theatricals in the loft (for which the audience sometimes paid not to come), and haunted Halloween houses in the barn."

Clifton was active in church, both teaching and singing in the choir, and serving as a church trustee. He was active in Masonry for 55 years. In his free time Clifton enjoyed classical music, and his wife says that one of their favorite relaxation's was reading to one another.

Their Children:
1. Sherideth Diana [15251887111] b. OCT 25, 1941 in Pittsfield, NH.; graduated from Pittsfield High School in 1959, receiving the Betty Crocker and Mood Kent Awards; after graduation m. AUG 15, 1959 to Richard Arthur SEELEY, s/o Joseph Harold and Laura Elizabeth (Richards) Seeley; he was b. APR 17, 1935; he holds a doctorate from Eastern Baptist Theological School; Sherry graduated from Rhode Island College in 1974 with a degree in early child education; she now has her master's degree in special education and teaches in two high schools in Endicott, NY. where the family resides;
    Their Children:
    1. Calvin Gordon Seeley (identical twin) b. FEB 15, 1961; m. Alisa Marie Sirrinia on OCT 17, 1992.
    2. Karl Richard Seeley (identical twin) b. FEB 15, 1961.
    3. Ruth Catherine Seeley; b. DEC 29, 1963; m. Stephen Chandler Smith, s/o Frederick and Miriam (Chandler) Smith of Plymouth, MA. on JUN 1, 1985; both Ruth and Stephen are graduates of Gordon College;
        Their Children:
        1. Stephanie Miriam Smith; b. MAR 3, 1990.
        2. Timothy Smith; b. APR 19, 1991.
2. Jennifer Lois [15251887112] b. OCT 31, 1943 at Pittsfield; graduated from Pittsfield High School in 1961; m.1. John ELKINS; m.2. John WARREN on NOV 25, 1977; they reside in Concord, NH.
    Children (all by first husband):
    1. John Clifton Elkins; b. FEB 4, 1963; d. SEP 23, 1983
    2. Joyce Anne Elkins; b. JUN 14, 1965.
    3. Jill Stephanie Elkins; b. OCT 23, 1966.
3. Linden Staniels [15251887113] b. DEC 29, 1945 in Pittsfield; graduated from Pittsfield High School in 1963; served in U.S. Army; currently employed at Yankee Book Peddler at Contoocook, NH.; m. Dagmar Jean ANDERSON, d/o Walter Olavi and Helen (Hergengroder) Anderson. at Chicester, NH. on AUG 1, 1970; Jean was b. JUN 3, 1952; she was a foster daughter of Clifton and Ruth Cram; Jean was an honor student at Pittsfield High School; Linden serves as organist at the Advent Christian Church in Pittsfield in his leisure time.
    Their Child:
    Matthew Scott [152518871131] b. MAY 3, 1977

Ruth Elizabeth CRAM (1912-)
[1525188712]

Ruth was born AUG 1, 1912 at Pittsfield, NH. She married first Robert Alexander HOOVER, son of Jarry J. Hoover, on APR 2, 1938 at Pittsfield. He was born in 1909 in Clearfield, PA. She later married a Mr. EMERSON.
    Her Child:
    1. Leone Louise Hoover; b. JAN 8, 1942 at Urbana, IL.

References:

Genealogical and Family History of the State of New Hampshire (p. 1391)
Letters to the Author from Ruth (Staniels) Cram (dtd. JAN 8, 1994 & JAN 21, 1994)
Who's Who of America's Crams
Unpublished Manuscript of Elmer Cram (files 113 & 235)

family of Ralph Adams CRAM [152532731]

Ralph Adams CRAM [152532731]
b. DEC 16, 1863
d. SEP 22, 1942

1. Mary Carrington [1525327311] b. NOV 9, 1901
m. SEP 20, 1900   2. **Ralph Wentworth [1525327312]** b. 1904
3. Elizabeth Strudwick [1525327313] b. 1912

Elizabeth Carrington READ
b. JUN 10, 1873
d. SEP 30, 1943

Mary Carrington CRAM (1901-1989)
[1525327311]

Mary was born NOV 9, 1901 and died JUL 4, 1989. She married Jerome C. GREENE in 1922. They became the parents of two children before divorcing. She married second Richard H. THURSTON about 1930. They later divorced, and she was married a third time to Edward M. NICHOLAS in 1936. She lived in the community of Dummerston, near Brattleboro, VT., and it was there that she died.
    Children by Jerome Greene:
        1. Jerome D. Greene II; b. MAY 27, 1923.
        2. Elizabeth Carrington Greene; b. MAY 1, 1925; m. Andrew S. Crichton in 1948;
            Their Children:
                1. Marc N. Crichton; b. 1948.
                2. Kyle C. Crichton; b. 1952; m. Jeannie Mandelker;
                    Their Children:
                        1. Andrew McLean Crichton; b. 1988.
                        2. Liza Carrington Crichton; b. 1991.
    Child by Edward Nicholas:
        3. Charlotte O'Brien Nicholas; b. 1937.

Ralph Wentworth Cram (1904-1973)*
[1525327312]

Ralph was born on SEP 8, 1904 and died SEP 28, 1973. In his youth he worked in his father's office as a draftsman. Later he became a salesman of medical supplies. Ralph was an avid sportsman. His great interests were hunting, the balance of nature, and the environment. He was one of the original members of the Southborough (MA.) Rod and Gun Club. He was well known as a free-lance contributor and columnist for magazines and newspapers on the subject of sports and hunting - particularly in the Stowe, VT. area where he spent a great deal of time during the latter years of his life.

Ralph married Ann HEATH. She had been born with the name Florence, but had it changed before her marriage (sometime in the 1920's). She was born DEC 28, 1903 and died DEC 3, 1972. Ann was the granddaughter of Ed Heath , who received a patent on JUL 20, 1874 for "caveat on an alleged improvement in grain binder." It is a family legend that he was found burned to death in his workshop, allegedly murdered to silence him and eliminate his "improvements" to the grain binder (which later became the thresher and reaper).

Ann owned and operated "The Crams" Ski Lodge in Stowe, VT. during the early 1950's, and served as secretary to the Dean of Admissions of Wellesley College during the 1960's. Ann was an avid environmentalist, more knowledgeable about botany than hunting. her daughter Sarah remembers that she was the person to whom people would bring sick and injured birds and animals for care and curing. She was a Siamese cat lover, a terrific cook and a voluminous reader, recalls her son.
    Their Children:
        1. Patricia Day [15253273121] b. DEC 8, 1930;
        2. Sarah Elizabeth Blake [15253273122] b. JUL 28, 1940;
        3. Ralph Adams, II [15253273123] b. JUN 9, 1941;

Elizabeth Strudwick CRAM
[1525327313]

Elizabeth was born about 1912 and died in 1967. Her son, David remembers her as someone who was active in amateur theatricals, a person who adored animals (especially cats), a good cook, and an employee in educational institutions and the government in a variety of positions. She was married three times, her first husband being Wallace McIlwaine SCUDDER, the second Armstrong deRouliac PRESCOTT and the Third Baxter POLK. She lived the last 12 to 14 years of her life in El Paso, Texas with her third husband.
Her Children (both by her first husband):
1. David W. Scudder; b. MAY 8, 1936; m. Marie Louise Sibley on JUN 14, 1958; he reports that his grandfather, Ralph Adams Cram, left his library to him despite a meaningful portion of it being destroyed several years later in a fire; perhaps half of his books remain in the collection
   Their Children:
   1. Claire W. Scudder; b. APR 12, 1960.
   2. Deirdre W. Scudder; b. DEC 5, 1962; m. Peter Martin; they reside in Needham, MA.
   3. Andrew W. Scudder; b. SEP 2, 1965.
2. Judith Carrington Scudder; b. MAR 26, 1939; m. William Robinson; later divorced;
   Their Child:
   1. William Robinson, Jr.; b. in 1969 or 1970.

References:

Letter to the author from Ralph Adams Cram II (dtd AUG 4, 1993)
Letter to the author from Elizabeth Crichton (dtd. AUG 20, 1993)
Letter to the author from David Scudder (dtd. AUG 16, 1993)
Letter to the author from Edward Wall (dtd SEP 1, 1993)

family of Victor Prescott CRAM [152573123]

Victor Prescott CRAM [152573123]
b. MAR 21, 1857
d. APR 19, 1927

m. DEC 17, 1879

Esther Almyra JOHNSON
b. MAY 2, 1868
d. JAN 13, 1919

1. Victor Dee [1525731231] b. OCT 6, 1880
2. Mark William [1525731232] b. MAR 18, 1882
3. Vivian Etta [1525731233] b. DEC 13, 1883
4. Paul Rufus [1525731234] b. 1885
5. Ada Bertha [1525731235] b. JAN 3, 1887
6. Lulu Prescott [1525731236] b. JAN 4, 1890
7. Charles Chester [1525731237] b. 1892
8. Eliza [1525731238] b. 1893
9. Alberta [1525731239] b. NOV 28, 1894
10. Woodruff Bryan [152573123A] b. AUG 11, 1897
11. Owen Prescott [152573123B] b. JUL 17, 1900
12. Thelma [152573123C] b. MAY, 1903
13. Alton Brooks [152573123D] b. MAR 21, 1905

Victor Dee CRAM (1880-)
[1525731231]

Victor Dee was born OCT 6, 1880 at Kanab, Kane County, Utah. He died at Salt Lake City. He married Emily Isabel RASBAND, daughter of Thomas Heber and Sarah Jane (Murdock) Rasband, ON JUN 22, 1910. She was born JAN 6, 1866 in Wasatch County, Utah.
    Their Children (all born in Salt Lake City):
1. Dee Raymond [15257312311] b. MAY 9, 1911; m.1. Edna OGZEWALLA, d/o Charles & Matilda Razine (Gernand) Ogzewalla, on JUL 6, 1929; she was b. JUL 20, 1910 in Tamaroa, Perry County, IL., and d. JUL 20, 1931 in Salt Lake City; m.2. Eva WRIGHT, d/o Bert Leonard Lewis and Salena (Einerson) Wright, on DEC 22, 1934 at Coalville, Summit County, UT; she was b. JUL 4, 1912 at Salt Lake City;
    Child by Edna:
    1. Carmen Rayola [152573123111] b. FEB 20, 1930 at Salt Lake City.
2. Heber Rasband [152573123112] b. SEP 22, 1912; d. AUG 7, 1936.
3. Lois [152573123113] b. NOV 6, 1914; d. in Salt Lake City on NOV 19, 1914.
4. Lorna Ruth [152573123114] b. NOV 2, 1915; m. Paul McFARLANE.
5. Rhea Ann [152573123115] b. DEC 17, 1917; m. Wesley L. STEFFENSEN, s/o Rasme Emanuel & Elizabeth (Checketts) Steffensen, on JUL 9, 1937; he was b. JUL 24, 1914 in Tremonton, Box Elder County, Utah, and d. JUL 9, 1937 in Salt Lake City;
    Their Children:
    1. Sonia Steffensen; b. JUL 21, 1938 in Santa Monica, Los Angeles.
    2. Carol Steffensen; b. APR 29, 1941 in Inglewood, Los Angeles.
    3. Linda Steffensen; b. FEB 24, 1945; in Inglewood, Los Angeles.
6. Victor James [152573123116] b. MAY 1, 1919; d. in Salt Lake City on MAY 2, 1919.
7. Mark Rasband [152573123117] b. MAY 22, 1921.
8. Sara Lesle (or Leslie) [152573123118] b. AUG 3, 1923; d. MAY, 1942;
    m. William A. POST.
9. Joy Rasband [152573123119] b. SEP 29, 1925.
10. Thomas Dale [15257312311A] b. MAY 6, 1928.

Mark William CRAM (1882-)
[1525731232]

Mark was born MAR 18, 1882 at Kanab, Kane County, UT. He married Rose STONEY, daughter of Robert and Sarah (Jakeman) Stoney, of Beaver, Beaver County, UT., on JUN 1, 1904. She was born APR 27, 1880. Mark was a high school teacher.
    Their Children:
1. Myrna [15257312321] b. FEB 18, 1905 at Provo, UT.; m. FEB 15, 1930 to John Franklin DAVIS.
2. LaRue [15257312322] b. FEB 23, 1907 at Beaver, UT.; d. APR 6, 1931.
3. Revo [15257312323] b. OCT 16, 1910 at Brigham, Box Elder County, UT.;

m. FEB 7, 1934 to Karl H. JARVIS.
4. Fay [15257312324] b. OCT 14, 1913 at Farmington, Davis County, UT.
5. Marva [15257312325] b. MAY 7, 1915 at Farmington, UT.

Vivian Etta CRAM (1883-)
[1525731233]

Vivian was born DEC 13, 1883 at Kanab, UT. She married Milton H. KNUDSEN, son of Herman and Amanda (Evert) Knudson, on NOV 22, 1905 at Salt Lake City. They resided in Provo, UT.
Their Children:
1. Vera Knudsen; b. OCT 2, 1906 in Provo, UT.; m. Oliver Martell Anderson.
2. Mildred Knudsen; b. NOV 26, 1907 in Provo; m. Frank E. Peterson.
3. Oran Milton Knudsen; b. NOV 14, 1909 in Provo; m. Marie Lillian Eccles.
4. Genevieve Knudsen; b. SEP 11, 1911 in Provo; m. George Grant Gardner.
5. Merle Knudsen; b. NOV 7, 1912 in Provo; m. John Albert Haigh.
6. Eudora Knudsen; b. AUG 13, 1914 in Provo.
7. Grace Knudsen; b. NOV 5, 1917 in Provo, and d. there NOV 5, 1917.
8. Ames Russell Knudsen; b. JAN 7, 1920 in Ames, Iowa; m. June Wakefield.
9. Jay Donald Knudsen; b. JUN 10, 1923 in Driggs, Teton County, ID.
10. Elaine Knudsen; b. JUN 10, 1925 in Ephriam, Sunpete County, UT.

Paul Rufus CRAM (1885-1885)
[1525731234]

Paul was born in 1885 at Huntington, Emory County, UT. He died at the age of two weeks.

Ada Bertha CRAM (1887-)
[1525731235]

Ada was born JAN 3, 1887 at Huntington, Emory County, UT. She married James NISBET, son of George and Marian (Air Lees) Nisbet on MAR 21, 1911 at Salt Lake City. James was born APR 21, 1889 at Galston Ayrshire, Scotland, and died MAR 9, 1944 at Salt Lake City.
Their Children (all born at Salt Lake City):
1. LeRoy Heber Nisbet; b. JAN 26, 1915 at Salt Lake City; m. Beryl Anderson.
2. Bert Cram Nisbet; b. FEB 25, 1917; m. Patricia Ann Hogan.
3. Frank James Nisbet; b. JUL 30, 1922 at Salt Lake City.
4. Mark Cram Nisbet; b. JUL 13, 1928 at Salt Lake City.

Lulu Prescott CRAM (1890-)
[1525731236]

Lulu was born JAN 4, 1890 at Huntington, UT. She married Angus ALLRED, son of Thomas Butler and Hannah (Stoddart) Allred, on JUN 26, 1918. He was born JAN 22, 1881 at Spring City, UT., and died NOV 30, 1931 at Delta, Millard County, UT.
Their Children (all born in Delta, Millard County, UT.):
1. Glenn Angus Allred; b. SEP 15, 1919 at Delta, Millard County, UT.; m. Lorraine Greek, d/o Hershel Thurmon & Ida Ola (Hall) Greek, on DEC 14, 1941; she was b. DEC 25, 1922 in El Paso, TX.
2. Thomas Boyd Allred; b. MAY 6, 1921.
3. Victor Dean Allred; b. SEP 13, 1922; m. Alice Jackson, d/o Victor Orin & Ada Estella (Rey) Jackson, on MAY 9, 1944 in Salt Lake City; she was b. MAY 9, 1923 in Driggs, Idaho.
4. Llanos Allred; b. APR 6, 1925.
5. Veda Allred; b. JUL 4, 1927 (twin)
6. Ada Allred; b. JUL 4, 1927 (twin)

Charles Chester CRAM (1892-1892)
[1525731237]

Charles was born in 1892 in Huntington, UT. and died at the age of two weeks.

Eliza CRAM (1893-1893)
[1525731238]

Eliza was born in 1893 and died at the age of four months.

Alberta CRAM (1894-)
[1525731239]

Alberta was born NOV 28, 1894 in Huntington, UT. She married Joseph Egbert DAVIS, son of Edwin Wooley and Matilda Elnora (Egbert) Davis, on JUN 3, 1921 in Salt Lake City. He was born in Kaysville, Davis County, UT. on NOV 2, 1879.
   Their Children:
         1. Joseph Egbert Davis; b. APR 2, 1922 in Salt Lake City.
         2. Edwin Victor Davis; b. SEP 29, 1924 in Salt Lake City.
         3. Ruth Davis; b. JAN 25, 1927 in Salt Lake City.
         4. Virginia Davis; b. JAN 31, 1931 in Salt Lake City.

Woodruff Bryan CRAM (1897-)
[152573123A]

Woodruff was born AUG 11, 1897 at Huntington, UT. He married Reva Ileta JACOBS, daughter of Swen Hopkins and Mary Emily (Thomas) Jacobs, on DEC 3, 1919 at Salt Lake City. She was born APR 20, 1902 at Salem, Madison County, Idaho. He was an attorney at Detroit, MI.
   Their Children:
         1. Naida Marie [152573123A1] b. NOV 21, 1921 in Salt Lake City.
         2. Jean Lorraine [152573123A2] b. SEP 26, 1926 in Detroit, MI.
         3. Donald Bruce [152573123A3] b. NOV 7, 1932 in Detroit, MI.

Owen Prescott CRAM (1900-1922)
[152573123B]

Owen was born JUL 117, 1900 at Draper, Salt Lake City, UT. He died MAY 22, 1922.

Thelma CRAM (1903-1903)
[152573123C]

Thelma was born in MAY, 1903 in Provo, UT. She died in 1903 in Provo.

Alton Brooks CRAM (1905-1905)
[152573123D]

Alton was born MAR 21, 1905 and died MAY 2, 1905 in Provo, UT.

References:

Records of Mrs. Angus Allred of Delta, UT.
Records of Mr. Victor P. Cram of Salt Lake City, UT.
Records of Mrs. W. B. Cram of Detroit, MI.
Records of Mrs. J. H. Freeman of Los Angeles, CA.
Records of Mrs. Milton H. Knudsen of Provo, UT.
Unpublished Manuscript of Elmer Cram (files 57, 294, & 295)

family of Ralph LaVenture CRAM [152593A15]

Ralph LaVenture CRAM [152593A15]
b. NOV 6, 1906
d. MAR 8, 1939

m. JAN 22, 1930 _____1. Ralph Archibald [152593A15] b. NOV 6, 1930

Doris ARCHIBALD
b.
d.

Ralph Archibald CRAM (1930-)
[152593A151]

Ralph Archibald was born NOV 6, 1930, in Seattle, WA. He graduated from high school in Moline, IL., and in 1948 obtained a B.S. in pre-medicine from Augustana College, Rock Island, IL. He received his M.D. degree from the University of Michigan in 1955. After interning at James Decker Munson Hospital in Traverse City, MI., he served in the U.S. Army Medical Corps from 1956-1958. While in the service he practiced in obstetrics and gynecology at the Fifth General Hospital in Stuttgart, Germany.

From 1958 to the present (1995) Ralph has been engaged in family practice in Albion, Michigan. He has delivered more than 3,500 babies, and now has seen a fair number of "second generation" cases - children he delivered a generation ago now becoming parents. His practice of medicine follows traditional lines - he makes housecalls, and attends to the medical needs of the elderly as well as younger members of the family unit. He comments that his patients still keep his family provided with venison, fish, jam, jellies and baked goods as tokens of their appreciation. Ralph is Board Certified in Family Medicine. He has served as president of the Calhoun County Medical Society (in 1980), and has been Chief of Staff of Albion Community Hospital on two separate occasions.

Described by a friend as a "Jeffersonian man," Ralph built the family's first home while in medical school. He has continued to design, wire, plumb and install heating in subsequent homes they have owned. Since 1959 the Cram family has lived in an 1870 Italianate Victorian home in Albion, situated on an acre of land maintained much as it was in the 19th century. They cultivate vegetable and flower gardens, fruit trees, and a vineyard, which Ralph says manages to produce a creditable Delaware wine. In his spare time he enjoys sailing, wind surfing, photography, and travel. He is a member of the Salem United Church of Christ in Albion, and was president of the church council in 1990. Ralph was named Michigan Family Practitioner of the Year 1993-1994, by the Michigan Academy of Family Practice.

Ralph married Mary Ellen NIELSEN on SEP 12, 1953, soon after she graduated from the University of Michigan with a B.S. degree in Nursing.
 Their Children:
  1. Virginia Susan [152593A1511] b. JAN 11, 1955 in Ann Arbor, MI;
    Bachelors degree in Comparative Cultural Studies from Governor's State University in IL. in 1975; MBA from University of Chicago in 1988, and Masters in Finance from the Universite Catholique de Louvain in Belgium; fluent in French and Spanish, she has been employed as Secretary General of International Data Exchange Association of Brussels, Belgium since 1989; the association is concerned with the exchange of standardized information used in international commerce; m. in 1990 to Walter Fernando MARTOS of Cajamarca, Peru; they live in Brussels;
      Their Child:
      1. Alexandra Irene Martos, was b. JAN 20, 1991.
  2. Katherine Celeste [152593A1512] b. OCT 23, 1956 in Fort Ord, CA.; Bachelors degree in Hospital Administration from Concordia College in MN., and MBA from Michigan State University; m. Thomas Franklin REEVES on AUG 19, 1978; they reside in Ypsilanti, MI.; both are employed in the health care field;

Their Children:
1. Margaux Allison Reeves; b. APR 19, 1987.
2. Kelley Elizabeth Reeves; b. APR 23, 1989.
3. Stephen Cram Reeves; b. AUG 19, 1990.

3. Ralph Nielsen [152593A1513] b. APR 2, 1962 at Albion, MI; B.A. degree from Kalamazoo College, MI., and Masters degree in Real Estate Appraisal and Investment Analysis from the University of Wisconsin in 1987; in 1990 he resided in Chicago, employed by Julian Poft & Downey; m. Carolyn Irene GIBBENS on May 18, 1991 at the First United Methodist Church in Evanston, IL.;

Their Children:
1. Nielson Gibbens [152593A15131] b. APR 5, 1993 in Evanston, IL.
2. John Nielsen Gibbens [152593A15132] b. in 1993.

References:

Letter to the author from Mary (Nielsen) Cram dtd. MAY 5, 1977
Letters to the author from Dr. Ralph Archibald Cram dtd. MAR 18, 1990 and DEC 3, 1990.
Letters to the author from Mary (Mrs. Ralph Archibald) Cram (dtd. JAN 20, 1991 & DEC 5, 1993)

family of Maynard Urlin CRAM [152593A21]

Maynard Urlin CRAM [152593A21]
b. AUG 17, 1897
d. JAN 6, 1957

m.1.   JUN 20, 1918

Dorothy KEMMERLY
b.
d. JAN 2, 1993

m.2.   1945

Edna WARWICK

1. John Charles [152593A211] b. 1919.
2. Margaret Elizabeth [152593A212] b. 1920.
3. Louise Mae [152593A213] b. 1926.

John Charles CRAM (1919-1994)
[152593A211]

John was born FEB 13, 1919 in Springfield, OH., and died JAN 21, 1994 at Troy, OH. The family lived in Fostoria, OH. for several years, and John recalled that although he had few memories of that time, two that stood out in the mind of a small boy were the rabbit hutches in his back yard and a next door neighbor who ate his pie with his hands.

"From Fostoria we moved to Mansfield where dad was employed for about the next ten years," John said. "I started school there and my ambition was to become a Linotype operator like my dad. That ambition was forgotten the day that grandfather Cram gave me a discarded battery operated radio. (I) don't know what happened to the radio, but it sparked my interest in electronics."

Maynard lost his job in Mansfield when John was in the eighth grade, and the family moved to Upper Sandusky. John graduated from Upper Sandusky High School in 1937. He did odd jobs at a local radio shop and was underfoot so much that the owner hired him to work on the service bench for $7.50 a week.

"A regular visitor to the shop was the projectionist at one of the local movie houses," he recalled. "I became his substitute, and after a time became the regular operator after he and the theater owner came to a parting of the ways."

In the fall of 1941 John applied for a job at the Fairfield Air Depot near Dayton, OH. and started work the day after Christmas as an aircraft electrician. In OCT of 1942 he enlisted in the Army Air Corps. After military training and technical schooling he left for duty with the Fifteenth Air Corps in southern Italy in DEC, 1943. John next attained the rank of technical sergeant, and was chief non-commissioned officer of the Power Gun Turret Shop of the Eighty-Eighth Depot Repair Squadron. Their assignment was to carry out major repair jobs on B-24 Liberator bombers which returned to the base with significant battle damage. John returned home in DEC, 1945.

He returned to Fairfield Air Depot in FEB, 1946, and after the Air Force became a separate arm of the military services, the depot became Patterson Field of the Wright-Patterson Air Force Base complex. In 1961 John transferred to another Dayton Air Force facility - which in 1962 became the Defense Electronics Supply Center (DESC). The primary task of the center is the procurement (and allied functions) of common electronic parts for issue to all military services and many non-military government activities. Initially he worked in an organization that supplied technical assistance and information to procurement. The last three years at DESC were spent as chief of a group of technical writers. He retired in APR, 1976.

On JAN 26, 1946 John married Lydia Lois WELBOURN, daughter of Lawrence Franklin (Frank) and Orpha (Brock) Welbourn. She was born OCT 24, 1919 near Union City, OH. After their marriage Lois ran a pre-school for children in Troy, OH. where they lived. John enjoyed his stereo and tinkering in his basement workshop where he fixed all manner of things for his family, friends, and neighbors. He and Lois traveled in Europe, Hawaii, Venezuela and Alaska following his retirement. John also enjoyed volunteering for the Troy Public Library. He was substitute driver for the library's Bookmobile, assisted with Friends of the Library projects, repairing balky audio and video cassettes from the library's collection.

On Wednesday, JAN 19, 1994 John suffered a massive stroke and was rushed to the hospital. Two days later doctors announced there was no brain activity and he was kept on life support long enough for surgery that resulted in the donation of his liver and eyes according to the provisions of his living will. The date of his death was JAN 21, 1994. His body was cremated and interred in Riverside Cemetery in Troy. A memorial service was held for him at the First United Methodist Church on JAN 26, the day that would have been his forty- eighth wedding anniversary

Their Children:
1. Suzanne J. [152593A2111] b. JAN 29, 1948 in Dayton, OH.; Suzi graduated from Troy High School and attended Ohio State University, studying education; m. on AUG 1, 1970 to Gary MATHES, s/o Glen & Helen Mathes; he was b. JAN 24, 1946 and graduated from Ohio State U. in 1969 with a BS. degree in agriculture; Gary served as a first Lt. with the Second Armored Div. at Ft. Hood, TX. from 1969-1971; he is currently (1991) District Conservationist for Richland County, OH. with the US Department of Agriculture Soil Conservation Service (USDA); Suzi is an administrative assistant with the USDA.

Their Child:
1. Anne Louise Mathes; b. JUN 9, 1977 at Millersburg, Holmes County, OH.

2. Charles Welbourn [152593A2112] b. JAN 29, 1952 in Dayton; he graduated from Troy High School and earned his BS degree from Purdue University in Electrical Engineering; he received a MA. degree from George Washington University in telecommunications operations; from 1974 to 1976 he was employed by the Federal Communication Commission, and from 1976 to 1983 by the Federal Aviation Administration in Washington, DC.; In March of 1983 he transferred to the Foreign Technology Division of the Air Force Systems Command at Wright-Patterson Air Force Base near Dayton; he m. Susan TARBUCK on OCT 4, 1974 at Hammond, IN.; they were divorced on MAR 8, 1990; Charles resides in Beavercreek, OH. with his children;

Their Children:
1. Kevin John [152593A21121] b. MAY 14, 1978 in Silver Spring, MD.
2. Erin Kathleen [152593A21122] b. MAR 13, 1981 in Silver Spring, MD.

Margaret Elizabeth CRAM (1920-) [152593A212]

Margaret (known as Betty) was born DEC 4, 1920 in Kenton, OH. The family moved to Fostoria, OH. shortly thereafter, and two years later to Mansfield. Betty recalls that her earliest memories are of having mumps, and being struck by a sled piloted by her brother John - necessitating her only trip to the doctor as a child to get four stitches. The family later moved to Upper Sandusky where she graduated from Upper Sandusky High School.

Betty claims to come by her interest in journalism honestly with her father, grandfather, and two uncles in the printing and newspaper business. She tells of visiting her grandfather Cram's printing shop in Marion, OH. when young having a fine time, and coming away with printer's ink all over her. In high school she was associate editor of the Senior Annual and a member of the school newspaper staff.

After graduation she worked for a local lawyer (and representative in the Ohio General Assembly), Harold L. Mason for the princely sum of $5.00 per week. In 1941 she married Harold SIMS, a farmer in Salem Township, Wyandot County, OH. He enlisted in the Army in 1942, and Betty enlisted in the Air Force. Harold was a glider trooper, and was killed in the invasion of France on JUN 12, 1944.

Following the war, Betty attended Ohio State University. It was there that she met and later married Crawford W. WELCH, son of Wesley and Ethel (Glover) Welch, on JUN 5, 1947. Crawford was born MAR 3, 1919 at Junction City, AR. They moved to Arkansas to be near Crawford's ailing father, and aside from Crawford's tours of duty in the military have lived there ever since. Crawford was a representative for Goodwill Publishing Co. for several years, and in 1948 became affiliated with Metropolitan Life Insurance Co.

Crawford began his military career during the Korean Conflict. He served a tour of duty with Army Ordnance in Germany and France, where Betty joined him for three years. Their daughter Cathy was born in Kaiserslautern, Germany, and Wendy in Verdun, France. Following this tour, Crawford remained in the reserves until his retirement in 1973, with 33 years of continual service including his active duty, reserve, and national guard service.

Betty retired as church secretary in North Little Rock in 1980, and Crawford dabbles in insurance and real estate these days. They are charter members of the First Baptist Church of Sherwood, AR., a bedroom community of Little Rock where they have lived for the past 47 years. Betty volunteers at the Baptist Memorial Medical Center. They enjoy the facilities of nearby Little Rock Air Force Base.

Their Children:

1. Roger William Welch; b. DEC 3, 1948 in Little Rock, AR; gr. from Sylvan Hills H.S. in 1966; served a four-year Navy enlistment in Spain and the Philippines; attended Captial City College in Little Rock; m. Jolene DeWeerd on AUG 5, 1973; she was b. NOV 4, 1954; he is employed by Kerr Paper Co., and she is a dental hygienist in Benton, AR, where they live;

   Their Child:

   1. Jeff William Welch; b. JAN 29, 1978 in Benton, AR.

2. Lizabeth Claire (Betsey) Welch; b. DEC 9, 1951 in Little Rock; gr. Sylvan Hills H.S. in 1969; attended Ohio State University and University of Arkansas at Fayetteville and Little Rock; she received her MA in Social Work in 1991; m. Arlin Fields in 1976; they divorced in 1986; Betsey m. Jeff Johnson in 1991; he is a mechanic specializing in electrical vehicles; she works with young children and adolescents at Bridgeway Psychiatric Hospital in North Little Rock.

   Children (both by first marriage):

   1. Laura Johanna Fields; b. OCT 1, 1979 in Little Rock.
   2. Jonathan Brendon Fields; b. OCT 3, 1981 in Little Rock.

3. Cathy Winona Welch; b. JUN 27, 1954 in Landstuhl, Germany; gr. Sylvan Hills H.S. in 1972; she worked for AR. State Rehab for 10 years; m. Tom Swift in 1973; divorced in 1982; Cathy m. Tim Lampe in 1983; they live in Cheyenne, WY. where he is stationed at F. E. Warren AFB as a general staff officer (Lt. Col.); Cathy received her BS degree in Accounting and CPA certification in 1992 in Omaha, NE.

   Her Children:

   1. Thomas Russell Swift; b. DEC 12, 1978 in Little Rock, AR.
   2. Jill Marie Lampe; b. JUL 24, 1984 in Omaha, NE.

4. Wendy Carole Welch; b. OCT 4, 1955 in Verdun, France; gr. from Sylvan Hills H.S. in 1973; attended the University of Arkansas at Fayetteville; while a student there she met and married Larry Clements; they divorced in 1993; Wendy recently married Monte Morris, an electrical engineer; he is employed at AP& L Nuclear Plant in Russellville, AR., where they reside.

   Children (both by first marriage):

   1. Rachel Elizabeth Clements; b. JUL 23, 1984 at Little Rock.
   2. Ashley Marie Clements; b. AUG 23, 1987 at Little Rock.

5. Marcy Ann Welch; b. OCT 19, 1960 at Ft. Leavenworth, KS. (where Crawford was attending Staff and Command College); gr. Sylvan Hills H.S. in 1978; received her B.S. degree in Elementary and Special Education at University of Arkansas at Little Rock in 1984; she has been teaching sixth grade at Sylvan Hills Elementary School; she is currently pursuing her master's degree at Univ. of Arkansas at Little Rock; unmarried.

Louise Mae CRAM   (1926-1985)
[152593A213]

Louise was born AUG 7, 1926 in Carey, OH. and died DEC 23, 1985 in Upper Sandusky, OH. She was reared in Upper Sandusky, graduating from Upper Sandusky High School in 1944. She attended Ohio State University, graduating in 1947 with a BS degree in Education. She taught in the Lorain, OH. school system until 1950, when she moved to Highland Falls, NY. to be near her fiancee, then a cadet in the United States Military Academy.

On JUN 13, 1951 Louise married Franklin Loeb WILSON, son of Winfield and Helen (Loeb) Wilson. He was born DEC 22, 1928 in Dayton, OH.., graduated from Columbus North High School in Columbus, OH. He attended Ohio State University in 1946-47 before entering the United States Military Academy in 1947. He graduated with a commission of second. Lt. of Infantry in 1951. The family lived at Army Posts in Georgia, Kentucky, Alabama, North Carolina, Kansas, Texas, Hawaii, and in Springfield, Virginia (while Frank was assigned to the Pentagon). Louise resided in Ohio to be near her family on two occasions - while her husband served wartime duty assignments in Korea and Viet Nam. Their last two assignments took them to the University of Connecticut, and NATO Headquarters in Brussels, Belgium. Frank retired from active duty in JUN, 1981 with the rank of Colonel. Upon retirement they moved to Upper Sandusky, where they were residing at the time of her unexpected death from heart failure in DEC 23, 1985. Louise is buried in the Old Mission Cemetery at Upper Sandusky. Frank presently resides in Ashland, OH.

Their Children:

1. Jennifer Louise Wilson; b. MAY 4, 1953 in Columbus, OH.; graduated from West Springfield High School, VA. and attended Northern Virginia Community College; m. to Thomas Kane Galleher, Jr., s/o Thomas and Elizabeth Galleher, on AUG 26, 1972; he was b. FEB 26, 1951 at Redwood City, CA.; he graduated from Annandale High School and attended Lynchburg College; In JUL, 1970 Jeni began work for the U. S. Government; she has worked as an analyst in the Office of the Deputy Chief of Staff for Intelligence, U. S. Army Materiel Command since MAR, 1985; her husband Tom is a supervisor in the Combat Service Support Branch, U. S. Army Personnel Command; they reside in Haymarket, VA., and have no children.

2. Joel William Wilson; b. OCT 18, 1954 at Ft. Bragg, NC.; he graduated from West Springfield High School in 1972 and earned his Bachelor's degree in Industrial Psychology from Bowling Green State University, OH. in 1976; in 1978 he was awarded his MBA degree, with a concentration in Business Logistics, from Ohio State University; Joel served in the U. S. Army from 1976 to 1983 with the 82nd Airborne Division and was stationed in Ft. Eustis, VA., and Ft. Bragg, NC.; He joined Procter and Gamble Co. and is presently Logistics Manager; he also maintains Active Reserve Status in the U. S. Army with the rank of Major; Joe m. Wendy Dilworth on JUN 12, 1977 in Elyria, OH.; they were divorced in OCT 1985; on MAY 20, 1989 he m. Linda Smith in Cincinnati, OH.; they live in Cincinnati;

    Children by Wendy:

    1. Kristen Michelle Wilson; b. JAN 19, 1982 in Fayetteville, NC.
    2. Lindsay Nicolle Wilson; b. APR 21, 1985 in Plano, TX.

    Child by Linda:

    3. Andrew Scott Wilson; b. FEB 14, 1990 in Cincinnati, OH.

3. John Franklin Wilson; b. SEP 6, 1956 at Ft. Sam Houston, TX.; graduated from James W. Robinson Jr. High School, Fairfax, VA on JUN 4, 1974; attended Miami University, Oxford, OH. 1974-1975; transferred to Kansas State University in AUG, 1975 to study landscape architecture and dance; m. Mrs. Pamela Jean (Roy) Garling on DEC 9, 1989; she was b. SEP 25, 1949; John is a graphic designer and production manager for The Daily Reporter newspaper, and Pam is typesetting coordinator for the Suburban News Publications; they reside in Galena, OH.;

Pam's children by her previous marriage:
1. Paul Robert Garling; b. JUN 10, 1970.
2. Jennifer Jean Garling; b. MAY 4, 1973.
3. David Randall Garling; b. JAN 6, 1985.

References:

Letter to the Author from Betty (Cram) Welch (dtd. APR 25, 1994)
Letter to the Author from John C. Cram (dtd. MAY 10, 1991)
Letter to the Author from Franklin L. Wilson (dtd. JUN 8, 1991)
Letter to the Author from Jennifer Wilson-Galleher (dtd. JUN 12, 1991)
Letter to the Author from Joel Wilson (dtd. JUN 17, 1991)
Letter to the Author from John Wilson (dtd. JUL 5, 1991)
Records of Michael Cram

family of Ramon Shoup CRAM   [152593A22]

Ramon Shoup CRAM [152593A22]
b. NOV 14, 1902
d. JAN 13, 1961

m. JUN 25, 1927 _____1. Michael Alan [152593A221] b. NOV 8, 1938

Helen Fern HOLLAND
b. AUG 22, 1902
d. MAR 5, 1971

Michael Alan CRAM (1938-)
[152593A221]

Michael was born on NOV 8, 1938 in Columbus, OH. He graduated from Mansfield Senior High School, Mansfield, OH., but when the family returned to Alabama he enrolled in Birmingham Southern College. There he majored in journalism and speech, was a member of Delta Sigma Phi social fraternity, on the staff of the college newspaper and year book and was a member of the inter-fraternity council. While attending college Mike worked in the advertising department of the Birmingham News and WBRC-TV television station. He received his BA degree in 1961.

Following graduation he was employed by the Alabama State Employment Service and Associated Industries of Alabama before being named Assistant Executive Secretary of the Jefferson County Medical Society, a position he held for three years.

In 1965 he joined Chrysler Corporation, first in their Space Division in Huntsville, AL., and later at the Detroit Tank Plant, Automotive Sales Group and Corporate Communication Staff in Detroit, Michigan. He wrote employee oriented publications, did personnel interviewing, and was involved in the administration of a number of benefit programs and other personnel activities. In 1970 he received his MA degree in mass communication from Wayne State University in Detroit, Michigan.

On AUG 26, 1967 Mike was married to Mary Esther Livingway, daughter of Emory and Cleo (Idema) Livingway, of Detroit, MI. She was born JUN 7, 1937. Esther was a high school teacher and librarian of the Redford Union High School library at the time of their marriage. She later became a full-time homemaker until their children were old enough to attend school.

The Cram family moved to Chagrin Falls, OH. in 1969 when Mike became labor relations/communication specialist with the Automotive Division of TRW, Inc. He later served as assistant personnel manager of the TRW Main Plant. Mike held personnel positions with the Allen Bradley Systems Division and Stock Equipment Company in suburban Cleveland before moving the family to Troy, OH. where he was Employee Relations Manager of the Fram Corporation Plant in nearby Greenville, OH.

IN 1981 Mike left Fram and purchased a family oriented franchised bookstore, Little Professor Book Center, in Troy. For the next seven years he managed the 2,000 sq. ft. store, serving local educational and religious organizations, as well as area businesses and the general public.

In 1989 Mike once again changed his career path when he entered the college bookstore business. He became manager of the University Campus Store of Southeastern Massachusetts University in N. Dartmouth, MA., and in SEP, 1991 he associated himself with the Follett College Stores Corp. when he took over management of the Old Town Hall Bookstore at Wheaton College (MA.). He later managed the Baruch College Bookstore in mid-town Manhattan (NY.) for one year. One year in New York City was enough for mike. He re-entered retail book selling in February, 1996 when he became manager of a 22,000 sq. ft. superstore for Barnes and Noble in Macon, Georgia, where he now resides

In 1980 Esther became Extension Coordinator of the Troy/Miami County Public Library in Troy, OH. - a position that she held until the family moved to New Bedford, MA. in 1988. At that time she was named

Branch Librarian with the New Bedford Public Library, but due to budget cuts she was laid off 1990. She currently resides in Rochester, MI. The Crams were divorced in 1991.

Most of Mike's spare time lately has been taken up with researching, writing and assembling this book. During his college years Mike enjoyed cave exploring (spelunking) underneath the mountains of Alabama. He qualified as a member of a cave rescue squad sponsored by Civil Defense organization in the early 1960's. Later he was a member of Toastmasters International for ten years, attaining the level of Able Toastmaster and holding every office in his local club and serving in offices at both the Area and District levels. He was a member of Kiwanis International for four years in Troy, OH. and served a two-year term on the club's Board of Directors.

Their Children:

1. Marc Andrew [152593A2211] b. NOV 7, 1970 in Cleveland, OH.; graduated from New Bedford High School, MA. in 1989; resides with his companion, Leslie Sweet (d/o James Sweet) in Bristol, RI. where he is a cook for a local restaurant; on JUN 24, 1993 they became the parents of a daughter, Abigail Sweet in Providence, RI.; Leslie also has a son, Jeffrey Sweet, who was b. SEP 17, 1990.

2. Matthew Alan [152593A2212] b. OCT 17, 1972 in Cleveland, OH.; graduated from New Bedford High School in 1991; entered the U.S. Marine Corps. on JUL 3, 1991; On FEB 4, 1995 he married Brenda Rios, d/o Leonardo and Nellie Rios;   She was b. APR 22, 1966; Matt currently works with the security force of a bank in Providence; Brenda is a secretary for a local firm.

Their Child:

1. Madison Elan [152593A22121] b. APR 18, 1995 at Pawtucket, RI.

Reference:

Records of Michael Cram

family of Rinaldo Orland "Nally" CRAM [152636142]

Rinaldo Orland CRAM [152636142]
b. JAN 1, 1864
d. JUL 11, 1940

m. DEC 31, 1890   1. Verl Orland [1526361421] b. NOV 3, 1891.
                                         2. **Leland Leslie [1526361422]** b. OCT 13, 1893

Lena JENKINS
b. SEP 11, 1873
d. JUN 14, 1954

Verl Orland CRAM (1891-1973)
[1526361421]

Verl was born NOV 3, 1891 at Undine, MI. and died OCT 12, 1973 at Jerome, AZ. Undine was located on the west shore of Walloon Lake in Bay Township, Charlevoix County, Michigan. The site of the Cram-Whitford mill is now part of Camp Michigana.

Verl married Florence HANSHEW, daughter of Alonzo and Eva (Descomb) Hanshew, at Flint, MI. She was born MAR 11, 1893 and died in 1962 in San Jose, CA.
        Their Children:
             1. Robert Leroy [15263614211] b. JAN 15, 1918 at Flint, MI.; m. Evon KRESS at Port Huron, MI. on OCT 14, 1940; she was b. JUN 6, 1921 at Port Huron; Robert worked for Michigan Bell Telephone Co. for 42 years; he started in Port Huron, and retired out of the Traverse City office in 1978;
                Their Children:
                    1. Leland Robert [152636142111] b. AUG 27, 1944 at Port Huron; m. Kathleen Faye BASCH on MAY 22, 1965 at Traverse City, MI.; Lee works for the Grand Traverse County Road Commission in Traverse City.
                        Their Children:
                            1. Eric Leroy [1526361421111] b. MAR 25, 1970 at Traverse City; m. Dana Marie SIMMONS on JUL 1, 1989 at Niagara Falls, NY.; Eric is presently (in 1991) in the U.S. Coast Guard, stationed on the "Mackinaw," an icebreaker mooring in Cheboygan.
                            2. Marc Leland [1526361421112] b. SEP 23, 1973 at Traverse City, MI.; Marc's name is a palindrome of the name Cram.
                  2. Linda Kay [152636142112] b. JUL 19, 1950 at Pontiac, MI; m.1. Jim SIMMONS on MAY 22, 1968; m.2. Henry WHITWORTH on SEP 8, 1973; m.3. John Raymond GRANT, III on OCT 26, 1978; m.4. Walter Eugene SPIERS in SEP, 1983;
                    Her Children:
                      1. Dana Marie Simmons; b. SEP 3, 1969.
                      2. Ryanna Danielle Simmons; b. MAR 6, 1972.
                      3. Rebecca Ann Shawn Whitworth; b. NOV 12, 1973.
                      4. Rueben Henry Whitworth; b. MAY 20, 1976.
                      5. Josiah Lee Ramon Grant; b. AUG 10, 1982.
                      6. Carrie Lin Bernie Spiers; b. JUN 24, 1984.
                      7. Jessica Marie Louise Spiers; b. NOV 3, 1985.
                      8. Jedidiah Daniel Lukas Spiers; b. APR 10, 1987.

Leland Leslie CRAM (1893-1928)*
[1526361422]

Leland was born OCT 13, 1893 at Undine, MI. and died APR 7, 1928 (Easter Sunday) at Port Huron, St. Clair County, MI. Leland worked in Flint for the Marshall Furnace Co., and just before his death he traveled to Port Huron to set up a new branch office of the firm. There he came down with pneumonia and died in a very short time.

He married Marguerite PRICE on FEB 20, 1915 at Petoskey, Emmet County, MI. She was born MAR 2, 1894 at Charlevoix, MI., and died JUN 26, 1975 at Cottonwood, AZ. Marguerite worked for the telephone office in Charlevoix before her marriage. After Leland's death, she and the children returned to Charlevoix where she worked as a beauty operator. There she met Walter Alexander, who was a junior high school principal. They were married AUG 20, 1932 in Petoskey. That fall he went to Central Lake as school superintendent. He accepted the position of superintendent at Northport in 1939 or 1940. While there, they rented rooms to summer tourists. Marguerite was injured and Walter died as the result of an automobile accident near Ann Arbor, MI. on APR 9, 1951, just after he had been appointed School Superintendent for Cheboygan County.
> Their Children:
> 1. Leslie Jayne [15263614221] b. JUL 17, 1916.
> 2. Willard Glenn [15263614222] b. JUN 30, 1918.
> 3. Marguerite Marie [15263614223] b. JUL 14, 1920.

Reference:

Letter to the Author from Anna Ruth Cram (dtd. JUN 7, 1991)

family of Adelbert CRAM [152636742]

Adelbert CRAM [152636742]
b. NOV 6, 1875
d. SEP 23, 1960

m. MAR 31, 1897

Ennes MINER
b. DEC 18, 1871
d. MAY 19, 1926

1. Cecil Marion [1526367421] b. FEB 7. 1898.
2. Donald Adelbert [1526367422] b. SEP 1, 1901.
3. William Miner [1526367423] b. DEC 22, 1903.
4. Clarence Findlay [1526367424] b. APR 5, 1905.
5. Harold Raymond [1526367425] b. JUN 19, 1909.
6. Randall Maurice [1526367426] b. APR 19, 1914.

Cecil Marion CRAM (1898-)
[1526367421]

Cecil was born FEB 7, 1898.

Donald Adelbert CRAM (1901-)
[1526367422]

Donald was born SEP 1, 1901.

William Miner CRAM (1903-)
[1526367423]

William was born DEC 22, 1903.

Clarence Findlay CRAM (1905-)
[1526367424]

Clarence was born APR 5, 1909.

Harold Raymond CRAM (1909-)
[1526367425]

Harold was born at Deep River IA. on JUN 19, 1909. He married Elena CHAVEZ on AUG 11, 1929 at the Little Brown Church in the Vale at Nashua, IA. She was born MAR 20, 1913 at Los Griegos, New Mexico, the daughter of Carlos and Crecenciana (Lopez) Chavez. Her mother died at the age of 21 from tuberculosis, less than two years after her birth . Elena was raised by her elderly grandmother. Later she was adopted without form of law by Mrs. Mary Elizabeth Johnston, director of the Harwood School for Girls, which she attended. Elena then used the name Elena Johnston until her marriage.

Harold graduated from Millersburg, IA. High School in 1926 wearing his first dress suit, complete with vest. He recalls, "Since I had no money for college, and no prospects of any, I decided to seek the only non-farm employment that was available in the community at that time. My decision was to take up rural school teaching. . . (Then) one could teach with a high school diploma providing an examination could be passed and normal school was attended for three summer months. This meant that if I could pass the spring examinations, which were in mathematics, history, geography, spelling, reading and civics, I could enroll in summer school and be ready to teach come September." For the next two years he taught children of all ages from kindergarten to eighth grade. "Rural teachers played many parts in a day's work. The day began with arriving at school an hour or so ahead of the first student. This allowed time for sweeping the floor, starting the coal or wood burning fire in the stove, carrying in a fresh bucket of water and generally getting things tidied up for the day's activities. School always began promptly at 9 o'clock and ended in the afternoon at four. There was a fifteen minute recess both the middle of the morning and afternoon."

It was while attending Epworth League at the local Methodist Church to meet young people of his age group that he met Elena. The problem was that she was a high school junior, only 16 years of age, and he was an "old man" of 20. They were very much in love, but the obstacles to their relationship seem insurmountable. "It was at this point that the wisdom of her missionary mother (Mary Elizabeth Johnston) came to the rescue. She said that since we both wanted to get married she would make a bargain with us. We would both enroll in a nearby private school which consisted of a four year academy and a four year college. Elena would complete her senior year in the academy and I would enroll as a freshman in the college. . . Mother Johnston would continue to work and help with our education and we in turn would promise her a home for as long as she lived. The bargain was made and kept and following college she lived with us for many years until she passed away in 1942 at the ripe old age of seventh-three."

When Harold received his BA degree in Business Administration from John Fletcher College at University Park, IA. in 1933, it was the depth of the depression. Rather than join the WPA, paying $60 a month (which he considered a "make work" project), he returned to rural school teaching at a salary of $40 per month. A year later he joined the staff of the Ottumwa, IA. Courier as a subscription salesman. In 1937 he became circulation manager of the La Cross, WI. Tribune. In 1945 he bought a small meat market and grocery store called Tiny Market in La Crosse, WI. He followed up on his successful investment by expanding his super markets, and building new ones, first in Wisconsin and later in Iowa.

In 1966 Harold became a pioneer of sorts when he built the first "Food Bonanza" warehouse market in Rochester, MN. Harold says, "Although our predecessors in the warehouse market business had dealt mostly in dry groceries because they were in the wholesale business, we decided to make them into complete stores with the addition of frozen foods, dairy products, bakery goods and frozen meats. . . The new warehouse was opened in late November with about four times as much business as we had anticipated. . . Our venture was a success beyond our fondest dreams, Volume the first year was near the four million mark and we were leading all food stores in that area in weekly volume." Over the next four years Harold was to build and open three more stores before selling the business in MAR, 1971. In 1973 he and Elena retired and moved to Naples, Florida, where they live today.

Harold's civic achievements parallel his business success. He has been a Mason since 1944, a member of both York Rite and Scottish Rite. He joined the Rotary Club in 1945 and remains active today. He was elected a Trustee of Vennard College, University Park, IA. in 1975. He has been a lifelong active member of the Boy Scouts of America. He served as a Scoutmaster in Iowa and was on the Area Council board in La Cross for many years. In 1976 Harold was presented the "Distinguished Service Award for Business" by the alumni of Vennard College. He is listed in Who's Who in the Middle West.

Their Children:
1. Harold Ramon [15263674251] b. DEC 2, 1931.
2. David Lee [15263674252] b. NOV 30, 1934.
3. Judith Mary [15263674253] b. NOV 18, 1938.
4. Roger Carlos [15263674254] b. JUN 30, 1943.
5. Norman Allen [15263674255] b. AUG 30, 1945.
6. Linda Elena [15263674256] b. NOV 14, 1949.
7. Marc Eric [15263674257] b. MAR 4, 1951.
8. Stanley Bruce [15263674258] b. AUG 4, 1952.

Randall Maurice CRAM (1914-)
[1526367426]

Randall was born APR 19, 1914.

References:

Tall Corn by Harold R. Cram
Letter to the author from Harold R. Cram (dtd. DEC 11, 1993)

Family of Sherman Mitchell CRAM [1526B8133]

Sherman Mitchell CRAM [1526B8133]
b. JUN 14, 1891
d. JUN 4, 1938

m. MAR 14, 1915

Bernice BENNETT
b. MAY 9, 1893
d. JAN 23, 1990

1. George F. [1526B81331] (1916-1987)
2. Robert L. [1526B81332] (1918-1979)
3. **Keith B. [1526B81333]** b. 1920
4. John M. [1526B81334] (1921-1953)
5. Bessie E. [1526B81335] (1922-1962)
6. Sherman, Jr. [1526B81336] (1924-1978)
7. Maude [1526B81337] (1925-1925)
8. Barbara [1526B81338] b. 1927

George F. CRAM (1916-1987)
[1526B81331]

George was born AUG 4, 1916 at Montville, ME. and died MAY 22, 1987 at Fairfield, ME. (of emphysema). George was a carpenter by trade, and a very good one. He attended Liberty High School, and was known as a very good baseball player. He married Lucille HEATH on APR 11, 1936. They resided at Camden, ME.

Robert L. CRAM (1918-1979)
[1526B81332]

Robert was born JUN 29, 1918 at Montville, ME., and died at Togus (?) on JUL 12, 1979. He was in the Postal Service before and during the war. He served overseas in the Navy Postal Department during World War II. Robert married Mary JONES on OCT 7, 1939, and they resided at Liberty, ME. They were divorced after the war. Robert was a member of the Veterans of Foreign Wars. He died of throat cancer.

Keith B. CRAM (1920-)*
[1526B81333]

Keith was born JAN 18, 1920 at Liberty, ME., and still lives in the house in which he was born. He attended Walker High School, graduating in 1939. Keith joined the Marine Corps on MAR 10, 1941 and didn't get home until OCT 15, 1945. He served in the South West Pacific for 42 months. Keith says he was aboard a ship in the first convoy to leave the United States for combat duty in 1941. He also served in the Korean War. Keith is a member of the Veterans of Foreign Wars.

He married Madeleine O. ROY, daughter of Adelon and Clara (Bolduc) Roy of Waterville, ME., on FEB 19, 1949. She was born MAY 16, 1924. They reside in Liberty, ME., and attend the Catholic Church in Belfast, ME.
>   Their Children:
>   1. Michael S. [1526B813331] b. FEB 12, 1953.
>   2. Roxanne [1526B813332] b. MAY 9, 1954.

John M. CRAM (1921-1953)
[1526B81334]

John was born JAN 13, 1921 at Liberty, ME., and died of cancer in the Navy Hospital in New York on FEB 1, 1953. He was a graduate of Walker High School, joining the Navy Air Wing during World War II. He was decorated for bravery during his service in the Eurpoean Theater. He married Claudia BROWN on JUN 29, 1946. They resided in Liberty, ME., but being a career Navy man, their residence was most anywhere in the United States. John was a member of the Elks Club in Augusta, ME.
>   Their Children (both died of diabetes at an early age):
>   1. John Jr. [1526B813341]
>   2. Gregory [1526B813342]

Bessie E. CRAM (1922-1962)
[1526B81335]

Bessie was born OCT 21, 1922 in Montville, ME. and died at the Belfast, ME. Hospital on SEP 23, 1962. She was a graduate of Walker High School. She married Joseph H. BOIVIN, and they resided in Liberty, ME. Bessie died of cancer at the age of 39, leaving her husband and six children.

Sherman CRAM, Jr. (1924-1978)
[1526B81336]

Sherman was born on OCT 24, 1924 in Montville, ME., and died of heart failure in Thayer Hospital on NOV 12, 1978. He married Shirley BROWN of Winsor, ME. on APR 28, 1944. They resided in Liberty, ME. where he was a member of the Masonic Lodge.

Maude CRAM (1925-1925)
[1526B81337]

Maude was born JAN 5, 1926 at Liberty, ME., and only lived a few hours. She died the same day.

Barbara CRAM (1927-)
[1526B81338]

Barbara was born AUG 16, 1927. She married Robie CREASEY on OCT 8, 1944. They reside in Liberty, ME. She was baptized in the Liberty Baptist Church. They have two daughters.

References:

Letter to the author from Keith Cram (dtd. MAR, 1991)
Records of Addie B. Moore
Records of Keith Cram

family of Henry Sergeant CRAM [153822211]

Henry Sergeant CRAM [153822211]
b. JAN 21, 1907
d.

m.1.   MAY 5, 1931 _____ 1. John Sergeant, III [1538222111] b. MAY 31, 1932
                                          2. A daughter who died at birth

Edith Kingdon DREXEL
b. NOV 18, 1911
d. 1934

m.2.   .

Ruthven VAUX
b. 1911
d. 198-

m.3. SEP 26, 1945 _____ 3. Henry Sergeant, Jr. [1538222112] b. JUN 12, 1945

Elouise FORREN
b. JUN 16, 1923
d. NOV 5, 1949

m.4. APR 20, 1950 _____ 4. Edith Clare Cooper [1538222113] b. FEB 5, 1954.
                                          5. Peter Cooper [1538222114] b. MAr 15, 1956.

Lucy (Ladd) GUEST
b. AUG 12, 1916
d. NOV, 1993

John Sergeant CRAM, III (1932-)
[1538222111]

John was born MAY 31, 1932 in New York City. The family called him "Jackie." He attended St. Paul's School in Concord, NH., graduating Magna Cum Laude. He attended Princeton University, but apparently did not graduate, leaving perhaps upon receiving money from his mother's inheritance.

He married first Sally STOKES in APR, 1960, in the Church of the Cross, Bluffton, SC. Hank Cram states that he believes the marriage was dissolved shortly thereafter in Mexico. There was no issue from this marriage. He married second Lady Jeanne Louise (Campbell) MAILER, daughter of Ian, 10th Duke of Argyll and Janette (Atkin or Akin) Campbell, daughter of Lord Beaverbrook. Lady Jeanne was one of the many wives of novelist Norman Mailer, and mother of Mailer's daughter Kate. She is also the mother of Cusi Cram, model.

Henry Sergeant CRAM, Jr. (1945-)
[1538222112]

Henry (known as "Hank" and the author of Notes on the Cram Family and Related Families)was born in Lenox Hill Hospital, New York City on JUN 12, 1945. In 1968 he was married in Tonbridge, Kent, to June Katherine (Dickson-Wright) JANIS, daughter of Arthur and Aileen Mary (Bath) Dickson-Wright. They were divorced in 1983.   She was born in London, England on JUN 17, 1930. June had previously been married to concert pianist Byron Janis. They are the parents of a son, Stephan Jude Janis, born in Chicago in 1955. The Janises were divorced in Mexico on AUG 14, 1964. He later married Maria Veronica Cooper, daughter of Rocky and Gary Cooper (the actor). Hank and June were later divorced.

Hank is a realtor in Bluffton, SC. where he has a home overlooking the shoreline. On APR 23, 1994 he married Rachael Julien GIROUX, daughter of Robert Joseph Giroux, at their "pink house" on Victoria Bluff Plantation.

Children of Hank & June (in the eleventh generation):
1. Henry Sergeant St. Jude [15382221121] b. FEB 17, 1966; d. FEB 20, 1966
2. Christina Elouise [15382221122] b. FEB 1, 1967 in St. Mary's Hospital at London, England; her early years were spent travelling with her parents, first in Italy, then England and later in the 1970's to Spain where she learned Spanish, French and Chinese; in DEC, 1979 she came to America for the first time; she spent three years in Bluffton, SC., but returned to live with her mother in London in MAR, 1984 following her parents divorce.

Edith Clare Cooper CRAM (1954-)
[1538222113]

Edith was born FEB 5, 1954 at Savannah, GA. Nothing further is known of her.

Peter Cooper CRAM (1956-)
[1538222114]

Peter was born MAR 15, 1956 in Savannah, GA. He was married JUN 16, 1958, to Leisa K. (Tracy) CZURA, daughter of William and Janice Tracy of Grosse Pointe, MI. Her mother, Janice, was born in Scotland. The wedding took place on the May River, Bluffton, SC. They also have a home at Victoria Bluff Plantation.

Their Children (in the 11th generation):
1. Peter Cooper [15382221141] b. JUL 1986, at Beaufort, SC.; is called "Coop."
2. William Tracy [15382221142] b. MAR 9, 1988, at Beufort, SC.; known as "Willie;" Hank Cram notes that some members of the family say he should be known as "Nick" since at the time of his birth his father was spending the night at the Knickerbocker Club, in New York City, having gone before the election committee the previous afternoon, the result of which was his election to the club.

Reference:

Notes on the CRAM Family and Some Related Families (p. 22)
Letters to the author from Hank Cram (dtd. 1990-1994)

family of James Edwin CRAM [161134231]

James Edwin CRAM [161134231]
b. OCT 6, 1858
d. APR 16, 1920

m. MAY 10, 1885

Ida FORREY
b. MAY 16, 1863
d. APR 26, 1949

1. Ole Robert [1611342311] b. MAR 22, 1887.
2. George Edwin [1611342312] b. OCT 5, 1889.
3. Hazel Eva [1611342313] b. MAR 27, 1892.

Ole Robert CRAM (1887-1979)
[1611342311]

Ole was born MAR 22, 1887 in Stockton, KS. and died JUN 5, 1979 at St. Francis, KS. His son tells that when Ole was born, a famous Norwegian violinist was touring in the United States and was featured prominently in the news media. His parents liked the name and used it. It also was passed to Ole's second son. Ole became an attorney, banker and farmer in St. Francis, Kansas. He read law in a local law office and was admitted to the bar in 1925. Ole twice served in the House of Representatives of the Kansas Legislature (1920-1922 and 1956-1966). He was a patron of the arts, world traveler and enthusiastic promoter of the Republican Party. "Bob" as he was known, learned to fly at the age of 59 and was piloting a plane until the age of 85. He married Elizabeth RINGO on JUN 30, 1914. She was a school teacher and piano teacher. Elizabeth died on JAN 3, 1953, and Ole died in St. Francis on JUN 5, 1979.

Their Children: (in the eleventh generation)
1. James Jacob [16113423111] b. JUL 3, 1916; served in WW II as a Lt.; m. Josephine FIRKINS, d/o Edwin & Margaret Firkins, on JUN 25, 1942, in St. Frances, KS.; she was b. JUN 27, 1919; he is a retired civil engineer from the USBR; she is retired from Accent Publications;
   Their Children (twelfth generation):
   1. Joann [161134231111] b. OCT 5, 1943; m. Robert W. JOSELYN;
   2. Jon Jacob [161134231112] b. DEC 10, 1949;
   3. Jeri [161134231113] b. JAN 7, 1955; m. Mr. HOWE;
2. Ole Robert, Jr. [16113423112] b. AUG 27, 1918 in St. Francis; he m. Margerie FIRKINS, d/o Edwin Delos Firkins, at the Methodist Parsonage at Kansas City on JAN 30, 1943; she was b. FEB 5, 1918; he is a retired family physician; they live in Larned KS.
   Their Children (twelfth generation):
   1. Patricia Sue [161134231121] b. SEP 15, 1944; she became a nurse; m. Michael NELSON, a pediatrician; they live in Albuquerque, NM;
      Their Children:
      1. Aimee Nelson; b. NOV 14, 1970.
      2. Chad Nelson; b. OCT 27, 1972.
   2. Charles Robert [161134231122] b. FEB 15, 1947 in Little River, KS.; m. Sandy ROBERTS on APR 2, 1969.
      Their Child:
      1. Douglas [1611342311221] b. NOV 9, 1969; he graduated from North Texas State University in May, 1993.
   3. James Edwin [161134231123] b. DEC 1, 1949; m. Becky SCHMIDT on May 27, 1972; he is a pharmacist, and she is an RN;
      Their Children:
      1. Marc [1611342311231] b. JUN 14, 1977.
      2. Scott [1611342311232] b. 1980.

4. Mary Margaret [161134231124] b. OCT 25, 1951; m. John
     MYERS on DEC 27, 1975; she taught several years before
     starting a family; they live in Longmont, CO.
      Their Children:
          1. David Myers; b. JUL 17, 1977.
          2. Kerri Myers; b. JUL 5, 1980.
          3. Wendy Kathleen Myers; b. JAN 1, 1985.
          4. John Andrew Myers; b. MAY 27, 1987.
5. Betty Jane [161134231125] b. OCT 27, 1953; m. Tom
     DICKERSON on JUL 8, 1978; the family resides in
     Albuquerque, NM.
      Their Children:
          1. Abigail Elizabeth Dickerson; b. MAY 28, 1981.
          2. Edward Charles Dickerson; b. 1986.
3. Ernest Richard [16113423113] b. APR 1, 1924; earned an MD degree from U. of
     Kansas in 1952, served as Cheyenne County Coroner 1954-92 while in private
     practice; he m. Bonnie Jean WATERS, d/o Lloyd & Ione (Page) Waters, on
     AUG 29, 1948; she was b. OCT 22, 1926; he is a retired physician and she is a
     homemaker; both are active in civic organizations, their church and the arts; they
     reside in St. Francis, KS.
      Their Children (twelfth generation):
          1. Richard Lloyd [161134231131] b. SEP 7, 1951; BS.
               degree in Civil Engineering from West Point;
               Masters in Economics, Kansas State, 1979; Law
               Degree, U. of Kansas, 1983; Chicago Art School,
               1992; currently a portrait and landscape artist in
               Chicago; divorced;
                His daughter:
                    1. Megan [1611342311311] b. about 1982.
          2. Ione Beth [161134231132] b. JAN 3, 1953; degree in
               Music and Ballet from U. of Indiana, 1974; Master of
               Music, Fort Hays St. Univ., KS., 1983; m. Michael
               SLATTERY in 1975; she is a teacher of music,
               Hays, KS. school system.
          3. Claudia Kay [161134231133] b. JAN 4, 1955; degree in
               English Literature U. of Kansas, 1978; m. Robert
               BUNKER in 1984; they are separated; she lives in
               Loveland, CO.; a professional folk harpist;
                Their Children:
                    1. Julian Bunker; b. 1985.
                    2. Joel Bunker; b. 1990.
          4. Ole Robert, III [161134231134] b. JAN 1, 1962; BS
               degree in electrical engineering, computer minor, U.
               of KS., 1985; m. in 1991; employed by Dept. of
               Navy at Seal Beach Naval Station, Ontario, CA.;
                His daughter:
                    1. Shannon Elizabeth [1611342311341]
                         b. in 1991.
          5. Adele Elizabeth [161134231135] b. JUN 1, 1971; currently
               (in 1993) in final year of a five-year Occupational
               Therapy program at U. of Kansas Medical Center in
               Kansas City.; she enjoys biking, hiking, dancing,
               singing, travel, and gourmet cooking.

George Edwin (1889-1969)
[1611342312]

George was born OCT 5, 1889 in Emporia, KS. He was in the automotive electric business in Boulder, CO. George married first Nettie BROWN of St. Francis on JAN 7, 1917. She was b. OCT 7, 1881 in Clyde, KS. the daughter of William and Sarah (Larr) Brown. They were divorced sometime after the birth of their four daughters. She died in Boulder CO. in 1955; Ole Robert Cram, Jr. relates that after her death George married a second time and spent some time in Corpus Christi, TX, but returned to Oregon to live out the last few years of his life. He died DEC 12, 1969 in Dayton, OR.

Their Children (eleventh generation):
1. Carol Vesta [161134233121] b. JUL 1, 1918; m. Franklin HAYES; resided in CA.;
2. Marda [161134233122] b. NOV 19, 1920; m. Carl KEETER on SEP 10, 1943 at St. John's Episcopal Church in Boulder; resided in Denver, CO., and Twin Falls, ID. Their Child:
    1. Gary Keeter; b. OCT, 1944.
3. Eva Mae [161134233123] b. JUN, 1922; she was disabled and had to attend special schoola; resided in Denver; died in Olathe, CO. in 1988.
4. Harriet Carol [161134233124] b. APR 11, 1924; m. Eugene E. LEIST; they resided in Boulder, CO., and later in Denver.

Hazel Eva (1892-1966)
[1611342313]

Hazel was born on MAR 27, 1892 in Emporia, KS. She married Cleveland WARD, and they resided in Cheyenne, Wyoming. Her husband was a mail clerk on the Union Pacific, running on a fast train between Cheyenne and Ogden, Utah. Hazel died FEB 8, 1966, in Cheyenne, WY.

References:

History of Roxbury, VT. (p. 450)

Who's Who of America's Crams

Letter to the Author from Dr. E. R. Cram (dtd. NOV 30, 1993)

Letters to the Author from Dr. Ole Robert Cram, Jr. (dtd. DEC 20, 1993 & JAN 5, 1994)

Letter to the Author from Gary Keeter (dtd. DEC 24, 1993)

Letter to Ralph W. Cram from Fred D. Cram (dtd. JAN 1, 1938)

Records of Myra Cram of Des Moines, IA. and Cedar Falls, IA.

Unpublished Manuscript of Elmer Cram (files 21, 28 and 250)

family of Archie Rice CRAM [161139193]

Archie Rice CRAM [161139193]
b. FEB 28, 1887
d. OCT 3, 1937

m. MAR 12, 1913   1. Reginald Maurice [1611391931] b. APR 29, 1914

Beatrice Mae CLEVELAND
b. FEB 10, 1896

Reginald Maurice CRAM (1914-)
[1611391933]

Reginald was born APR 29, 1914 at Northfield, VT. He received his BS. degree from Norwich University in 1936 and did post graduate work at Boston University Law School in 1937-38. Reginald was awarded an honorary Doctorate of Military Science in 1974.

He entered the Air Force Intelligence School in 1943 and made the the armed services his career. He was assigned to the office of the Adjutant General of VT. in 1938-41. During World War II he participated in the anti-submarine campaign of the USAAF during 1941-42, and served in the Asiatic-Pacific Theatre with the United States Marine Corps. from 1943-45. He was attached to NATO in the early 1950s, and later to the Supreme Headquarters of Allied Powers in Europe. Reginald was named Commander of the Orientation Group for the USAF in 1957, and joined the Organization of the Joint Chiefs of Staff in 1961. He retired from Air Force active duty in 1964. From 1964 to 1966 he served as Deputy Adjutant General for the State of VT. and as Adjutant General from 1967-1981. He was promoted to Major General in the USAF in 1968. Throughout his military career he received a number of commendations including: Decoration of Legion of Merit; Air Medal D.S.M.; Air Force Joint Commendation Medal; Air Force Commendation Medal; and the Army Commendation Medal.

He has been active and held numerous offices in many civilian organizations. He is past president of the Long Trail council of Boy Scouts of America; national delegate in the American Cancer Society; trustee of Norwich University; chairman of disaster services for the northern VT. chapter of the American Red Cross. He has been the recipient of the Vermont Distinguished Service Medal and the Distinguished Service medal of the National Guard Association of the U.S. In 1990, Reginald was awarded the St. George Medal for distinguished service from the VT. Division of the American Cancer Society. He is a member of the American Legion, the VFW, the VT. Historical Society, Rotary International, Theta Chi and Pi Sigma Alpha fraternities, and a Mason.

Reginald married Kathryn Elizabeth MOSHER, the daughter of Kenneth Ellister and Mildred Mosher, on JUN 29, 1937. She was born on JAN 31, 1918 in Brattleboro, VT.
   Their Children:
      1. Robin Carol [16113919331] b. MAY 5, 1938 in Brookline, MA.; m.
          Paul LUALDI on NOV 24, 1961 in Washington, DC.;
             Their Children:
                1. Paul L. Lualdi; b. JAN 25, 1964, Washington, DC.
                2. John Cram Lualdi; b. MAR 31, 1966, in Boston
                3. Sarah Luisa Lualdi; b. APR 29, 1967, in Boston
      2. Marilyn Jane [16113919332] b. OCT 12, 1939 in Montpelier, VT.; m.
          Vcevold Otis STREKALOVSKY on DEC 23, 1961 in Washington, DC.
                1. Elisabeth Cram Strekalovsky; b. APR 12, 1965, Boston.
                2. Katherine Otis Strekalovsky; b. AUG 14, 1967, Boston.
                3. Anna Brooks Strekalovsky; b. DEC 12, 1974, Boston.

References:

Who's Who in America 1988-89 (p. 660)
Letters to the author from Reginald Cram (dtd. SEP 16, 1990 & OCT 18, 1990)

family of Osceola Canel CRAM [161634611]

Osceola Canel CRAM [1616341611]
b. MAR 24, 1870
d. AUG 24, 1961

m.1. NOV 10, 1898

Laura Edna McCLIMANS
b. DEC 24, 1876
d. MAR 2, 1920

m.2.   1925

Alice (Torrey) HUFFMAN
b. MAY 10, 1889
d. DEC 13, 1931

1. Richard Wilbur [1616346111] b. JUL 11, 1899
2. Julia Maria [1616346112] b. FEB 14, 1901
3. Mabel Elsie [1616346113] b. JUN 30, 1902
4. **John Conrad [1616346114]** b. JUN, 1903
5. Honor Lucile [1616346115] b. MAR 27, 1907
6. Bernice Irene [1616346116] b. MAR 5, 1913

7. Fred Lee [1616346117] b. OCT 25, 1930

Richard Wilbur CRAM (1899-1950)
[1616346111]

Richard Wilbur (who was known as "Dick") was born JUL 11, 1899 at Sargent, NE. and died OCT 28, 1950. He was buried at Burwell, NE. He married Viola CORNELIUS on NOV 11, 1926, in Marengo, IA. She was born in 1905, in Maquoketa, IA.
>   Their Child:
>> 1. Louis Jerome [16163461111] b. JUL 18, 1935; m. MAY 4, 1968 in Genesco, IL., to Mary Kay RADUE.

Julia Maria CRAM (1901-)
[1616346112]

Julia Maria was born FEB 14, 1901 in Loup County, NE.   She married Thomas M. McNEELY on JUN 11, 1933, in Boise, Idaho. He was born on OCT 22, 1905, in Abbeville, Mississippi.
>   Their Children:
>> 1. Thomas M. McNeely, Jr.; b. SEP 16, 1934, in Los Angeles, CA.; m. JUL 22, 1967, to Glen DeTucci who was b. NOV 19, 1942; one child: Jennifer Louise McNeely was b. MAR 12, 1971, in Natchez, MS., and d. AUG 11, 1978.
>> 2. Osa L. McNeely; b. OCT 19, 1937, in Glendale, CA.; m. NOV 29, 1963, to Joseph Tillman, III in New Orleans, LA.; he was b. DEC 7, 1936, Charlottesville, VA
>>> Their Child:
>>>> 1. Joseph Dean Tillman, IV; b. SEP 10, 1965, Orlando, FL.

Mabel Elsie CRAM (1922-)
[1616346113]

Mabel Elsie was born JUN 30, 1902, in Loup County, NE. She married Joy Stephen BROMWICH on OCT 15, 1922. He was born JUN 21, 1899, in Kent, NE. and died FEB 18, 1926, in Ord, NE. (he was buried in Kent Cemetery).
>   Their Children:
>> 1. Ava Lauretta Bromwich; b. APR 16, 1924 in Kent, NE; m. SEP 1, 1947, Robert C. Hastert who was b. APR 28, 1923, in Shelby, NE.
>>> Their Children:
>>>> 1. Joyce Elizabeth Hastert; b. APR 28, 1956.
>>>> 2. Laura Rose Hastert; b. MAY 15, 1960.
>>>> 3. Paul Louis Hastert; b. MAY 21, 1965.
>> 2. Joyce Ella Bromwich; b. APR 16, 1926; died the same day, in Kent, NE.

John Conrad CRAM (1905-)*
[1616346114]

John Conrad has been known as "Jack" during his lifetime. He was born JUN 26, 1905, in Loup County, NE., and was raised on a cattle ranch there. In 1929 he moved to Idaho. Jack married Leola Mae OLSON on APR 11, 1937. She was born MAY 9, 1912, at Round Valley, NE. In 1990 he resides in Melba, Idaho. He writes: "We live about 4 1/2 miles southeast of Melba about 1 1/2 miles from the Snake River. I have what you would call a small dairy, and milk about 50 cows."
>   Their Children:
>   1. Mary Opal [16163461141] b. JAN 20, 1938, at Boise, ID., m. Homer BROWN on OCT 8, 1955.
>   2. David Samuel [16163461142] b. JAN 30, 1940, at Nampa, ID.; m. AUG 30, 1959, to Delores ROBINSON.
>   3. Francis Orrin [16163461143] b. FEB 4, 1941, at Melba, ID.; m. DEC 21, 1963 to Dalla BRADY.
>   4. Martha Elizabeth [16163461144] b. APR 8, 1944, at Melba, ID.; m. Sterling BURTON on AUG 25, 1961.
>   5. Alma Jonathon [16163461145] b. SEP 14, 1945, at Nampa, ID.
>   6. Edward Nephi [16163461146] b. DEC 28, 1947, at Nampa, ID.; d. AUG, 1966.
>   7. Bryan Paul [16163461147] b. MAR 11, 1950, at Nampa; d. MAR 30, 1965.
>   8. Abigail Kathryn [16163461148] b. OCT 3, 1951, in the car on the way to Nampa.
>   9. Phillip Matthew [16163461149] b. APR 12, 1953, in Nampa; d. AUG, 1971.
>   10. Michael Benjamin [1616346114A] b. MAR 11, 1955, at Nampa.
>   11. Laura Rose [1616346114B] b. JUN 16, 1956, at Nampa.

Honor Lucile CRAM (1907-)
[1616346115]

Honor Lucile was born MAR 27, 1907, in Loup County, NE. She married Frank W. DUELKS on JUN 24, 1933. He was born JAN 23, 1908, in Los Angeles, CA.
>   Their Child:
>   1. Donald Wayne Duelks; b. JUL 19, 1936 in Los Angeles, CA.; m.1. Kay Dianne Williams on MAR 23, 1956 (they divorced); m.2. Bernice Helen Patterson on APR 9, 1961; they adopted a daughter, Doreen Carol, who was b. AUG 14, 1964; m.3. Susan A. Evans on FEB 14, 1971.

Bernice Irene CRAM (1913-1916)
[1616346116]

Bernice was born MAR 5, 1913 in Loup County, NE., and died AUG 10, 1916, in Custer County, NE.

Fred Lee CRAM (1930-)
[1616346117]

Fred Lee was born OCT 25, 1930 in Custer County, NE. He married Rosetta Belle DILSAVER on OCT 14, 1951. She was born FEB 3, 1932 in Loup County, NE. Their children were all born in Burwell, NE.
>   Their Children:
>   1. Alisa Collette [16163461171] b. SEP 20, 1952.
>   2. Teddy Morris [16163461172] b. DEC 26, 1953.
>   3. Jacky Lee [16163461173] b. NOV 5, 1955.
>   4. Kerry Sue [16163461174] DEC 15, 1957.

References:

Cram (pp. b-18, b-19 and b-20)
Letter to the author from John C. Cram (dtd. NOV 16, 1990)

family of Albert Irvin CRAM [161634612]

Albert Irvin CRAM [161634612]
b. NOV 16, 1871
d. JUN 21, 1957

1. Besse Iola [1616346121] b. SEP 22, 1898
m. SEP 1, 1897
2. Jay Irvin [1616346122] b. JUL 23, 1900
3. **Roy Spencer [1616346123]** b. FEB 3, 1903
Effie Violet WILSON
4. Honor Elva [1616346124] b. FEB 3, 1906
b. DEC 4, 1876
d. JAN 1, 1958

Besse Iola CRAM (1898-1943)
[1616346121]

Besse Iola was born SEP 22, 1898 in Burwell, Nebraska, and died JUL 16, 1943 in Denver, Colorado. She was buried in Fairview Cemetery in Craig, Colorado. Besse married Frank William BIESER on OCT 9, 1922. He was born SEP 9, 1897 in Odeboldt, Iowa, and died NOV 27, 1981 at Concordia, KS. The family resided in Inglewood, Simla, Craig, and Steamboat Springs, Colorado. They also lived for a time in Washington, DC.
    Their Children:
        1. Joyce Mary Bieser; b. AUG 14, 1923 in Denver, CO.; m. John B. Ferguson on
                OCT 22, 1944 in Craig, CO.; four children: Cynthia, Patricia, Linda, Shirlyn.
        2. Frank William Bieser, Jr.; b. NOV 3, 1924 at Denver, CO.; d. JAN 13, 1927 in
                Simla, CO. of pneumonia; he is buried there.
        3. Marilyn Candace Bieser; b. APR 4, 1927 in Aurora, CO.; m. John Bolchunos in
                Craig, CO. on SEP 24, 1955; he was b. SEP 10, 1926 in Kenosha,
                WI.; four children: Valerie, Julie, Thomas, Bradley.
        4. Albert Howard Bieser; b. JAN 31, 1932 in Steamboat Springs, CO.; m. Barbara Strait
                of Ft. Collins, CO. in 955; she was b. JUL 5, 1926;
                two children: Scott, Frank.
        5. Shirley Besse Bieser; b. JAN 17, 1935; m. Claude Merton Higgins, Jr. in Boulder,
                Co. on NOV 19, 1954; he was b. JUN 30, 1935;
                two children: Gayle, Michael.

Jay Irvin CRAM (1900-1905)
[1616346122]

Jay Irvin was born JUL 23, 1900. He died DEC 20, 1905, in Burwell, NE., of meningitis.

Roy Spencer CRAM (1903-1989)*
[1616346123]

Roy Spencer was born FEB 3, 1903, in Burwell, NE. and died there AUG 4, 1989. He married first, Edith Marie FREASE on AUG 12, 1926 in Ravenna, NE. She was born JUN 26, 1903 in South Omaha, NE. and died APR 19, 1955 in Pasadena, CA. She and Roy Spencer were divorced JUN 20, 1941. He married second Pearl Theresa SIGNER on SEP 1, 1941 in Reno, NV. She was born MAR 17, 1909 in Primrose, NE. and died JUL 7, 1989. Roy was a physician, described by others as a "good old fashioned country family doctor." Roy had two children by each wife.
    Children by Edith:
        1. Roene Ruth [16163461231] b. FEB 8, 1928.
        2. Jean Marie [16163461232] b. SEP 18, 1933.
    Children by Pearl:
        3. Albert Edwin [16163461233] b. OCT 23, 1942.
        4. Roy Spencer, Jr. [16163461234] b. DEC 31, 1945.

Honor Elva CRAM (1906-)
[1616346124]

Honor Elva was born FEB 3, 1906, in Burwell, NE. She married Charles A. FREASE, Jr. on JUN 9, 1929. He was born DEC 12, 1905 in South Omaha, NE. and died MAR 13, 1959. Charles was Honor's second husband, records do not reveal any details of her first marriage.

Their Child:

1. Sharon Honor Frease; b. JAN 4, 1933 in N. Hollywood, CA; m.1. Robert A. Rich on AUG 28, 1955; he was b. DEC 29, 1932 in New York; they were divorced in DEC, 1961; she m.2. L. Roper on SEP 4, 1963, from whom she was divorced in MAR, 1964; she was m.3. on MAY 29, 1969 to Richard A. Chute, who was b. MAR 17, 1934 in San Franciso; they divorced in SEP, 1979; she and Richard remarried on JUN 7, 1980 - divorcing for the second time in MAR/APR, 1982; she m.4. Murlin Dale Street on FEB 4, 1986; he was b. FEB 23, 1927 at St. Louis, MO.; no issue from any spouse.

One adopted daughter:

1. Stacy Honor Rich; b. FEB 23, 1960 in Oxnard, CA.; m. APR 1, 1978 to Lynn Dennis who was b. FEB 28, 1956; they have three children.

References:

Cram (pp. b-21, b-22 and b-23)
Letter to the author from Jean (Cram) Hannon (dtd. DEC 20, 1993)

family of Matt Arthur CRAM [161634625]

Matt Arthur CRAM [161634625]
b. JUL 23, 1885
d.

                                      1. John Marion [1616346251] b. FEB 15, 1915

m.1. JAN 14, 1911 _____2. Betty Claire [1616346252] b. NOV 30, 1920

Maude B. HARRIS
b.
d. JUN 26, 1948

m.2. DEC 23, 1955

Hazel F. FOSTER
b.
d. MAY 26, 1964

m.3. DEC 24, 1968

Alice B. ALEXANDER
b.
d. AUG/SEP, 1978

John Marion CRAM (1915-1947)
[1616346251]

John Marion was born FEB 15, 1915 in David City, NE., and died APR 2, 1947 in Oklahoma City, OK.
He married Lillian E. STUART in JUN, 1939 in Greenville, TX. John was a Lieutenant J.G. in the United
States Navy and was killed in an auto wreck.
        Their Children:
            1. John Stuart [16163462511] b. FEB 8, 1941 at Ft. Madison, IA.;
                m. Clara Sue THOMASSON;
                    Their Children:
                        1. John Stuart, Jr. [161634625111]
                        2. Michelle Lee [161634625112] b. MAY 12, 1972.
            2. Karen Elizabeth [16163462512] b. JUN 6, 1944 at Ft. Lauderdale, FL;
                she d. JUL, 1962.

Betty Claire CRAM (1920-)
[1616346252]

Betty Claire was born NOV 30, 1920 in Plainview, TX. She married Morris W. ALFORD on DEC 27, 1943.
        Their Children:
            1. Claire Ann Alford; b. APR 18, 1947 in Lubbock TX.; she m. Gerald G. McNew, Jr.
                Their Children:
                      1. John Michael McNew; b. AUG 8, 1967.
                      2. Ryan Patrick McNew; b. FEB 7, 1973.
            2. Katherine Elizabeth Alford; b. OCT 10, 1951 in Littlefield TX.; m. --- Freye;
                they were divorced by the time <u>Cram</u> was written in 1980.

Reference:

<u>Cram</u> (pp. b-13 and b-14)

family of Timothy Blaisdell CRAM [163121226]

Timothy Blaisdell CRAM [163121226]
b. APR 26, 1870
d.

m. MAY 22, 1894   1. Kenneth Blaisdell [1631212261] b. FEB 22, 1897
                                                    2. Virginia L. [1631212262] b. AUG 12, 1904

Georgia SHORES
b. MAR 11, 1872
D.

Kenneth Blaisdel CRAM (1897-)
[1631212261]

Kenneth was born FEB 22, 1897 at Chicago, IL. He married Helen DONNELLY, the daughter of Judge
Charles H. and Nina (Blakelee) Donnelly, on JAN 26, 1922. She was born AUG 22, 1898 in Woodstock,
IL.
   Their Children:
      1. Charles Donnelly [16312122611] b. 1924.
      2. Kenneth Blaisdel [16312122612] b. NOV 7, 1926 at Evanston, IL.

Virginia L. CRAM (1904-)
[1631212262]

Virginia was born AUG 12, 1904. She married Thomas O'SULLIVAN of New York. They resided in New
York City.
   Their Children:
      1. Thomas O'Sullivan; b. in New York City.
      2. Peter O'Sullivan ; b. in New York City.
      3. Virginia O'Sullivan; b. in New York City

Reference:

Unpublished manuscript of Elmer Cram (file 58)

family of Walter Burkhart CRAM [163121228]

Walter Burkhart CRAM [163121228]
b. JAN 10, 1874
d. DEC 23, 1949

m. APR 13, 1898 _____1. Charles Hilliard [1631212281] b. AUG 29, 1900

Nina del VALLE
b. FEB 16, 1873
d.

Charles Hilliard CRAM (1900-)
[1631212281]

Charles was born AUG 29, 1900, in Carniolos, CA. He married Susan Barret PRESLEY, daughter of
Walter A. Presley, in MAY, 1925, at Riverside, CA. She was born APR 1, 1901 at Bay City, MI.
Charles was employed by the Department of Agriculture. Politically it is said he was a Republican.
    Their Children (in the eleventh generation):
        1. Charles Hilliard [16312122811] b. MAR 15, 1926; m. Joan Elizabeth Smith, d/o
            Ray Eldon & Mable Smith; she was b. SEP 16, 1929 in Omaha, NE.
            Their Children (in the twelfth generation):
                1. Michael Linden [163121228111]
                2. Candace Denise [163121228112] b. MAR 17, 1955.
      2. Susan Elisa [16312122812] b. FEB 27, 1927; m. Charles A. Weireter.

Reference:

Unpublished manuscript of Elmer Cram (files 58 & 60)
Who's Who of America's Crams

Tenth American Generation

family of Elmer Herbert CRAM [1524332133]

Elmer Herbert CRAM [1524332133]
b. SEP 25, 1865
d.

m. NOV 11, 1891 _____ 1. Theodore Francis [15243321331] b. SEP 29, 1892

Abbie LOUISE KELLEY
b.
d.

Theodore Francis CRAM (1892-1918)
[15243321331]

Theodore Francis was born SEP 29, 1892 at Providence, Rhode Island. He married Marion G. DUDLEY, daughter of George and Grace (Bartlett) Dudley, on SEP 29, 1918. She was b. NOV 18, 1895 at Lee, NH. Both were graduates of New Hampshire University (in 1915 and 1916 respectively). He died at Greenwood, MA. on JAN 8, 1918.

     Their Child (twelfth generation):

        1. Barbara Louise [152433213311] b. NOV 17, 1917; she was a graduate of the University of New Hampshire in 1939. She was a member of Kappa Delta Sorority; she married Elliott WHALEN of Boston on SEP 13, 1942 at Savannah, Georgia; he was the son of Elliott and Ruth (Craigen) Whalen of Boston, MA.; Elliott served with the Marines in World War II at Bouganville, Guam, and Emirau.

References:

Unpublished manuscript of Elmer Cram (files 144 and 215)

family of Ralph Wentworth CRAM [1525327312]

Ralph Wentworth CRAM [1525327312]
b. SEP 8, 1904
d. SEP 28, 1973

m._____

Ann HEATH
b. DEC 28, 1903
d. DEC 3, 1972

1. Patricia Day [15253273121] b. DEC 8, 1930
2. Sarah Elizabeth Blake [15253273122] b. 1940
3. Ralph Adams, II [15253273123] b. JUN 9, 1941

Patricia Day CRAM (1930-1994)
[15253273121]

Patricia Day was born DEC 8, 1930 in Hollywood, CA. and died in 1994. She married Donald Gale of Stowe, VT. They lived in Morganton, NC.
Their Children: Peter Gale (twin); Charles Gale (twin); Jennifer Gale; Deborah Gale.

Sarah Elizabeth Blake CRAM (1940-)
[15253273122]

Sarah was born JUL 28, 1940 in Concord, MA. She was named for Ralph Adams Cram's wife. She grew up in Stowe, VT. Sarah is a 1962 graduate of Western College for Women, Oxford, OH. with a BA. in Art History. Health and Human Services Secretary, Donna Shalala was a classmate there. Sarah says she has been an interior decorator, a fashion coordinator, and during her earlier years a waitress at Longfellow's Wayside Inn in Sudbury, MA. She has lived in Arlington, VA. for 17 years.

In her spare time she indulges in pastel painting of landscapes, seascapes, and portraits. She loves the sea - in all seasons and presenting its many moods. She also likes reading, gardening and entertaining, although she hates cooking. She married a Mr. GIBSON. They are divorced.
Her Children:
1. Forrest Earl Gibson; b. MAR 18, 1968 in Athens GA.; grad. of West Virginia U. in 1992 with a degree in landscape architecture; on presidents list and earned Award of Merit from American Society of Landscape Architects; employed with the firm of Derk and Edson, landscape architects in Lititz, PA.; he is an assistant Scoutmaster there; also enjoys golf skiing and other outdoor activities.
2. Robert Andrew Gibson; b. JUL 2, 1975 in S. Weymouth, MA.; he is an Eagle Scout; in high school he was on the football team and co-president of the environment club; plans to study environmental engineering in college.

Ralph Adams CRAM, II (1941-)
[15253273123]

Ralph was born JUN 9, 1941. He has been in the architectural profession for 30 years, specializing in the health care industry. He considers himself "semi-retired" preferring to drive to the office only three or four days a week. Ralph married Sandra TREMBLAY on JUN 9, 1974. They have been living on a small farm near Hopkinton, MA. since 1979, where he admits, "we try to keep one step ahead of the termites and carpenter ants." In their spare time they "rough" board horses. They own two of their own and board up to four others. Both Ralph and Sandi are cat lovers, sharing the premises with six at present. Sandi is assistant librarian with the Research Library of the Federal Reserve Bank of Boston. They have no children.

References:

Letter to the author from Ralph Adams Cram, II (dtd AUG 4, 1993)
Letters to the author from Sarah C. Dawson (dtd. SEP 6, 1993 and SEP 19, 1993)

family of Leland Leslie CRAM [1526361422]

Leland Leslie CRAM [1526361422]
b. OCT 13, 1893
d. APR 7, 1928

m. FEB 20, 1915

Marguerite PRICE
b. MAR 2, 1894
d. JUN 26, 1975

1. Leslie Jayne [15263614221] b. JUL 17, 1916.
2. Willard Glenn [15263614222] b. JUN 30, 1918.
3. Marguerite Marie [15263614223] b. JUL, 1920

Leslie Jayne CRAM (1916-1977)
[15263614221]

Leslie was born JUL 17, 1916 at Flint, Genesee County, Michigan and died JUN 3, 1977 at Cottonwood, Arizona. She married first R. B. McCUTCHAN on NOV 28, 1935 at Central Lake, MI. She married second Robert O'Dell TYLER on NOV 6, 1937 at Lansing, MI. She married third Paul Raymond FRAME on OCT 27, 1962 at San Dimas, CA. Paul was born MAR 4, 1913 in Nebraska and died NOV 21, 1988 in Hershey, NE.

Her Children (all by her second husband):
1. Barbara Jayne Tyler; b. MAY 23, 1938 at Vermontville, Eaton County, MI.; she m. Gerald Lyttle on MAY 11, 1957 at Hastings, MI.
    Their Children:
    1. Laura Jean Lyttle; b. MAR 2, 1958.
    2. Robert Lloyd Lyttle; b. MAY 22, 1959.
    3. Lisa Lyttle; b. AUG 13, 1964.
2. Betty Jean Tyler; b. JAN 11, 1940 at Lansing, Ingham County, MI.; m.1. Bud Matheny; m.2. Stanley Cook on SEP 3, 1966;
    Her Child:
    1. Darla Jo Matheny; b. MAY 12, 1958.
3. Bonnie Joan Tyler; b. APR 10, 1941 at Hastings, Barry County, MI.; m.1. Darrell Jones on JUL 27, 1957; m.2. Laverne Rohm;
    Her Children:
    1. Dennis Lee Jones; b. JAN 20, 1958.
    2. Vickie Lynn Jones; b. APR 21, 1959; m. Michael A. Hartman.
    3. Debra Jones; b. JUL 17, 1960.
    4. Patsy Ann Jones; b. JAN 23, 1962.
    5. Jennifer Rohm.
4. Brenda Joyce Tyler; b. OCT 21, 1945 at Hastings, Barry County, MI.; m. Loren Cook on OCT 5, 1963;
    Their Children:
    1. Douglas Leslie Cook; b. MAY 11, 1964.
    2. Carol Ann Cook; b. APR 18, 1965.
    3. Dean Scott Cook; b. AUG 28, 1967; m. Teresa Jo Jamison.
    4. Christina Gail Cook; b. JUL 5, 1970.

Willard Glenn CRAM (1918-)
[15263614222]

Willard (known as Bill) was born JUN 30, 1918 in Flint, Genesee County, Michigan. He attended Bay City Business College 1937-1939. Following his marriage to his first wife, Marian, the family moved to Lansing where he worked for a roofing company. The following year found them in Traverse City doing business as "Cram Roofing Company." Because of an unsettled world political climate, they moved to Detroit where Bill worked for Hudson Tool And Die Co. Their first child Marianne was born there. Bill enlisted in the armed forces in MAY, 1944 serving in the European Theater during World War II with the 42nd "Rainbow" Division. He was discharged APR 5, 1946.

After the war, Bill entered the retailing field. He was employed by Smallegan and Smith General Store in Central Lake, MI., and Market Basket Foods in southern California. He later maintained family apartment buildings in San Jose. Bill re-entered retailing operating a toy store in Jerome, Arizona. He worked as a salesman for Cactus Craft of Tucson, sold jewelry for Ed Youngs of Albuquerque, and operated an office supply store in Cottonwood. The Crams now live in "retirement" in Jerome, Arizona.

Willard married first Marian Louise SMITH on DEC 31, 1939 at Central Lake, MI. She was born OCT 30, 1920 at Central Lake. He married second Anna Ruth WORKMAN on NOV 26, 1954 at Atwood, Michigan. She was born JUN 21, 1927 at Chicago, Illinois.
>   Children by Marian:
>   1. Marianne Lee [152636142221] b. DEC 15, 1941 at Detroit, MI.; m.1. Richard Wallace JACKSON on DEC 16, 1961 at San Jose, CA.; he was b. NOV 2, 1936 at Stockton, CA.; m.2. Dennis Harold GREEN on NOV 2, 1969 at Reno, Nevada; he was b. AUG 1, 1945 at Wenatchee, WA.; m.3. Willard Earl PINER, Jr. on DEC 3, 1983 at Reno, NV.; he was b. JUN 29, 1948 at Dallas, TX.
>   2. Carolyn Jo [152636142222] b. MAR 25, 1947 at Petoskey, MI.; m. Barry James SHODA on JUN 17, 1967 at San Juan Bautista, CA. he was b. SEP 21, 1947 at San Jose, CA.
>   >   Their Children:
>   >   1. Bartholomew James Shoda; b. DEC 20, 1967, at San Jose, CA.
>   >   2. Theresa Ann Shoda; b. JUL 11, 1971, Salt Lake City, UT.
>   >   3. Matthew John Shoda; b. MAY 17, 1976 at Salt Lake City.
>   >   4. Adam Joseph Shoda; b. JAN 27, 1979 at Cottonwood, AZ.
>   >   5. Levi David Shoda; b. FEB 17, 1981 at Coalville, UT.
>   3. Janet Sue [152636142223] b. JUN 29, 1949 at Petoskey, MI.with the Marines
>   Children by Anna Ruth:
>   4. Rodger Bruce [152636142224] b. MAR 9, 1956 at Pasadena, CA.; m. Susan Kay DICKSON on JUN 24, 1978 at Ridgefield, CT.; she was b. DEC 3, 1955 at Schenectady, NY.
>   >   Their Children:
>   >   1. Adam Rodger [1526361422241] b. JAN 17, 1984 at Waterbury, CT.
>   >   2. Tyler Robert [1526361422242] b. MAY 19, 1987 at Willingboro, NJ.
>   5. Rebecca Gail [152636142225] b. FEB 4, 1958 at Pasadena, CA.; m. Brian Richard LEWIS on NOV 22, 1975 at Jerome, AZ. he was b. MAY 1, 1959 at Grand Junction, CO.
>   >   Their Children:
>   >   1. Heather Jannine Lewis; b. APR 23, 1976, at Cottonwood, AZ.
>   >   2. Janel Lauren Lewis; b. AUG 21, 1982 at Cottonwood.
>   6. Philip Dean [152636142226] b. JUN 30, 1961 at San Jose, CA.

Marguerite Marie "Peggy" CRAM (1920-) [15263614223]

Marguerite was born JUL 14, 1920 at Flint, Genesee County, Michigan. She married first Albert COCKAYNE on NOV 21, 1944 at Thomasville, Georgia. She married second John McCALL on JUN 28, 1946 at Traverse City, MI. John was born AUG 28, 1920 at Kalkaska, MI.
>   Children of Marguerite and John:
>   1. John McCall; b. SEP 20, 1948 at Grayling, MI.; d. six hours later; buried at Gaylord.
>   2. Patricia Anne "Patsy" McCall; b. FEB 20, 1948 at Petoskey, MI; adopted by the McCalls on FEB 25, 1948; m.1. John Harmon; m.2. Wayne Livingston on JUN 2, 1977;

Patricia's Children:
     1. John Harmon
     2. Melissa Harmon; b. SEP 8, 1967.

3. Willard John McCall; b. SEP 27, 1949 at Grayling, MI; m.1. Dawnette Ferry; m.2. Patricia Rzepka on JUN 10, 1977;
     Children of John and Patricia:
          1. Timothy Rzepka McCall; b. JUL 5, 1967
             at Coldwater, MI.
          2. Tammy Rzepka McCall; b. AUG 18, 1969 at Coldwater.
          3. Nathan Willard McCall; b. OCT 3, 1979
             at Kalamazoo, MI.

4. Donald J. McCall; b. AUG 20, 1951 at Coldwater, MI.; m. Karen ----
     Their Child:
          1. Donald McCall; b. OCT 16, 1978 at Coldwater, MI.

Reference:

Letter to the author from Anna Ruth Cram (dtd. JUN 7, 1991)

family of Keith B. CRAM [1526B81333]

Keith B. CRAM [1526B81333]
b. JAN 18, 1920
d.

m. FEB 19, 1949 _____ 1. Michael S. [1526B813331]
                                               2. Roxanne [1526B813332]

Madeleine A. ROY
b. MAY 16, 1924

Michael S. CRAM (1953-)
[1526B813331]

Michael was born FEB 12, 1953 at Waterville, ME. He married first Karen SANBORN. No children.
They were divorced. He married second Cynthia TRUNDY on MAR 31, 1984. They reside in Glenburn,
ME.
    Their Children:
        1. Benjamin Keith [1526B8133311] b. DEC 8, 1984.
        2. Samuel Ira [1526B8133312] b. APR 18, 1988.
        3. Katherine Rose [1526B8133313] b. NOV 20, 1990.
    Two children by Cynthia's previous marriage:
        4. Rachel Young
        5. Rebecca Young

Roxanne CRAM (1954-)
[1526B813332]

Roxanne was born MAY 9, 1954 in Belfast, ME. She married Ronald NEWTON, Jr. on JUN 17, 1972.
They reside in Monteville, ME. Roxanne is a home maker and workes part time in the Liberty, ME. post
office.
    Their Children:
        1. Bethany Lynn Newton; b. JUN 10, 1973; graduated from high school in 1991.
        2. Lisa Marie Newton; b. JUL 29, 1975.

References:

Letter to the author from Keith Cram (dtd. MAR, 1991)
Records of Keith Cram

family of John Conrad CRAM [1616346114]

John Conrad CRAM [1616346114] b. JUN 26, 1905 d. m. APR 11, 1937 Leola Mae OLSON b. MAY 9, 1912 d.	1. Mary Opal [16163461141] b. JAN 20, 1938 2. David Samuel [16163461142] b. JAN 30, 1940 3. Francis Orrin [16163461143] b. FEB 4, 1941 4. Martha Elizabeth [16163461144] b. APR 8, 1944 5. Alma Jonathan [16163461145] b. SEP 14, 1945 6. Edward Nephi [16163461146] b. DEC 28, 1947. 7. Bryan Paul [16163461147] b. MAR 11, 1950 8. Abigail Kathryn [16163461148] b. OCT 3, 1951 9. Phillip Matthew [16163461149] b. APR 12, 1953 10. Michael Benjamin [1616346114A] b. MAR, 1955 11. Laura Rose [1616346114B] b. JUN 16, 1956

Mary Opal CRAM (1938-)
[16163461141]

Mary Opal was born JAN 20, 1938 in Boise, Idaho. She married Homer BROWN on OCT 8, 1955. He was born NOV 18, 1936.
> Their Children:
>> 1. Terryl Andrew Brown; b. NOV 9, 1963.
>> 2. Michael Dean Brown; b. MAY 4, 1965.

David Samuel CRAM (1940-)
[16163461142]

David Samuel was born JAN 30, 1940 in Nampa, ID. He married Delores ROBINSON on AUG 30, 1959. She was born DEC 1, 1941.
> Their Children:
>> 1. Yvonne Lorita [161634611421] b. Jun 30, 1960.
>> 2. Zane Conrad [161634611422] b. DEC 30, 1967,

Francis Orrin CRAM (1941-)
[16163461143]

Francis Orrin was born FEB 4, 1941 in Melba, ID. He married Dalla BRADY on DEC 21, 1963. She was born JUL 5, 1939.
> Their Children:
>> 1. Mary Ruth [161634611431] b. SEP 9, 1964.
>> 2. David Oran [161634611432] b. SEP 8, 1965; twin of Daniel, below.
>> 3. Daniel Paul [161634611433] b. SEP 8, 1965; twin of David.
>> 4. Laurie Ann [161634611434] b. APR 19, 1967.
>> 5. Alisa Renee [161634611435] b. FEB 3, 1969; twin of Ole, below.
>> 6. Ole Rodney [161634611436] b. FEB 3, 1969; twin of Alisa.

Martha Elizabeth CRAM (1944-)
[16163461144]

Martha Elizabeth was born APR 8, 1944 in Melba, ID. She married Sterling BURTON on AUG 28, 1961. He was born MAR 11, 1941.
> Their Children:
>> 1. Beverly Ann Burton; b. FEB 2, 1962.
>> 2. Pamela Kay Burton; b. MAR 22, 1972.

Alma Jonathon CRAM (1945-)
[16163461145]

Alma Jonathon was born SEP 14, 1945 in Nampa, ID. He married Carol Marie JENKINS on FEB 23, 1968. She was born AUG 20, 1947. They were divorced before 1980.
> Their Child:
>> 1. Camille Sue [161634611451] b. AUG 29, 1972.

Edward Nephi CRAM (1947-1966)
[16163461146]

Edward Nephi was born DEC 28, 1947 in Nampa, ID. He died AUG 17, 1966. Nothing more is known about him.

Bryan Paul CRAM (1950-1965)
[16163461147]

Bryan Paul was born MAR 11, 1950 in Nampa, ID. He died MAR 30, 1965. There is no additional information on his life.

Abigail Kathryn CRAM (1951-)
[16163461148]

Abigail Kathryn was born OCT 3, 1951 in Nampa, ID. She married Rodney McDOWELL on JUN 9, 1972. He was born JUN 12, 1950.

Phillip Matthew CRAM (1953-1971)
[16163461149]

Phillip Matthew was born APR 12, 1953 in Nampa, ID. He died SEP 11, 1971. There is no further information concerning him.

Michael Benjamin CRAM (1955-)
[1616346114A]

Michael Benjamin was born MAR 11, 1955 in Nampa, ID.

Laura Rose CRAM (1956-)
[1616346114B]

Laura Rose was born JUN 16, 1956 in Nampa, ID.

Resource:

Cram (pp. b-18 and b-19)

family of Roy Spencer CRAM [1616346123]

Roy Spencer CRAM [1616346123]
b. FEB 3, 1903
d. AUG 4, 1989

m.1. AUG 12, 1926 _____ 1. Roene Ruth [16163461231] b. FEB 8, 1928
                                          2. Jean Marie [16163461232] b. SEP 8, 1933

Edith Marie FREASE
b. JUN 26, 1903
d. APR 19, 1955

m.2. SEP 1, 1941 _____ 3. Albert Edwin [16163461233] b. OCT 23, 1942
                                          4. Roy Spencer, Jr. [16163461234] b. DEC, 1945

Pearl Theresa SIGNER
b. MAR 7, 1909
d. JUL 7, 1989

Roene Ruth CRAM (1928-)
[16163461231]

Roene Ruth was born FEB 8, 1928 in South Omaha, NE. She married John Lee MOONEY in Altadena,
CA. on AUG 22, 1948. He was born NOV 11, 1924 in Detroit, MI.
   Their Children:
   1. Mary Catherine Mooney; b. DEC 9, 1949; m. Rory Kevin O'Connor; div., no issue
   2. William Ford Mooney; b. APR 25, 1953 in Altadena, CA.; m. Patricia
        Louise Condit; they are divorced, no children.
   3. Thomas Glen Mooney; b. FEB 1, 1957 in San Diego, CA.; m. Susan Dawn Winberg
        on APR 4, 1979; she was b. JUL 8, 1954; three children.
   4. Cheryl Ann Mooney; b. AUG 23, 1959 in LaMesa, CA.

Jean Marie CRAM (1933-)
[16163461232]

Jean Marie was born SEP 18, 1933 in Grand Island, NE. She married first Roger Charles Andre
ROBITAILLE on JUL 19, 1952 in Altadena, CA. He was born DEC 5, 1930. They divorced in MAR 15,
1963. She married second Bruce Moody BARRON on APR 29, 1967. He was born JAN 14, 1926 in Los
Angeles, CA. They were divorced AUG 11, 1982. She married third Dr. Thomas Allen HANNON on JUN
4, 1983. He was born OCT 10, 1931 at Phoenix, AZ. They reside in Chino Valley, Arizona.   Jean had
five children by Andre, but no issue by Bruce or Thomas.
   Children by Andre Roger Robitaille:
   1. Paul Martin Robitaille; b. DEC 21, 1952 in Altadena, CA.; m.1. Deborah Sue
        Woodford; they divorced SEP 1, 1981; m.2. Carolyn Alice Schroeder; they
        divorced APR 5, 1989; m.3. Patricia Mae Ruby on MAY 4, 1991; no children
        from any marriage..
   2. Anne Marie Robitaille; b. APR 30, 1954 in Santa Monica, CA.; m. Paul David
        Jenkins; three children.
   3. Denise Jan Robitaille; b. FEB 9, 1956 in Santa Monica, CA.; m. Michael Edward
        Lierman; three children.
   4. Elaine Therese Robitaille; b. MAY 1, 1957 in Santa Monica, CA.; m. Donald
        Eugene Boroff; three children.
   5. Alan Spencer Robitaille; b. JAN 4, 1959 in Santa Monica, CA.; m. Paula Burdette
        Lloyd; two children.

Albert Edwin CRAM (1942-)
[16163461233]

Albert Edwin was born OCT 23, 1942 in Omaha, NE. He married first Eva Jo WUNDERLICH on NOV 17, 1962. She was born NOV 25, 1944 . They were divorced in MAR, 1986. He married second Ellen (VanVark) KIBEE on JUL 11, 1987. She was born JAN 2, 1952 in Dubuque, IA. Ellen holds RN. and MA. degrees and is Director of Cirtical Care Nursing Services at the University of Iowa Hospitals and Clinics.

Albert graduated from the University of Nebraska Medical School in 1969. He trained in general surgery at the University of Iowa, completing his training in 1974, and taking the certifying examination in 1975. Following a tour of duty with the Navy he taught at the U. of Iowa, and acted as director of the burn unit until 1985. After taking a sabbatical to complete a plastic survery residency at the U. of Chicago, he returned to the U. of Iowa where is is Director of Plastic and Reconstructive Surgery. His avocation is autocross racing. He says he is hoping to improve on his seventh place finish in the 1993 Nationals.

Their Children:
1. Michele Monique [1616341612331] b. MAY 19, 1963 in Lincoln, NE.; received BS. in Forestry at Iowa State U. and a Master's degree at the U. of Michigan; at this writing she lives in Asheville, NC. where she is a plant pathologist with U.S. Forestry Service.
2. Michael Raymond [1616341612332] b. MAY 31, 1964 in Lincoln, NE.; graduateded from U. of Iowa Medical School in 1993; entered Ohio State U. to take an urology residency; he won Iowa State Championship in men's doubles and mixed doubles in tennis in 1982.
3. Ross [1616341612333] b. APR 2, 1981; Ellen's son, adopted in JAN, 1989.

Roy Spencer CRAM Jr. (1945-)
[16163461234]

Roy was born DEC 31, 1945 in Omaha, NE. He was married on SEP 6, 1975 to Reba Muriel (Cade) BARNES. She was born JUN 3, 1945 in Shreveport, LA. He is a pharmacist. The family lives in Tishomingo, OK. There are two children of Ms. Barnes by a previous marriage.

Children of Reba by previous marriage:
1. Allen Barnes; b. JUL 2, 1964 at Clainda, IA.
2. Bryan Barnes; b. MAY 9, 1967 at Clainda, IA.

Their Children:
3. John Edwin [161634612341] b. JUN 3, 1976 in New Orleans.
4. Amanda Sue [161634612342] b. DEC 9, 1979 at Ardmore, OK.

References:

Cram (pp. b-22 and b-23)
Letter to the author from Dr. Albert Edwin Cram [dtd. NOV 30, 1993]
Letter to the author from Jean (Cram) Hannon [dtd. DEC 20, 1993 & JAN 28, 1994]

Selected Bibliography

Adams, Andrew N. Genealogical History of Henry Adams of Braintree, Massachusetts and his descendants; also John Adams of Cambridge, Massachusetts 1632-1897. Rutland, Vermont: Tuttle & Company State Printers, 1898.

Andrews, Carol. Letters to the author, dtd. APR 8, 1990 and JUN 27, 1990.

Baer, Mabel Van Dyke. Cram, Cressy, Gove and Wadleigh Families. Manuscript (ts.) in the DAR Library, Washington, DC. (109 pp.)

Bailey, Richard. Records of the Merrimack Valley.

Balch, Galusha B., M.D. Genealogy of the Balch Families in America. Salem, Massachusetts: Eben Putnam Publishing Co., 1897.

Bass, H. Royce. History of Braintree, Vermont. Rutland, Vermont: Tuttle & Company State Printers, 1883.

Behme, Margaret. Letter to the author, dtd. MAR 10, 1990.

Bell, Charles H. History of Exeter, New Hampshire. Boston: press of J. E. Farwell & Co., 1888.

Black, George F. Surnames of Scotland - Their Origin, Meaning, and History. New York: New York Public Library, 1946.

Brown, Carol A. Letter to the Author. MAY 2, 1978.

Brown, Howard Morton. "Cram Family of Carleton Place." ts. Ottawa, Canada (1977)

Brown, John, Jr. History of San Bernardino and Riverside Counties. (3 Vol.) Chicago: Lewis Publishing Co., 1922.

Brown, Warren. History of the Town of Hampton Falls, New Hampshire 1640 - 1900. Manchester, New Hampshire: John B. Clarke Co., 1900.

Carter, Rev. N. F. History of Newfields, New Hampshire 1638-1911. Concord, NH.; Rumford Printing Company, 1912.

Carter, Rev. N. F. History of Pembroke, New Hampshire. Concord, NH.: Republican Press Association, 1895.

Carter, Rev. N. F. Native Ministry of New Hampshire. Concord, NH.: Rumford Printing Company, 1906.

Cemeteries, Deerfield, New Hampshire, Second & Third Ranges. Comp. by Joanne F. Wasson. (ts.), 1989.

Chandler, Charles Henry. History of New Ipswich, New Hampshire 1735 - 1914. Fitchburg, Massachusetts: Sentinel Printing Company, 1914.

Chapman, Rev. Jacob and Rev. James H. Fitts. Lane Genealogies. (Vol. 1) Exeter, NH.: Newsletter Press, 1891.

Chase, Benjamin. History of Old Chester, New Hampshire from 1719-1869. Auburn, NH.: Published by the author, 1869.

Cochrane, Rev. W. R. History of Antrim, New Hampshire. Manchester, NH.: published by the town, 1880.

Cochrane, Rev. W. R. and George K. Wood. History of Francestown, New Hampshire from its Earliest Settlement April, 1758 to January 1, 1891. Nashua: J. H. Barker, 1895.

Cogswell, Rev. E. C. History of Nottingham, Deerfield and Northwood. Manchester, NH.: printed by John B. Clarke, 1878.

Colonial Families of the United States of America. (7 Vol.) Ed. George Norbury Mackenzie. Baltimore: Genealogical Publishing Company, 1966.

Colonial Gravestone Inscriptions in the State of New Hampshire. Comp. Mrs. Charles Carpenter Gross. Dover, NH.: Genealogical Publishing Company, 1974.

Contemporary Authors. (Vol. 49-52) Detroit, MI.: Gale Research Company, 1975.

Coolidge, A. J. and J. B. Mansfield. History and Description of New England, General and Local. (2 Vol.) Boston: Austin J. Coolidge, 1860.

Coues, William P. Letter to the author, dtd. JUL 3, 1990.

Cram, Charles M. Genealogical Outline of the Cram, Walker and Weeks Families. Boston: 1934.

Cram, Daniel H. History of the Family Von Cramm. ts. New England Historic Genealogical Society, Boston, about 1880.

Cram, Ernest Richard. Sainty's Dick Cram. St. Francis, Kansas: Privately printed by the author, 1994.

Cram, Elmer H. Cram Family Papers. Manuscript 200, ts. New England Historic Genealogical Society, Boston.

Cram, Fred D. Letter to Ralph W. Cram dtd. JAN 1, 1938.

Cram, George William. Letters to Daniel H. Cram dtd. FEB 15, 1875; APR 30, 1875; SEP 26, 1875.

Cram, Hank. Notes on the CRAM Family and Some Related Families. ts. (57 pages) Bluffton, South Carolina.

Cram, Harry W. Letter to the author, dtd. FEB 2, 1991.

Cram, John C. Letter to the author, dtd. JAN 20, 1977.

Cram, John G. Personal family records.

Cram, Dr. John W. Letter to Ralph W. Cram, dtd. DEC 6, 1923.

Cram, Laura E. Letter to the author, dtd. OCT 6, 1981.

Cram, Mary (Nielsen). Letter to the author, dtd. MAY 5, 1975.

Cram, Melvin D. Letters to Ralph W. Cram, dtd. MAY 28, 1905 and MAR 4, 1925.

Cram, Myra. Personal family records.

Cram, Dr. Ralph Archibald Letters to the author, dtd. MAR 18, 1990 and DEC 3, 1990.

Cram, Ralph Adams. Letter to Baron Burchard von Cramm, dtd. JUL 17, 1929.

Cram, Ralph Adams. Letter to Ramon S. Cram, dtd. APR 18, 1935.

Cram, Ralph Adams. Letter to Mrs. D. H. Sheehan, dtd. FEB 7, 1919.

Cram, Reginald. Letters to the author, dtd. SEP 16, 1990 & OCT 2, 1990.

Cram, Roy S. Cram. Burwell, Nebraska: privately published book, about 1980.

Cram, William H. "One Cram Family in Canada and U.S.A." ts. Indian Head, Sask., Canada

Cram, Wilson. Letters to Hilda Cram., dtd. MAY 17, 1918; JUL 6, 1918; JUL 7, 1918.

Cramb, Dr. John. Letter to Mrs. Cora Cressey Crowe, Modesto, CA., dtd. JUN 28, 1924.

Cramb, Dr. John. Letter to Ralph W. Cram, dtd. JAN 19, 1925.

Cramm (von), Burghard Freiherr. Letters to the author dtd. FEB 21, 1972 and APR 21, 1977,

Cross, Lucy R. H. The History of Northfield, New Hampshire 1780 - 1905. Concord, NH.: Rumford Printing Co., 1905.

Currier, John J. "Ould Newbury" Historical and Biographical Sketches. Boston: Damrell & Upham, 1896.

Curtis, John Gould. History of the Town of Brookline, Massachusetts. Cambridge, MA.: Riverside Press, 1933.

Cutter, Elizabeth A. Personal family records.

Dearborn, John Jacob. The History of Salisbury, New Hampshire from the Date of Settlement to the Present Time . . . Eds. James O. Adams and Henry P. Rolfe. Manchester N.H.: William E. Moore, 1890.

Directory of the Ancestral Heads of New England Families - 1620-1700. Comp. Frank R. Holmes. Baltimore: Genealogical Publishing Company, 1964.

Donovan, Dennis and Jacob Andrews Woodward. History of Lyndeborough, New Hampshire 1735 - 1905. Medford, MA.: Tufts College Press, 1906.

Dow, Joseph. History of the Town of Hampton, New Hampshire. Salem, MA.: Salem Press Publishing and Printing Co., 1893. Two Volumes.

Doyle, Arthur Conan. Complete Original Illustrated Sherlock Holmes. Secaucus, NJ.: Castle Books, 1976.

Freeman, Kathe F. Letters to Elmer H. Cram dtd. JAN 29, 1946 and APR 26, 1946.

Fullonton, Joseph. The History of Raymond, New Hampshire. Dover: Morning Star Job Printing, 1875.

Galt, Iola Lalley. "Exeter Through the Years." The Exeter, New Hampshire, Story - 1975. (3rd Ed.) Exeter, NH.: published by the Exeter Area Chamber of Commerce and produced by Exeter News-Letter Co., 1975.

Gazetteer of Orange County, Vermont 1762-1888. Comp. by Hamilton Child. Syracuse, N.Y.: Syracuse Journal Co., 1888.

Gazetteer of Washington County, Vermont. Comp. by Hamilton Child; ed. by William Adams. Syracuse, NY.: Syracuse Journal Co., 1889.

Genealogical and Family History of the State of Maine. (4 Vol.) Ed. George Thomas Little. New York: Lewis Historical Publishing Co., 1909.

Genealogical and Family History of the State of New Hampshire. (4 Vol.) Ed. Ezra S. Stearns. New York: Lewis Publishing Company, 1908.

Genealogical and Personal Memoirs Relating to the Families of the State of Massachusetts. (4 Vol.) Ed. William Richard Cutter. New York: Lewis Historical Publishing Company, 1910.

Genealogical Register of the Descendants of George Abbot of Andover, George Abbot of Rowley, Thomas Abbot of Andover, Arthur Abbot of Ipswich, Robert Abbot of Branford, CT. - and George Abbot of Norwalk, CT. Comp. by Rev. Abiel Abbot, D.D., and Rev. Ephraim Abbot. Boston: James Munroe & Co., 1847.

Genealogies of Rhode Island Families. (2 Vol.) Baltimore: Genealogical Publishing Co., Inc., 1989.

Gove, William Henry. The Gove Book. Salem, MA.: Sidney Perley, 1922.

Hadley, George Plummer. History of the Town of Goffstown 1733 - 1920. (2 Vol.) Published by the town. Concord, NH.: Rumford Press, 1924.

Hammond, Rev. Charles. History of Union, Connecticut. New Haven, CT.: Press of Price, Lee & Adkins Co., 1893.

Hartman, Francis B. Records from Historical Registry and Dictionary of the U.S. Army from 1789-1903.

Hawke, David Freeman. Everyday Life in Early America. New York: Harper & Row Publishers, 1988.

Hayward, William Willis. History of Hancock, New Hampshire 1764 - 1889. Lowell, MA.: Vox Populi Press, 1889.

Hazen, Rev. Henry A. History of Billerica, Massachusetts with a Genealogical Register. Boston: A. Williams & Co., 1883.

Hertman, Francis B. Records from Historical Registry & Dictionary of the United States Army 1789-1903.

Historical Collection of the Essex Institute. Vol. 10. Salem, MA.: published by Essex Institute, 1870.

History of Acworth, With the Proceedings of the Centennial Anniversary, Genealogical Records, and Register of the Farms. Springfield, Maine: S. Bowles, 1869.

History of Barnard, Vermont With Family Genealogies 1761-1927. (2 Vol.). Montpelier, VT.: Vermont Historical Society, 1928.

History of Jackson County, Iowa. Chicago: Western Historical Co., 1879.

History of Litchfield, and an Account of the Centennial Celebration - 1895. Augusta, ME.: Kennebec Journal Printing Co., 1897.

History of Littleton, New Hampshire. Ed. by James R. Jackson. Cambridge, MA.: published by the town, printed by University Press, 1905. Three Volumes.

History of Marietta and Washington County, Ohio

History of Rockingham & Strafford Counties, New Hampshire. Comp. by D. Hamilton Hurd; 1882.

History of Shiawassee and Clinton Counties, Michigan. Philadelphia: D. W. Ensign & Co., 1880.

History of the First Century of the Town of Parsonsfield, Maine, Incorporated August 29, 1785, and Celebrated with Impressive Ceremonies at North Parsonsfield, August 29, 1885. Ed. by Jeremiah Wadleigh Dearborn. Portland: Brown Thurston, 1888.

History of the Town of New London, New Hampshire 1779 - 1899. Concord, NH.: Rumford Press, 1899.

History of Washington, New Hampshire 1768-1886. Claremont, N.H.: Claremont Manufacturing Co., 1886.

Hurd, D. Hamilton. History of Merrimack & Belknap Counties, New Hampshire. Philadelphia: J. W. Lewis & Co., 1885.

Hurd, Duane Hamilton. History of Rockingham & Strafford Counties, New Hampshire, With Biographical Sketches of Many of its Pioneers & Prominent Men. Philadelphia: J. W. Lewis, 1882.

Keeter, Gary Lynn. Cram Family History. (42 pages) Vacaville, CA.: Privately printed by the author, 1994.

Knowles, Martha. Personal family records.

Lane, Edmund J. and James P. Lane. Lane Genealogies. (3 Vol.) Exeter, N.H.: Newsletter Press, 1891.

LeMay, Peggy (Cram). Letter to the author, dtd. SEP 9, 1986.

Leonard, Rev. Levi W. History of Dublin, New Hampshire. Dublin, N.H.: Published by the town of Dublin; 1920.

Lewis, Mary Jane Sanborn. Letter to the author, dtd. AUG 21, 1989.

Little, William. The History of Weare, New Hampshire 1735 - 1888. Lowell, MA.: published by the town, printed by S. W. Huse and Co., 1888.

Livermore, Abiel Abbot and Sewall Putnam. History of The Town of Wilton, Hillsborough County, New Hampshire. Lowell, MA.: Marden & Rowell Printers, 1888.

Lord, C. C. "Trouble With The Minister." The Life and Times of Hopkinton, New Hampshire. Concord, N.H.: Republican Press Association, 1890.

Maine Historical and Genealogical Recorder. Portland, ME.: S. M. Watson, Publisher (1884-1889).

Meredith, New Hampshire Annals and Genealogies. Arranged by Mary E. Neal Hannaford. Concord, NH.: Rumford Press, 1932.

Miller, James Alfred Locke. Letter to the author, dtd. MAR 19, 1990.

Miller, Mary Deming (Cram). Letter to the author dtd. OCT 14, 1971.

Morison, George Abbot. History of Peterborough, New Hampshire. (2 Vol.) Rindge, NH.: Richard R. Smith, 1954.

Morrison, Leonard. History of Windham, New Hampshire 1719 - 1883. Boston: Cupples, Upham & Co., 1883.

Morrison, Leonard Allison. Lineage and Biographies of the Norris Family in America from 1640 to 1892. Boston: Damrell & Upham, 1892.

Muddy River and Brookline Records 1634 - 1838. By The Inhabitants of Brookline, in Town Meeting. Boston: J. E. Farwell & Company, 1875.

Mullen, Joan Norton. Letter to the author, dtd. SEP 11, 1990.

Nicholas, Mary Carrington (Cram). Letters to the author dtd. FEB 21, 1972, and MAR 11, 1972.

Noyes, Sybil, Charles Thornton Libby and Walter Goodwin Davis. Genealogical Dictionary of Maine and New Hampshire. (2 Vol.) Portland, Maine: Southworth-Anthoensen Press, 1939.

Noyes, Sybil, Charles Thornton Libby and Walter Goodwin Davis. Genealogical Dictionary of New Hampshire. Portland, ME.: Southworth-Anthoensen Press, 1939.

Old Records of the Town of Fitchburg, Massachusetts. (8 Vol.) Comp. Walter A. Davis, City Clerk. Fitchburg: Sentinel Printing Company, 1903.

Owen, Thomas McAdory. History of Alabama & Dictionary of Alabama Biography. (3 Vol.) Spartanburg, South Carolina: Reprint Company, 1978.

Pierce, Frederick Clifton. Batchelder, Batcheller Genealogy. Chicago: Press of W. G. Conkey Co., 1898.

Provincial Papers - Documents and Records Relating to the Province of New Hampshire. (7 Vol.) Edited by Nathaniel Bouton, D.D. Nashua, NH.: Oren C. Moore State Printer, 1873.

Putnam, Eben. A History of the Putnam Family in England & America. Salem, MA.: Salem Press Publishing & Printing Co., 1891.

Ramsdell, George Allen. The History of Milford. . . Family Registers by William P. Colburn. Published by the town - Committee of Publication: George A. Worcester, Clinton S. Averill, Concord, NH.: Rumford Press, 1901.

Ransom, Anna M. "Ransom (Harlow-Cram) Family Bible - Copied in 1935 by Anna M. Ransom, Denver, Colorado, from a Bible Then in Her Possession." DAR Magazine. Vol 91, p. 992.

Read, Benjamin. History of Swanzey, New Hampshire From 1734 - 1890. Salem, MA.: Salem Press Publishing and Printing Co., 1892.

Records of the Families of California Pioneers. Comp. by California State Society of Daughters of American Revolution, ts. DAR Library, Washington, DC., 1954.

Report of Genealogical Records Committee of Rhode Island NSDAR, 1941. Manuscript (ts.) in the library of the Rhode Island Historical Society, Providence, RI.

Report of Genealogical Records Committee of Rhode Island NSDAR, 1944. Manuscript (ts.) in the library of the Rhode Island Historical Society, Providence, RI.

Ridlon, G. T. Sr. Saco Valley Settlements and Families. Rutland, VT.: Charles E. Tuttle Co. (1969) Originally published in 1895 in Portland, ME.

Rietstap, Johannes B. Armorial General. (2 Vol.) Baltimore: Genealogical Publishing Co., 1965.

Riga, Brad. Letter to the author. JUL 17, 1989.

Roylance, Ward Jay. Remingtons of Utah with their Ancestors and Descendants. Salt Lake City: 1960.

Sanborn, Channing. "Lincolnshire Origin of Some Exeter Settlers." New England Genealogical and Historical Register. Vol 68, pp. 64-68. Boston: 1914.

Sanborn, F. B. Recollections of Seventy Years. (2 Vol.) Boston: Gorham Press, 1900.

Sanborn, V. C. Genealogy of the Family of Samborne or Sanborn in England and America, 1194-1898. Concord, NH.: Rumford Press, 1899.

Saunderson, Henry H. History of Charlestown, New Hampshire, The Old No. 4. Claremont, NH.: Claremont Manufacturing Co., 1876.

Sawyer, Rev. Roland D. History of Kensington, New Hampshire 1663-1945. Farmington, ME.: Knowlton & McLeary Co.

Secomb, Daniel F. History of the Town of Amherst, Hillsborough County, New Hampshire. Concord: Evans, Sleeper & Woodbury, 1883

Seward, J. L. The History of Sullivan, New Hampshire 1777 - 1917. (2 Vol.) Keene, NH.: J. L. Seward, Est., 1921.

Sieman, Margaret (Cram). Letter to the author, dtd. NOV 12, 1971.

Smith, Danny D. Letter to James Alfred Locke Miller, dtd. APR 25, 1990.

Somers, Rev. A. N. The Town History of Lancaster, New Hampshire. Concord, N.H.: Rumford Press, 1898.

Stackpole, Everett Schermehorn. History of the Town of Durham New Hampshire - 1913. Somersworth, N.H.: New Hampshire Publishing Co., 1973.

Stearns, Ezra S. History of Plymouth, New Hampshire. (2 vol.) Cambridge, MA.: Printed for the town by University Press, 1906.

Stearns, Ezra Scollay. History of the Town of Rindge, New Hampshire from the Date of the Rowley Canada or Massachusetts Charter to the Present Time, 1736-1874. Boston: George H. Ellis, 1875.

Stearns, Ezra Scollay, William Frederick Whitcher, and Edward Everett Parker. Genealogical & Family History of the State of New Hampshire: a Record of the Achievements of Her People in the Making of a Commonwealth and the Founding of a Nation. New York: Lewis Publishing, 1908.

Stewart, Janet M. Letters to the author, dtd. OCT 11, 1989 and MAY 4, 1990.

Stone, Arthur F. Vermont of Today. (4 vol.) New York: Lewis Publishing Co., 1929.

Tenney, M. J. The Tenney Family; or The Descendants of Thomas Tenney, of Rowley, Massachusetts, 1638-1904. Boston: Rumford Press, 1904.

Tibbals, Ralph Howard. Genealogical Records of Antrim, New Hampshire Families. Edited by Rose Wilkinson Poor, Concord: Bridge & Byron, 1967.

Town Papers of New Hampshire 1638-1784. (9 Vol.) ed. by Nathaniel Bouton, D. D., 1875.

Town Papers of New Hampshire 1706-1760. Ed. by Issac W. Hammond. Concord, NH.: Parsons B. Cogswell State Printer, 1893.

Tyler, Lorraine N. The Cram Family of New Hampshire. ts., Washington, D.C., Unpublished Essay, 1988.

Tyler, Lorraine N. Letter to the author, dtd. SEP 11, 1989.

Upton, Harriet Taylor. Twentieth Century History of Trumbull County, Ohio. (2 Vol.) Chicago: Lewis Publishing Co., 1909.

Vital Records of Newburyport, Massachusetts to the End of the Year 1849. (2 Vol.) Salem, MA.: Essex Institute, 1911.

Webster, J. C. Memorial Poems and Brief Ancestral Record of the Webster Family and Descendants. Hartford, CT: Press of the Hartford Printing Co., 1904.

Wheelwright, Edmund March. A Frontier Family. Cambridge: John Wilson & Son, University Press, 1894.

Who's Who in America 1988-1989 (45th. ed. - 2 Vol.) Wilmette, IL.: Macmillan Directory Div., 1988.

Who's Who in New England (2nd. ed.). Edited by Albert Nelson Marquis. Chicago: A.N. Marquis Co., 1916.

Who's Who in the North East. (3 Vol.) Edited by Albert Nelson Marquis. Chicago: A. N. Marquis Co., 1938.

Young, E. Harold. History of Pittsfield, New Hampshire. Concord, NH.: New Hampshire Bindery, 1953.

INDEX

Cram, Carol Marie (Jenkins)
    132
        Carol Vesta   115
        Caroline (Evans) 82
        Caroline (Stevens) 4
        Carolyn (Gibbens) 97
        Carolyn Jo   128
        Carrie E.   72
        Carrie Ida   70
        Carroll Albion 4
        Cecil Marion   55, 107
        Charles   70
        Charles Albert 82
        Charles Arthur 10
        Charles Chester 35, 95
        Charles Donnelly 122
        Charles H.   1
        Charles Hilliard 79, 80,
    123
        Charles Maurice 4
        Charles N.   74
        Charles O.   65
        Charles Robert 113
        Charles Sanborn 37
        Charles Wallace 34
        Charles Warren 24
        Charles Wayland 1
        Charles Welbourn 99
        Charlesetta Prescott 35
        Charley   65
        Charley P.   65
        Chauncey J.   65
        Chloris (Hamblin) 37
        Christina Elouise 112
        Christine (Macauley) 73
        Christopher Vernon 66
        Claire (Rhodes) 51
        Claire L.   51
        Clara   38, 79
        Clara (Hanson) 51
        Clara (Thomasson) 121
        Clara E.   65
        Clara L.   39
        Clara Smith   37
        Clare (Foss)   60
        Clarence Findlay 55, 107
        Claude Bunting 38
        Claudia (Brown) 109
        Claudia Kay   114
        Cleo Amy   29
        Clifford Harlan 28
        Clifton Swett   30
        Clifton Swett   89
        Clyde Allen   64
        Cora (Cousins) 10
        Cora (Howe)   2
        Cora (Neidig)   80
        Cora A.   63
        Cora Ann   19
        Cuba   69
        Cusi   111
        Cynthia (Trundy) 130
        Dagmar (Anderson) 90
        Dalla (Brady)   118

Dalla (Brady)   131
Dana   64
Dana Marie (Simmons)
    105
Daniel Paul   131
Daniel W.   53
Darlene   52
Daryle 64
David Lee   108
David Oran   131
David Samuel   118
David Samuel   131
David Smith   6
Deanna   39
Dee Raymond   93
Del Bert   39
Delia (Gilbert)   53
Della (Lockwood) 67
Delores (Robinson) 118,
    131
Dennis Gary   52
Deryl Leroy   39
Dianna (Shadduck) 27
Dolly (Langley)   16
Dolly Maude   8
Don Prescott   37
Donald Adelbert   55, 107
Donald Bruce   95
Donald Bunting   38
Donald Deming   47
Donald E.   52
Donald Gene   52
Donna 64
Dora (Fahrney) 53
Dora (Wolf)   28
Dora Eunice   29
Doreen Carol   118
Doris (Archibald) 44
Doris (Shelton)   38
Doris E.   52
Dorothy (Kemmerly) 45
Dorothy (Winslow) 16
Dorothy Dale   52
Douglas   113
Earl St. John   28
Earle Albert   66
Edith (Drexel)   61
Edith (Frease)   119
Edith (Swett)   30
Edith Bryce   62
Edith Clair Cooper 62, 112
Edith Julia   50
Edith Maybelle   28
Edna (May)   65
Edna (Ogzewalla) 93
Edna (Warwick)   45
Edward Nephi   118, 132
Edwin Clay   68
Edwin G.   83
Edwin James, Col. 9
Edwin Lincoln 2
Effie (Paine)   2
Effie Violet (Wilson) 75
Eldred John   38

Eleanor   86
Elena (Chavez)   107
Elinor Kittredge 22
Elinor Mary   41
Eliza   35, 95
Elizabeth (Henderson)   34
Elizabeth (Miller) 10
Elizabeth (Millikin) 74
Elizabeth (Read) 33
Elizabeth (Ringo) 113
Elizabeth Strudwick 33, 92
Ella (Carter)   24
Ella (Dickenson) 65
Ella Flora   18
Ella L. 10
Ella May (Burner) 53
Ellen (Kibee)   134
Ellen (Smith)   22
Ellery Maynard   65
Ellis Gilbert   53
Elmer E.   51
Elmer Elsworth   27, 28
Elmer Frank   70
Elmer Herbert   16
Elmer Herbert   87
Elmer Lockwood   67
Eloise Blaine   42
Elouise (Forren) 61
Elsie (Cecil)   63
Elsie (Miller)   51
Elva (Plant)   63
Emily (Marston)   1
Emily (Rasband)   93
Emily (Stackpole) 16
Emily Ann   20
Emily Frances   16, 87
Emma Belle   16
Emma Frances   18
Emma Maria   9
Enness (Miner)   54, 55
Ennis Chauncey   63
Eric Leroy   105
Erin Kathleen   99
Ernest Richard   114
Ernest Victor   84
Ervin John Leroy 63
Ervin L.   64
Ervin Leslie   63
Esmond   2
Esther 73
Esther (Anderson) 29
Esther (Johnson) 35
Esther (Livingway) 103
Esther (Longshore) 29
Esther (Sanborn) 33
Ethel   24
Ethel (Ketcham) 65
Ethel (Thompson) 34
Ethel Marie   34
Etta (Estabrook) 22
Etta M.   65
Eugene   51
Eugene Charles   59
Eugene Douglass   59

9 780788 404603